THE ENDLESS APPLE®

THE ENDLESS APPLE®

How to maintain state-of-the-art performance on your Apple® II and IIe

Drawings by Rick van Genderen

CHARLES RUBIN

MICROSOFT PRESS

PUBLISHED BY
Microsoft Press
A Division of Microsoft Corporation
10700 Northup Way, Box 97200,
Bellevue, Washington 98009

Library of Congress Cataloging in Publication Data
Rubin, Charles, 1953-
The Endless Apple
Includes index.
1. Apple II (Computer) 2. Apple IIe (Computer) I. Title.
QA76.8.A662R82 1984 001.64 84-16558
ISBN 0-914845-27-6

Printed and bound in the United States of America.

1 2 3 4 5 6 7 8 9 FGFG 8 9 0 9 8 7 6 5 4

Distributed to the book trade in the United States and Canada by Simon and Schuster, Inc.

For my son Daniel,
who has a seat on the rocket.

C O N T E N T S

ACKNOWLEDGMENTS

This book is the result of a group effort. Hundreds of people, most of whom had never heard of me, answered my phone calls, fielded my questions, gave the best answers they could give, and directed me to others for information they could not, themselves, provide. They were almost universally courteous and helpful, but there were a few dozen who went out of their way for me.

I would first of all like to thank Tracy Smith, Salley Oberlin, Karen-Lynne de Robinson, Barry Preppernau, and especially JoAnne Woodcock, of Microsoft Press, whose diligence and consideration have made this the most pleasant writing project I've ever undertaken.

At Apple Computer, Linda Merrill and Jeni Sall were invaluable in providing me with contacts within the Apple II Group. Among the contacts themselves, I am grateful to Jim Armstrong, Susan Berman, Lee Collings, Chris Espinosa, Harlan Felt, Bruce Friesen, Bill Kershaw, Dave Larson, Rod Riggenbach, Bill Schjelderup, Kin Seto, Joe Shelton, Doug Solomon, Louise Stanley, Bruce Tognazzini, Lisa Van Horne, and Hal Winfield. Like everyone at Apple, these people are incredibly busy, but they were never too busy to help.

Lee Thé of *Personal Computing* magazine got a disproportionate share of annoying phone calls from me, and always managed to be cheerful as well as helpful.

Among my hundreds of contacts with third-party manufacturers, retailers, and consultants, a few stand out as having been particularly generous with their help. Among those who spent a lot of time explaining things were Don Stokes at Titan Technologies, Bill Leineweber from Videx, Jennifer Gardner and Tim Gill at Quark, Tom Crosley and Ron Lichty from Softwest, Neil Gabbert and Dale Heatherington from Hayes Microcomputer Products, Dave Grabel at Digital Research, and Gary Carlston from Broderbund. Brad Roth of Infomax Computers in San Francisco unpacked a lot of new equipment for product illustrations. Donald Elman gave the manuscript a thoughtful technical review. And Steven Wong came through with a computer in a pinch.

While these people and many others deserve the credit for providing me with information, I accept the responsibility for any omissions or inaccuracies that may have occurred in the translation.

Charles Rubin
Oakland, California
September, 1984

INTRODUCTION

The Apple II is the personification of an idea—that the best of human technology is at our service to do what we want, when we want, the way we want it done. The same Apple that took your hand and led you into the world of computing now performs the most intricate calculations for you. The same Apple that can help your four-year-old learn to read can monitor experiments in outer space.

In a marketplace where newer, bigger, or faster is often confused with better, the Apple II has remained one of personal computing's greatest success stories for nearly eight years. It has done so in competition with some of the most formidable marketers and some of the cleverest engineers in the world, because the Apple II has always had something no other computer had—a personality. When we speak of my Apple, or your Apple, we're talking about more than a mass of plastic, metal, and silicon. We're talking about a device so approachable, obedient, and flexible it becomes a part of our lives in a way we may never have thought possible.

The Apple's personality—that feeling of its being *your* computer—isn't even approached by other products. Maybe it's the Apple's flexibility that makes us believe the Apple does what we want, not that we do what it wants. Or maybe the Apple's personality comes from Apple Computer's attitude toward personal computing: That it really can change the world, and that a computer should be willing and flexible enough to be as much (or as little) a part of our lives as we like, rather than dominate our desks like an oversized calculator.

This personality is as much a part of the Apple II as any of its other components. Yet unlike the computer's more physical aspects, its personality cannot be overshadowed by the march of mere technological progress or dimmed with the passing of years. This is why the Apple II has the most diverse and loyal following of any computer that has ever been (or is ever likely to be) brought to market.

The many devoted users who jumped on the Apple II bandwagon from the beginning have formed what is still the largest and finest assemblage of microcomputer user groups in the world. They publish magazines. They hold Apple-only product expositions. Many of them know the Apple II inside out, and almost all are more than willing to share that knowledge with newcomers. Just about anywhere in the Western Hemisphere, Apple users can get answers to technical questions anytime, day or night.

FINDING YOUR WAY AROUND

This book is for Apple II lovers who are no longer completely happy with their machine's capabilities. The initial yen for enhanced capabilities is almost always linked with a specific application (you don't like the way your word processor formats text, or you wish your spreadsheet would recalculate faster, for example), so this book is divided up by application, rather than by type of product.

Each chapter will explore a different application area and present options for improving Apple II performance. Often, a particular product or type of solution in one application area is also useful in other application areas, so some products appear in several chapters.

Within each chapter, the products are discussed in terms of their advantages in that particular area: how the product improves the application, how it works, what it does to your Apple, and how it measures up against other products as a solution in terms of price, performance, and ease of use. When the performance or operation of products differs among the Apple II, II+, or IIe, the differences will be explained.

Since there is more than one way to solve most computing problems, the end of each application chapter will contain two or three Showcase Systems that feature specific products. These Showcase Systems will also give you an idea of the price of an optimally configured system (containing several types of products) for that application.

In addition, there's a List of Products that shows the major manufacturers of product categories mentioned throughout the book. This guide is not meant to be an exhaustive listing, because such a list would change daily. The index lists the page locations of products and technologies wherever they occur. This way, you can find descriptions of specific products or brand names if you want to zero in on something in particular. There's also a Glossary defining some advanced terms that are used, in case you're not familiar with them.

This book is not meant to be a complete guide to the operation and technical makeup of every enhancement product made for the Apple II. Such a book, if it could indeed be compiled, would probably dwarf the *Encyclopaedia Brittanica.* Rather, the purpose is to suggest different approaches to Apple II enhancement and provide you with enough information to decide which ones to explore further.

The specific products mentioned in this book are examples, not ironclad recommendations. It's entirely possible that different reviewers or experts will suggest products other than those discussed here. And if you are interested in one of the products mentioned, please remember that in this fast-moving industry, the prices and even the product names are always subject to change.

One final question that can be addressed in advance is, "Why isn't there a chapter on education?" The reason is that this is a guide to maintaining state-of-the-art performance on Apple II computers, and the plain, unenhanced Apple II is and has always been the premier educational computer. It offers about five times as much educational software as its nearest competitor, and virtually all of that software will run on a bare-bones Apple with 48K or 64K of RAM, one disk drive, and a standard green monitor.

In schools, Apples can benefit from networking hardware and software, special input devices for the handicapped, video-projection hardware for large audiences, and voice synthesis and recognition systems, but these applications go far beyond the needs of the individual user. Since this book was written for individual users, institutional enhancements aren't covered.

This book is a celebration of the Apple's utility, its approachability, and its limitless appeal. In these pages, you'll learn why the Apple II has been the greatest microcomputer in the world, and why it will continue as such well into the future. If you yearn for the latest technological twist, you'll see how your Apple can give it to you. If you want to expand your computing horizons, you'll see where your Apple can lead you. And if you simply want to know just what makes this computer different from all others, what makes the Apple II every bit as exciting now as it was in the dawn of microcomputing, then this book is for you.

C H A P T E R

1

THE BEGINNING

It all began in April, 1977, at the Civic Auditorium in San Francisco, California. It was the first day of the first West Coast Computer Faire. Microcomputers were very new, but not so new that they hadn't already begun to light a few fires in the imaginations of technically adventurous, but otherwise ordinary, citizens who wanted to see just what these new boxes were all about. So, along with the calculator-carrying hobbyists who talked incessantly about PROMs and breadboards, the fair attracted business people who wanted to know about organizing their customer files, and other people who were just plain curious.

All the giants of the new industry were there: MITS and Processor Technology and IMSAI were showing their computers. And there were also a lot of small outfits selling plug-in circuit boards that made computers do various things that were of questionable utility, but nevertheless seemed interesting.

Each of these exhibitors had staked out a few card tables in the auditorium, and they had computers up and running for the public to see. But for the most part, what the public saw at each booth was a box covered with switches and blinking lights, a display showing a program listing, and one or two nervous company representatives who were scared stiff that a curious passerby would throw one of the switches or unplug the computer and thereby necessitate a lot of reprogramming.

And the business people who wanted to get some computer help with inventory or accounts payable found instead that they had to love fiddling with computers for its own sake to do anything even remotely useful. The idea that application software could be commercially available was a radical one.

But there was another company there that day, a relative newcomer called Apple Computer. The Apple display was hard to miss, because it stood right inside the main doors of the auditorium and featured a black Plexiglas tower with the Apple logo on it.

Slim, beige boxes with built-in keyboards, called Apple II computers, were displayed on counters around the booth, and large display monitors showed the computers at work. Instead of program listings, the screens displayed games and color graphics. Instead of nervous technicians, the booth was staffed by young, easy-going people who were having the time of their lives talking to visitors and playing the games. And the Apple people were inviting the passersby to pick up game controls and play the games themselves. Apple made the rest of the computer companies look like a bunch of amateurs, at least where marketing was concerned.

Even if you'd never seen a microcomputer before that day, you could go to the Apple booth, get your hands on a computer, and make it do something. And that was when the promise of computing power for people like you and me—something called personal computing—really began to unfold.

Figure 1-1
The Apple II

A SENSE OF POWER

The Apple II, which you can see in Figure 1-1, was by today's standards a very primitive device. It came with 4K or 16K of RAM that could be expanded—at great expense—to 48K. The basic model cost $1298. This early Apple II used a cassette player to store and load programs. It displayed uppercase letters only, in 40 columns across the screen, and you would probably use a television to display them. But it was shipped with Applesoft BASIC and a checkbook-balancing program (real software!), and this was pretty much the state of the art back then.

Of Course, Apple didn't quite have the field all to itself. Commodore was hot on Apple's heels with the PET, which had a built-in monitor as well as a built-in keyboard; Processor Technology had the Sol, with its built-in keyboard; and Radio Shack would soon have its TRS-80 Model I which, at its cheapest, cost less than half of what an Apple cost.

But maybe because of the futuristic booth that completely eclipsed any other display that day, or because of the easy-going attitude of the Apple employees, there was a sense of power, of stability and support, behind the Apple name. Customers felt as if they were betting on a company and a product that would still be around when their checks cleared the bank. They were right.

The Apple II began shipping in early January, 1978, and Apple Computer, Inc., had its first month of million-dollar sales in June, the same year. MITS, IMSAI, and Processor Technology all went out of business by mid-1979, and the Commodore PET and the TRS-80 Model I have long since disappeared from computer stores, but an upgraded, yet eminently recognizable version of the original Apple II is still selling some 50,000 units a month six years later.

There are many reasons behind these continuing sales, and a lot of them are probably the same as those that prompted you to buy your Apple. That sense of stability and support that Apple Computer projected from its beginning in 1977 has strengthened continuously since then. While other computer companies go through products as if they were Kleenex, Apple has steadfastly supported and upgraded the Apple II.

Many of the upgrades are made possible by the II's highly flexible design. As computer technology improves, Apple incorporates the improvements into its Apple II products. The main logic board has been enhanced over a dozen times. The disk operating system has been improved three times. The keyboard, the disk drives, the monitor, the power supply—all have been upgraded, so that the Apple II can continue to offer performance consistent with the rest of the industry.

Apple's support and the II's flexible design have been richly complemented and exploited by third-party developers, who have given the II more software and more hardware enhancements than exist for any other single microcomputer. And every time better software or better hardware appears for another computer, either Apple or some clever third-party manufacturer figures out a way to make it available for the II. The finest spreadsheet display you can get on any microcomputer is available exclusively on the Apple II. The best telecommunications products, graphics devices, and business software are all available for the Apple II.

In short, thanks to all this continuing innovation and support, you can do just about anything you can do with any personal computer with an Apple II. As Apple says—and it's not kidding—there are more people doing more things with Apple IIs than with any other personal computer.

A QUESTION OF ATTITUDE

Remember when you first got your Apple? Chances are it was your first personal computer. Remember your sense of delight and wonder as you opened the boxes and set everything up for the first time? This wasn't just a new toaster or television set. This was a computer: It was something that just might change your life, and would, at the very least, offer an endless and exciting new territory for you to explore. Maybe you got so excited you stayed up half the night with your new machine, plugging in peripheral devices, diving into manuals, watching words and pictures on the screen change at the touch of a key. For hours, days, or perhaps even weeks, your new Apple was the most amazing thing you'd ever seen.

Then something sad, but rather inevitable happened: You got used to your Apple. Like anything new, the Apple didn't stay new forever, and that sense of wonder and excitement faded. You got up to speed on your word-processing or spreadsheet program. You began concentrating on the work you'd bought the Apple to do, and the once endless possibilities of your Apple were buried under specifics, such as keeping the books, writing letters, and charting investments. You forgot about what your Apple *could* do, and formed a concrete opinion of what it *did* do. In effect, you put your Apple back into a box—in this case, a mental box—only days or weeks after you first unpacked it.

People like to put things in boxes: We tend to form an opinion of what something will and won't do, and then forever after we think of it in those terms. This attitude is convenient and perfectly harmless with a toaster or a television, because they don't do much anyway. But it's asking for trouble with a computer, particularly with an Apple. Putting your Apple into any kind of mental box or boxes means you're turning it into an unchanging object. If you think of an Apple as you do a television set, you'll feel the same way about improving it—if you want something different, you buy a new one. And that's a shame, because flexibility has kept the Apple II new for all these years. And it's a flexibility that could, with a little imagination, keep you computing happily forever.

OUT OF THE BOX

Renewing and maintaining a love affair with an Apple II is a three-part process:

1. You change your attitude about your Apple.

2. You change your attitude about the computing you do.
3. You change your Apple.

The first two parts of this process are required; the third part is optional. This book will help you through the whole journey. Just thumbing through each chapter will open your eyes to the variety of things an Apple II can do, and the variety of ways it can do them. You'll begin pulling your computer back out of that mental box it's in.

You and Your Apple

One totally untrue but perfectly understandable attitude you may have about your Apple is that, as a seven-year-old computer, it isn't worth enhancing. You could point to the growing percentage of new products devoted to other computers. You could cite the trend toward larger, more elegant programs that require a 16-bit processor. You could be worried that your aging Apple isn't physically up to being enhanced, much as an engine with 100,000 miles on it isn't up to being supercharged. You might even mention the new Apple IIc as proof that Apple's support for the old II is finally evaporating.

This attitude is reasonable, but unsupportable. If you want a 16-bit processor, you can go out right now and get one for your Apple II. In fact, you may soon be able to replace your Apple's 8-bit processor with a 16-bit version that will still run your old 8-bit programs *and* give you access to more RAM. As for physical infirmity, electricity is not gasoline. Electronic devices last a lot longer than mechanical ones, and most of your Apple is electronic. Except for the monitor, disk drives, and perhaps the power supply, it's entirely possible that your Apple will outlive you.

And as for the new IIc filling the IIe's shoes, that's like saying Cadillac will stop making big cars because it now makes a little one. As conceived, the IIc fills a niche in the Apple II product line; it doesn't become the product line itself. Apple's marketing people see the IIc as a smaller, lighter, easier-to-learn, and *less expandable* version of the Apple II.

The IIc was designed as a sealed unit into which users can plug exactly one mouse, one modem, one external disk drive, one printer, and one monitor. The IIc costs less than a IIe equipped with an 80-column card, disk drive, and monitor, but it costs more than a IIe by itself. The IIc is fine for people who can confidently predict that they'll never need more than what it offers, but it isn't as well suited as the IIe for individuals, small businesses, and schools that want to keep their options open. And for beginners with the least amount of money to spend, a "stripped" IIe is still the cheapest way to Apple computing.

If all this sounds like the folks at Apple plan to keep the expandable II around for awhile, it's because they do. Recent additions to the Apple II line, such as ProDOS (an enhanced operating system), the Apple Mouse, and AppleWorks (integrated software), all point to the future. Ongoing work by Steve Wozniak and others will soon result in products that will make the Apple II look and work amazingly like the Macintosh and Lisa, and this enhancement work shows no sign of abating.

When the IIc was announced in April 1984, Apple Computer took great pains to reposition the entire II product line as a family with a future. The Apple II line now has an installed base of over two million units, so the market is simply too big to walk away from. Indications from every sector of the personal computer market are that the Apple II will continue as a viable product through at least 1990. For individual computing needs, some would say it has never been bettered.

Enough Is Enough

This brings us to the second stage of the process—a change in your attitude toward the computing you do. A little more difficult, but no more expensive, it's a matter of stepping back from your computing and considering the difference between meeting your needs and buying products that go well beyond them.

Because computer technology changes so quickly, and because we're constantly exposed to advertisements for new hardware and software, we tend to think our problems can be solved only by buying something new. If we're not happy with the spreadsheets we design, we're more inclined to go shopping for new software than we are to consider re-reading the manual to get more out of our existing software. If we don't like the way our word-processed text is displayed, we'll consider getting a new computer before we explore other options. Part of this attitude comes from a lack of awareness of our other options (this book will help a lot in that department), but a lot of it is just plain consumerism and a desire for something new.

The proof of this is that we often find ourselves lusting after new products when our old ones are still perfectly good. A neighbor gets an IBM PC, and suddenly we're unhappy with our Apple. An increasing percentage of new software seems to have been written for MS-DOS, and we worry about being outdated, forgetting that our Apple is as useful and as reliable as ever. We are dazzled by 16-bit technology, even though it has virtually no effect on the quality of our word processing. We fall in love with huge spreadsheet/graphics programs, knowing that we never create large spreadsheets and never use graphics. We get carried away by doodads, such as screen icons and larger disk drives, whether we need them or not.

The first thing to consider in evaluating a change in computers or a change to your Apple is the difference between what you want and what you need. But assuming you've got all the money in the world and can switch computers whenever you like (and you don't care whether you really need a new one or not), there are other reasons to resist the temptation. You've got a lot of learning time invested in your Apple, in both the hardware and the software. You've also got a considerable amount of personal data stored on Apple disks. You're comfortable with your Apple and can make it do your bidding quickly and easily. A new computer might temporarily quell your lust for the latest, but it will also force you to invest a lot of time in learning a new system, finding ways to transfer your Apple disk files, figuring out new software, and generally getting comfortable again. The transition is difficult to make, and should only be undertaken as a last resort. As you'll see, it won't be necessary in most cases.

When Enough Isn't Enough

Realistically, though, there are times when it's better to get a new computer than it is to enhance your Apple. Perhaps your computer is part of a system of computers, and you need greater compatibility. Perhaps you absolutely must have a program that isn't available for the Apple—although there aren't many of these—and your need outweighs the disadvantages of making the change. If so, you'll have to face the music.

If you decide to enhance your Apple, you'll need to learn the how, why, and what of making the enhancement. You'll want to consider your options. These might be exclusively a matter of price or of features that differ between specific products, or they might involve significant differences between types of solutions.

Then, too, there's the Kludge (pronounced klooj) Effect to consider. A kludge arises from a situation in which modifying or enhancing your Apple causes more problems than it solves. Sometimes (usually after looking at too many hardware advertisements) I have a nightmarish vision of my Apple with all sorts of wires dangling from it, smoke rising from the motherboard and seeping through the case. My vision is of a kludge: an inelegant, inefficient, and generally troublesome computing device.

An Apple II is by no means a kludge. It takes some doing to make it one—but it can be done. Sometimes, a product that enhances one application will mess up another application. A speed-up circuit board that helps spreadsheet recalculation renders your favorite arcade game unplayable, or a monitor that does wonders for graphics makes text harder to read. In presenting hardware and software solutions throughout this book, I have tried to keep a sharp eye out for the Kludge Effect, and to cry foul when it rears its ugly head.

What's far more likely is that an enhancement product is simply more trouble to use than it's worth. If you have to start your Apple with a modification disk and then enter half a dozen control-character strings every time you want to use your favorite software, it simply might not be worth the trouble. You might well be tempted to give the Apple to the kids and get another computer instead. This is entirely reasonable in some cases—it will depend on your particular circumstances.

But, if you're a typical Apple owner, you've barely begun to tap the potential of your system. There are thousands of products on the market that can make your computer easier or more fun to live with, and there are products yet to be announced and capabilities yet to be exploited that will be truly mind-boggling. There's a lot of computing power and convenience still locked up in your Apple. Here's to unleashing it.

C H A P T E R

2

WORD-PROCESSING WONDERS

The Apple II has been much maligned as a word-processing machine, invariably by people who do their word processing on computers other than Apples. One critic will point to the keyboard, another to the display, a third to the capacity of the disk drives, and another to the quality of software as proof that the Apple II isn't even in the same league as other word-processing systems.

Some of this criticism is justified; some of it is bunk. But none of the word-processing limitations of an Apple II are permanent, and that's the news that really counts. In fact, the Apple is more able to adapt to your particular word-processing needs than any other computer on the market, regardless of what those needs might be.

The trouble with word processing on a microcomputer starts with the widespread popularity of this application and the individual ways in which we apply it. Everyone processes words once in a while. We've done it for centuries, and most of us have been using some kind of machine (a typewriter or a dedicated word processor) for years. Each of us got used to processing words in a certain way, and we carried that experience with us when we set about processing words on an Apple. A typewriter gave us total control over the location of letters on a page; we expected the same from the Apple. A word-processing machine had special keys that said Insert or Delete or Store; we expected the same on the Apple.

And on top of the presence or absence of specific features, we had prejudices about the way they were implemented. No one writes just the same as anyone else does—we each have our own likes and dislikes about keyboard feel and display size, our own needs in terms of format capabilities or printing attributes, our own sets of priorities when it comes to file-management features or cursor control.

Most of these preferences went begging with a dedicated word processor or a typewriter, because there was only one way to do things, and we adapted. Once we came over to a personal computer, though, we found nothing but options, and consequently had nothing but complaints, if things weren't just the way we wanted them to be.

Everyone wants something a little different when it comes to word processing, and this explains why software and hardware makers are continually reinventing ways to do the same thing.

There are dozens of word-processing programs, instead of the handful of really major programs we find in the spreadsheet world. Perhaps three spreadsheet programs can claim supremacy, but it seems as though everyone's word processor claims to be the best there is. The funny thing is that everyone's word processor probably *is* the best, for someone.

BEHIND THE EIGHT BALL

Software aside, there are hardware differences among personal computer systems that affect their suitability for word processing, and at first glance, the Apple seems to be rather toward the bottom of the heap. Even back in 1979 and 1980, when the first Apple word processors appeared, the "standard" requirements for serious word processing were a typewriter-like keyboard, an 80-column display, and as much disk storage space as possible. With these features in mind, let's see why the Apple II began its word-processing days from behind the eight ball.

The original Apple keyboard was modeled after a teletype machine, so its layout and responsiveness reflected the needs of that application, rather than those of a word processor or a typewriter. Teletype machines printed their output immediately on paper tape or roll paper. You couldn't correct mistakes once you'd made them, so there was no point in moving back to lines already printed. Hence, there were no up or down arrow keys on the Apple keyboard.

Likewise, teletype machines would only print uppercase letters, so there really wasn't any point in having a keyboard that could produce lowercase letters, as well. Thus, the Apple II keyboard and display featured nothing but uppercase letters.

Finally, the teletype keys were electromechanically connected to the print head. Teletyping was more a matter of push-typing than it was touch-typing, so the keys were a little closer together than they are on a typical typewriter (allowing typists to mash them with the necessary force). The Apple's keys were similarly close together, even though the computer had no print head to drive directly.

In the display department, the Apple was designed well before personal computerized word processing existed. It was considered more important for a person to be able to view a smaller amount of text (program lines containing big, 40-column letters) easily, than it was for a person to see lots of text (80 columns of smaller letters) slightly less easily. The 40-column display didn't matter much with spreadsheets: There hadn't ever been spreadsheets on microcomputers before, so there was no "standard" display size with which to compare. With word processors, though, the dedicated machines had set the standard—80 columns by 24 lines, or about half a page at a time—and the Apple display suffered in comparison.

Under these circumstances, it's easy to see why the Apple II looked like a bush-leaguer in the word-processing department. Oh, sure, it was okay for writing to your Aunt Martha, but for real, businesslike word processing, the Apple II was considered a dud.

But even if the unadorned Apple II begins as a second-rate word processor for many, it can easily be enhanced to equal or surpass the capabilities of any other word-processing system. The Apple's flexibility is the key, of course, but just as importantly, in the current world of 16-bit technology, its 8-bit processor is no handicap. Fundamentally, there's no word processing you can do on an existing 16-bit computer that you can't do on an 8-bit computer.

Word processing is about the simplest of applications in terms of the demands it makes on a computer's processor. Most word-processing programs are small enough to fit comfortably in an Apple's 48K or 64K of RAM, and the processing demands of displaying, printing, or relocating a bunch of text characters are an absolute cakewalk for a computer in comparison to recalculating a spreadsheet or sorting through a data base. You'll find that aside from an occasional bell or whistle, there's absolutely no difference among word processors that's due to the type of processor you're using.

If the quality of word processing between the 8-bit world and the 16-bit world is fairly even, however, the quality of word processing over time has changed quite a bit. Such features as on-line spelling checks, split-screen editing, searching and replacing in either direction, or even simpler things, such as automatic word wrap and on-screen formatting, are light years away from the first Apple word-processing capabilities. If you haven't upgraded your capabilities at all, you could still be living in the Dark Ages.

Of course, this might not matter if you're the only person using your system and your needs haven't changed. I know people who are still quite content using a 1979 version of Apple Writer I on a 40-column display. I know people who use 80-column displays for other programs, but prefer a 40-column display for word processing because it's easier on the eyes. Maybe you don't want to invest the time to learn a new program, or take advantage of a new peripheral device. It might very well be that the time you'll have to spend isn't worth the benefit you'd gain. The purpose here isn't to steer you into enhancements you don't need, but rather to offer them as possibilities in the event that you're looking to upgrade.

TOO MUCH SUCCESS

Suppose you're a successful author of gothic romances. You picked up an Apple II+ in 1981, just as your career was getting under way. Since then, your career has blossomed. You're doing eight books a year. What seemed like limitless word-processing power with your Apple Writer I program now makes you wonder whether it's really better than the old Underwood typewriter you used before.

The pressure of hectic editing has made you wish you could see more of a page on the screen at once. The clumsy uppercase/lowercase shifting is slowing you down. Then again, those Disk II disk drives only store about 70 pages of text per diskette, so you have five diskettes per novel. With the volume you're cranking out, there's a lot of disk swapping and confusion. You want to have quicker access to your growing library of boilerplate plot elements. Split-screen editing would also be nice. And, of course, your editor is complaining about typos in your manuscript, so you're also thinking about adding a spelling checker to your repertoire.

As if the act of creation weren't difficult enough, you have to spend hours each week waiting for your printer to crank out the finished product. Your Apple Writer I program doesn't let you chain files together, so you have to sit up into the wee hours of the morning feeding file after file to your slow, but trustworthy, daisy-wheel printer. It's so boring that you've taken to reading your own books.

And all this, of course, has begun to blunt your creativity, so you're thinking of hiring a secretary to do your word processing. You wonder whether a secretary would rebel at your Apple keyboard or your puny 40-column display. You're tempted to start all over again with a new computer—to make a clean break with the past.

On your next trip to the bank, you spot an IBM PC XT in a store window. It's love at first sight. You go inside. You drool over the hard disk. You tremble at the touch of the keyboard. Your pulse quickens when you see the advanced formatting capabilities on the crisp, 80-column display. You feel the color rise in your cheeks as you ask about the price. The salesperson responds in a husky voice. You faint. . . .

A wealthy and charming stranger whisks you home in a chauffeured limousine. You decline an offer of further assistance and stagger inside, plopping yourself down before your Apple. You look regretfully at the old warhorse. Is it really goodbye, at last?

Come, come. Kissing off your Apple for the sake of better word processing is like jilting a bride because you don't like the cut of her dress. There are so many ways to enhance an Apple for word processing that your biggest problem is likely to be choosing what you like best.

SOFTWARE

Word processing began on the Apple II in 1979 with two programs that appeared at about the same time: EasyWriter and Apple Writer. EasyWriter was written by John Draper, a brilliant telecommunications hacker who began calling himself Cap'n Crunch after discovering how to access and manipulate the American telephone system without paying for it, all with the aid of a giveaway bosun's whistle found in boxes of a popular breakfast cereal. (Ah, but that is another story entirely.) At about the same time, Apple itself was getting edgy about the absence of word-processing software for its computer, so it hired a fellow named Paul Lutus to write Apple Writer.

Neither of these programs was exactly what you would call elegant. Apple Writer, for example, didn't have word wrap, it didn't produce lowercase letters, it wouldn't display formatted text on the screen, and it forced you to hit ESC twice if you wanted to move the cursor to another part of a paragraph during text entry.

But despite these and lots of other shortcomings, using Apple Writer or EasyWriter was like magic compared to using a typewriter. You could actually delete whole words or paragraphs at a time with just two keystrokes. You could search for and replace words throughout a document with a few more keystrokes. And once you had perfected your text, you could print it out flawlessly at what seemed like lightning speed.

This was really living in those days, but things are a lot better now. For one thing, a number of word processors now offer dynamic formatting, which means that you can enter or edit text and you can format it in the same processing mode, at the same time. Many word processors separate editing and formatting into two procedures: You enter unformatted text with formatting or special "dot" commands; then, if you want to see what the printed text will look like, you have to exit the editor part of the program and display the formatted file on the screen. In contrast, word processors with dynamic formatting can format text as you enter or edit it, so you always see just what your document will look like. Dynamic formatting was originally the feature that separated dedicated word processors from microcomputer word processors, but a fairly sizable group of products offers it today.

In fact, the variety of programs available today is truly staggering. Since everyone's needs are different, it is impossible to recommend any program or programs as the best, across the board. Nevertheless, we can look at some programs that are very good at different things.

IIe or Not IIe

Is it IIe or not IIe? That is the first question to be answered when considering the virtues of various word processors. The IIe is nearly two years old now, and a growing number of software houses are making their programs a little easier to use by taking advantage of the IIe's two function keys, its Delete key, and its four arrow keys. Two particular programs that come to mind are AppleWorks and Word Juggler IIe. Both of these programs offer features or ease of use that go beyond the competition in some ways, but neither is available for the II/II+ series.

AppleWorks

NOTE: *AppleWorks is discussed in detail in Chapter 5, Integrated Applications.*

AppleWorks is Apple's integrated software package for the IIe. It combines a word processor, a file manager (much like the Quick File program), and a spreadsheet on one disk. The program uses the Open Apple and letter keys in combination to perform most of its commands; the letter keys are often mnemonic—F is Find, S is Save, D is Delete, and so on. The commands are very similar, regardless of the application you're in, so AppleWorks can be learned quickly. The program retails for $250.

The best things about AppleWorks' word processor are its dynamic formatting capability and its "Desktop" file-manipulation system, and of these, the latter is what really separates AppleWorks from the crowd. The Desktop system allows you to have several files in RAM at once by treating the available RAM space in the Apple as a work area where you can temporarily store files. You can also switch quickly from one file to another. Depending on the amount of RAM you have available (64K or 128K), you can bring up to twelve files into RAM (onto the Desktop).

For example, suppose that you are writing a report. You're entering the text of the report into one file, but you have three other files on the Desktop that contain information needed in the report. To move to another file on the Desktop, you simply press the Open Apple and Q keys at the same time to display a Desktop Index in the middle of your screen. The names of all files currently on the Desktop are listed, and the one you are working with is highlighted. (You can see it all in Figure 2-1.) To choose another file, you use the arrow keys to move the highlighted bar down to the name of the file you want to look at and then press Return. In a second or two, the file you highlighted replaces the report draft you

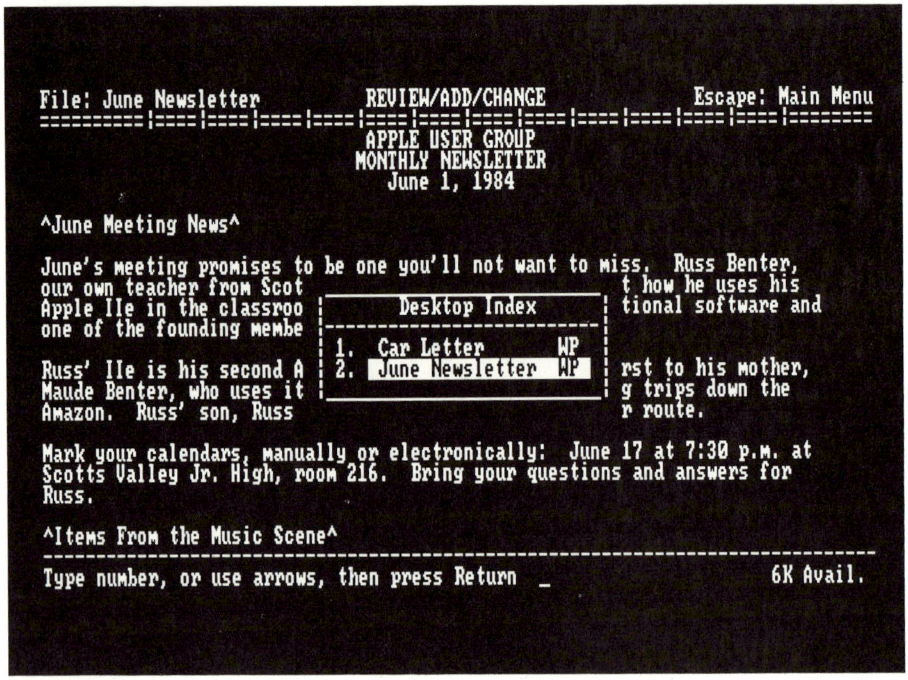

Figure 2-1

AppleWorks display, showing the Desktop Index

were working on. You can then look up the information you needed, and just as quickly switch back to enter the information in your report.

On the other hand, if the information is particularly complex or is formatted a certain way and you don't want to retype it, you can bring the file up on the screen, highlight the area of the file you want to copy, copy it to a buffer called the Clipboard, recall your report text, and then "paste" the contents of the Clipboard into the report at the location you select. This kind of information transfer is very quick and easy with AppleWorks. With 128K of RAM, you have about 55K of file space available on the Desktop, or enough for about 25 double-spaced pages of text. A 64K Apple will give you only about 10K of Desktop space, or about 4 double-spaced pages of text.

AppleWorks runs under Apple's enhanced ProDOS operating system (discussed later in this chapter). This enables it to use the Apple's RAM as it does, and speeds up loading and saving program and data files an average of 600 percent. But it also makes the files incompatible with DOS 3.3 files. If you want to use DOS 3.3 text files with AppleWorks, you have to use a special utility program on the ProDOS User's Disk to convert the DOS 3.3 files to a usable form. The conversion will only work, however, if your files are already stored in ASCII format—in other words, if your word processor has stored the files in the standard code known as ASCII, without automatically inserting non-standard characters of its own for formatting or other purposes.

Word Juggler IIe

Word Juggler IIe is a version of the most popular Apple III word processor, brought over to the IIe environment. Word Juggler IIe is made by Quark, Inc., which is recognized as an innovative software developer with a very close working relationship with Apple. Word Juggler IIe was the first ProDOS application program to appear (even before AppleWorks), and it is one of the most powerful programs you can buy for the Apple. Word Juggler IIe doesn't offer dynamic formatting, but it gives you an integrated spelling checker and tremendous form-letter capabilities in a product that can be mastered almost completely within a couple of hours.

Word Juggler IIe uses a special circuit board (installation instructions are included) to enhance the keyboard and a set of replacement keytops to make operation easier. The keytops have labels on their sides for many Word Juggler functions. The rest of the program functions are available by pressing the ESC key, followed by one of the keys in the top row. A command strip is included to remind you of what each top row key does when used with ESC. The result of all this labeling is that you have nearly every Word Juggler command right in front of you, and it's a lot like using a dedicated word processor. There are no special formatting commands to remember, because functions such as centering, line spacing, and margins are handled with labeled keys.

Power-wise, Word Juggler IIe's most startling feature is its form-letter capability. You can create up to 127 different variables to insert in letters, and you can then use an IF command and conditional statements (equal, not equal, less than, and so on) to cause the program to use certain values in one copy of a letter, and completely different values in the next copy. A billing letter, for example, might link the amount due to the addressee's name, so that you could print out customized billing letters, each with a different person's name, address, and billing amount. Variable values in Word Juggler can even be entire paragraphs, so you could print letters with entirely different contents for each person on a list.

Many form-letter programs limit document size to a few pages, but Word Juggler has no such limit. Individual documents can be about half a standard diskette (34 double-spaced pages) in length on a 128K machine, but there's also a file-linking feature that lets you link as many files as you like to create documents as long as you like.

Lexicheck, the spelling side of the program, uses a 50,000-word main dictionary to check documents, and it will also let you create as many personal dictionaries as you like. Since Word Juggler itself loads completely into the Apple's RAM, there's no need for it to access the program disk once you've got it up and running. Thus, you can load the Word Juggler program, remove the program diskette, and insert the Lexicheck diskette in your main drive. Once you've done that, you can check a document at any time simply by hitting the Open Apple and the 7 keys together. The spelling checker takes over; checks the document; provides a word count; shows you the misspelled words in context; lets you correct them, skip them, or add them to a personal dictionary; and returns you automatically to text editing mode after you correct the last word. Many spelling programs are fairly slow (and get a lot slower when the document gets longer), but Lexicheck can check a 7200-word document (that's the equivalent of about 29 double-spaced pages) in 78 seconds.

Word Guess Plus is another attraction of Lexicheck. If you're entering text and forget how to spell a word, you can check Lexicheck's main dictionary for words whose spelling is close to that of the one you just entered. With the cursor on the suspect word, you just press Open Apple and 8, and the program goes out to the Lexicheck dictionary on disk and finds words with spellings close to the one you typed. More than likely, the correctly spelled version of the word you're unsure of will appear in Lexicheck's display of similar words. You simply move a highlighted bar down through the list of displayed words until the correct spelling is highlighted, and then press Return. Presto! The word in your document is automatically replaced by the correct one.

Because of the keyboard enhancer, ProDOS, and some clever programming, Word Juggler is also very fast. Everything you do—whether it's moving from the beginning to the end of a file, displaying formatted text on the screen, or printing a document—happens without the usual delays for disk access or processing. There's also a built-in utility that will let you insert DOS 3.3 text files into Word Juggler documents. If you really want to upgrade your word-processing software with a minimum of retraining time and you don't mind converting to ProDOS, you should definitely check out Word Juggler IIe. I know of a similar program for the IBM PC that requires 256K of RAM and costs $495; Word Juggler IIe and Lexicheck together retail for $189.

II and IIe

If you're a II or II+ owner and have read the preceding sections on AppleWorks and Word Juggler, all this talk of Open Apple keys and ProDOS can be scary. It shouldn't be. ProDOS is as much at home on your computer as it is on a IIe. Furthermore, many of the all-time favorite word-processing programs for the Apple work on any II-series Apple. Some programs are available in either DOS 3.3 or ProDOS versions.

Apple Writer II (or IIe)

This all-time, best-selling word-processing program for the Apple II line is available in versions for either the II or IIe. Apple Writer doesn't have the dynamic formatting of AppleWorks, and isn't quite as easy to use, but it's much more powerful. The latest rendition of Apple Writer has a lot of advanced features for heavy-duty word processing. You can split the display to edit two parts of a file at once. You can create customized form letters of any length. And there's also a glossary that lets you store words or phrases under individual keys and recall them quickly.

Beyond this, there's Apple Writer's Word Processing Language, WPL, which is actually a programming language you can use for lots of useful functions. The Apple Writer disk comes with prewritten WPL programs for generating form letters, printing multiple files in succession, or as one continuous document, counting words in a document, moving files from one disk to another, and converting formatting commands from previous Apple Writer versions so they work in the current version.

But this is only the beginning. With WPL and some determination, you can also use Apple Writer to perform calculations, execute word-processing functions automatically, and create your own menu-driven Apple Writer programs. A report-generating program, for example, could automatically load a file, calculate some numbers in it, save the result as a new file, copy the result into a master report, and print the report, all without your being around. Of course, using WPL creatively requires either a lot of practice or programming expertise. Unless you have lots of long, complex, and repetitive word-processing functions to perform, WPL may not be worth learning if you don't already have some programming experience or simply enjoy this sort of thing for its own sake.

Nevertheless, Apple Writer II or IIe is a very capable program on its own. It does some things a little more slowly than other programs (counting words in a document takes about five minutes), and at $195 it isn't the cheapest program on the block, but it's a good, solid choice.

PIE: Writer

This program has been a favorite of diehard Apple aficionados since 1980. It's not the friendliest program around, nor the easiest to learn, but for raw formatting, editing, and file-manipulation power at a reasonable price, it's hard to beat. PIE: Writer costs $149.95, but is frequently discounted below $100. It has been upgraded a few times since it was introduced, and a new version, due out in late 1984, will add still more features. Here's a preview of the newest release of PIE: Writer, Version 3.0: It is not copy protected, and it is available in either ProDOS or DOS 3.3 versions; it can be custom-configured for Apple II, II+, or IIe machines using either 40- or 80-column displays, or the UltraTerm expanded displays discussed later in this chapter; and it can use and create either text or binary-number data files.

PIE: Writer is what a friend of mine calls a "novice-hostile, expert-friendly program." It doesn't hold your hand with cute tutorials or detailed help menus or lots of screen prompting, so it's fairly difficult to learn (you should probably allow yourself a few weeks to adjust). Once you've learned PIE: Writer, though, you'll find it does things most other programs don't do: It lets you create double-width documents (for printing in 132-column formats). It offers split-screen editing, and it works with a spelling checker called The Speller that can be invoked directly from the editor and is the fastest spelling program around. (The Speller costs an extra $49.95.)

PIE: Writer's file-management and editing capabilities are particularly exciting. It uses a virtual memory technique (which means swapping portions of files from disk to memory, and back again) to let you create and edit files larger than available RAM space. It lets you append sections of documents to other files on disk, or bring disk files into a current document. It has a form-letter capability (but not as nice or as easy to use as Word Juggler's). It counts the words in a document, regardless of the file's length, in nothing flat. It searches and replaces both backward and forward, and moves around a file fairly quickly.

If you can live with some initial hostility then, PIE: Writer is about the most flexible word processor you can buy for the Apple II or II+ without resorting to a programming language, such as WPL, or a coprocessor board (in addition to your Apple's main processor) and a far more expensive program (WordStar, for example). Once you master an admittedly large number of control-key commands, you'll find PIE: Writer lets you get the copy out as quickly as any program, anywhere.

Format-II

This relative newcomer is notable for its ease of use and its dynamic formatting and form-letter capabilities. Format-II does away with format dot commands and most control-key commands by using separate text entry and formatting modes. Because most of the formatting is done in a separate mode, commands such as center, justify, and so forth are accomplished with single keystrokes, most of which are mnemonic. You should be using this program productively within half an hour at most. Format-II is not copy protected, and it retails for $150.

Format-II's form-letter capabilities start with the ability to create and store a card-file type of database, which can then be sorted by the program and merged with letters. The database entries can have up to 16 different "slots," or fields, for data, so you can have quite a variety of information in a given file. Format-II can sort on any field, and it uses conditional statements to let you merge specific data into individual letters. You need to use a separate diskette for the database file.

The big tradeoff with Format-II is in the way it handles files. A Format-II document consists of a series of one-page files linked together. When you want to move around a document, or do global searches, you have to save the page you're on and get the next page from disk. This shouldn't be a problem if you create short documents most of the time, but it could be tiresome otherwise.

Another potential drawback is the dual-mode feature that lets Format-II eliminate format dot commands. Dot commands may be hard to remember, but at least you can enter them as you enter text and can thus format and create your document at the same time. With Format-II, you have to switch back and forth between the editor and the formatter. It's only a matter of hitting the ESC key, but the routine can be a real disruption if you're used to a program that handles these functions in a single mode.

WordStar

The granddaddy of all microcomputer word-processing programs, WordStar has probably sold more Z-80 cards to enable Apple owners to use the CP/M operating system than any other package. For a long time, Apple owners have been made to feel that they weren't really serious about word processing unless they were using WordStar. Let's look at this old-timer against its newer competition.

The pluses about WordStar are its extensive formatting capabilities, dynamic formatting, help menus, and virtual memory system that lets you create and edit documents larger than available memory. These are nice features, but I submit that PIE: Writer has equal formatting capabilities, is certainly no more difficult to learn, also uses virtual memory, and costs one-third as much (not counting the Z-80 card). Apple Writer has equivalent help menus and comparable formatting power, and it is far easier to learn and use.

What about spelling checkers? WordStar's is optional. There's a new spelling checker for IBM machines (the spelling program requires 192K of RAM), but Apple owners are relegated to SpellStar, which is a slow and clumsy example of the genre. Word Juggler IIe, PIE: Writer, and doubtless a few other native-Apple programs also feature spelling checkers, most of them products of second- or third- (as opposed to first-) generation software design. The Word Juggler spelling checker is included with the program at no extra cost.

WordStar also has a form-letter option called MailMerge. This is an extra-cost option (one that, cleverly enough, is required if you want to chain files together for printing) and it doesn't offer as much flexibility as those for Word Juggler, Apple Writer, or Format-II.

WordStar has lots of immediate, on-line help. True enough, but the program is so large it doesn't all fit into the Apple's memory, which means the program is constantly going out to the disk drive when you perform different functions. This disk accessing makes WordStar slower in execution than any of the programs mentioned earlier. PIE: Writer, Word Juggler IIe, Apple Writer II, and AppleWorks all have on-line help, too; and none of them needs it as desperately as WordStar.

So, WordStar was once a lot more powerful than native Apple word-processing programs, but no more. It isn't easy to use, it isn't cheap, and it isn't fast. You can do at least as well for a lot less money, and without buying a Z-80 card. If you really want WordStar or use it a lot at the office, if you need a Z-80 card and CP/M for other applications, or if you can think of at least one other CP/M program you really want to use, then the added capabilities of the CP/M operating system and some of the specific coprocessor cards being offered today may make such a move worthwhile.

Spelling Checkers

In almost every case, people new to spelling-checking programs overestimate the programs' powers. We expect that, like some electronic

English teacher, a spelling checker will seek out and correct spelling errors we make, supplying the ability to spell words wherever we lack it. But in reality, a spelling checker can do only one thing: It can compare the words in a document with a collection of words (or word roots and suffixes) in a dictionary on a diskette. When it finds words that don't match anything in its dictionary, the spelling checker marks the word in context (in the text itself) or lists the word in a special place so you can isolate the errors easily. The more advanced spelling-checking programs will let you create your own dictionaries in addition to the program's main dictionary, so the program will be aware of words (computer terms, medical terms, and so forth) that are unique to your profession and that the program's general dictionary would normally not contain. In addition, the more advanced programs not only identify words that are not matched by dictionary entries, they will help you replace the misspellings with correctly spelled words and even suggest the correct spellings for you.

This is all fine as far as it goes, but remember that checking spelling isn't the same as making sure you've said what you wanted to say in a document. You could, for example, make a typing mistake and spell "it" as "at." The spelling program wouldn't catch such a mistake, since both words would be in its dictionary. On the other hand, a spelling checking program will almost always balk at proper names, addresses, and the like, so there will always be such "mistakes" in your documents, whether they really are mistakes or not.

Matching words in a document against words on a diskette is a time-consuming operation, and some spelling checkers take several minutes to scan a 20-page document. In an effort to speed things up, some software developers have filled their spelling dictionaries with roots and suffixes of words, instead of the words themselves. This lets them make smaller dictionaries, which reduces the scanning and matching time. The problem with this approach is that some combinations of roots and suffixes aren't correct. A system like this might scan a word like "spellation," for example, and not identify it as a mistake, because the word would be composed of a correct root (spell) and a correct suffix (-ation).

On the other hand, having the biggest dictionary of complete words on the block isn't the answer, either, because the more words to check against, the longer the checking takes. One compromise some developers make is to have one small dictionary composed of 1,000 to 2,000 of the most commonly used words, and then an auxiliary dictionary with 20,000 to 50,000 less common words. The program checks the whole document against the small dictionary within a minute or so, eliminating perhaps

90 percent of the text in the document by matching the common words, and then scans the remaining 10 percent of the document against the entries in the larger dictionary. With fewer words to scan against the big dictionary, the process goes much faster. And when it comes to spelling checkers, the name of the game is checking the most words in the least amount of time.

But even the best programs aren't perfect. No matter how large the dictionaries, these programs will always miss something, so you end up proofreading the document by yourself anyway. Nevertheless, spelling programs can catch a lot of errors you'd overlook even when proofreading yourself, and the best programs will suggest some possible alternative spellings of words for you, so you don't have to refer to a dictionary as often when you're stumped.

Some of the finest spelling programs around are available for the Apple. The two major programs that work with most word processors are The Speller and THE SENSIBLE SPELLER. In shopping for a spelling program, be sure your choice will work with your word processor (take your program into a store and try checking a document from it), and then look for speed of checking, ability to create personal dictionaries, and whether or not the program shows you the suspect words in context. It's also nice to have a program that you can invoke from within your word processor, but for the most part this limits you to combination packages, such as Word Juggler, or packages made by the same company, such as PIE: Writer and The Speller. You can spend anywhere from $50 to $150 for a spelling program.

KEYBOARDS

NOTE: *IIe owners can skip this section.*

By far the most serious hardware limitation of an original Apple II or II+ for word-processing applications is the keyboard. While it has its Shift and Return keys in the normal places, it doesn't allow you to use the Shift key to produce both upper- and lowercase letters. Depending on the software being used, this limitation requires some interesting contortions from those who want uppercase letters at the beginnings of sentences and proper names. In the original Apple Writer program, for example, you have to press the Escape key before typing the letter you want capitalized. The next letter is then capitalized, and the program returns you to lowercase mode.

Shift-Key Modification

The remedy to this situation is either to buy or make a Shift-key modifier, which installs a wire "jumper" in one of the Apple's keyboard input circuits and gives the Shift keys their traditional capabilities. You can make your own Shift-key modification with about two dollars' worth of wire and IC connectors (clips designed for easy connection to circuit boards) from a local electronics shop. There'll probably even be somebody there—or certainly at an Apple dealer where on-site repairs are done—who can show you just where the wire connectors go. If you're not the adventurous type, you can buy a plain Shift-key modifier from your local Apple dealer for about $12 to $15. These are very simple products, usually sold to dealers by local electronics firms or hobbyists, so don't expect fancy packaging or typeset instructions.

There are also deluxe Shift-key modifiers available from a couple of sources. Usually, you see these advertised in Apple-specific magazines for anywhere from $25 on up. Most of the lower-end models give you an auto-repeat function on each key without making you hold down the REPT key. The best known (and most expensive) of these products is the Videx Enhancer II. It retails for $149, but it does a good deal more than activate your Shift keys. It modifies the Shift keys for upper- and lowercase, and adds Caps Lock (which shifts letter keys only), Shift Lock (which shifts the entire keyboard), and auto-repeat capabilities to the keyboard as well. The auto-repeat function has two speeds, either 15 characters per second or 50 characters per second. To repeat characters at the slow speed, you just hold down the character key. The 50 cps repeat speed is activated when you hold down both the character key and the REPT key at the same time.

What is potentially the best feature of the Videx Enhancer II, though, is its 1K of built-in RAM that lets you store up to 510 characters' worth of keystrokes and their definitions. You can assign a definition—a command sequence, a string of text, or whatever—to an individual key or a combination of keys and then recall it by hitting the key, or keys, when you want to use it. For example, if you were writing a report about Chronifundabulistic Widgets and got sick of typing that name over and over, you could assign it to a combination of keys that wasn't being used by your word-processing program. Then, you could recall the name whenever you wanted to insert it in text, just by hitting those keys.

You can also buy an optional Function Strip from Videx that gives you an additional 16 keys to define. The strip sticks onto your keyboard above the number keys. The strip costs an extra $30 if you buy it with the Enhancer II.

The Enhancer and other keyboard-modification products have no effect on any software you might run, and they connect to the keyboard rather than using up an expansion slot. They are particular, however, about which version of the Apple II you install them in. The dozen or so versions of the Apple II main logic board, or motherboard, fall into two groups: revision numbers 0 through 6, and revisions 7 and up. To determine which revision of the motherboard your Apple contains, remove the lid (with the power off!) and look along the left side of the motherboard (that green, flat thing at the bottom with all the chips attached to it). In the left-hand row of chips, look for a socket named MEMORY SELECT next to a letter E. If your motherboard has this socket, you have a revision 6 or under. If, instead of this, you see a white rectangle with three holes in it, your Apple is in the revision 7-and-up group.

In addition to these differences, the Apple II and II+ keyboards came in two distinct varieties, one with a "piggyback" keyboard encoder board (a circuit board that tells the Apple's processor which key is being pressed) that was attached underneath the main keyboard unit, and one that was all in one piece. You can spot the encoder board easily if you look for it. If you have a piggyback-style keyboard and a revision 7 or greater Apple, you'll have no problem installing the Videx Enhancer II or other keyboard modifiers. If you have a one-piece keyboard and/or a revision 6 or lower Apple, your ability to install a store-bought keyboard modifier will depend on the brand, so be sure to check this out.

Detachable and Replacement Keyboards

Another complaint hurled at the Apple II in attempts to declare it unsuitable for word processing is that the keyboard isn't detachable. Somehow, detachable keyboards have come to represent the ultimate in computing comfort. We have visions of ourselves reclining on the patio with a keyboard, while the computer hums away inside at the other end of a 50-foot coiled cord. At first blush, the idea of typing from an easy chair seems terrific, but it has its drawbacks. One problem is that using a keyboard anywhere except on a properly elevated typing platform invariably forces you into an uncomfortable position: Your hands are either too high or too low, or your arms are too close together (because they're squeezed in an armchair, for example). Another problem may be that you're too far away from the screen to read what you're typing.

The primary purpose of a movable keyboard is to give you flexibility in relation to the display screen. Everyone's eyesight is different, and the distance from the display screen with which different people are most comfortable is bound to vary. Many computers built in the past few years are one-piece units that incorporate the keyboard and display in the same housing and thus make it impossible to vary the distance between the keyboard and screen. The Apple, however, is not one of them. You can (and should) place your Apple's monitor as far away from the keyboard unit as you need to for comfort. Don't be afraid to experiment with different distances.

Until 1984, Apple IIe Starter Systems were shipped with a stand designed to hold the monitor directly above the keyboard unit, but this stand should only be used if the location is comfortable for you. I like the monitor a little farther away and a few inches higher than the Apple-supplied stand puts it. At any rate, the Apple's design gives you all the flexibility you could want in terms of relative placement of the keyboard and the monitor, so there's really nothing to improve upon there.

The only other benefit to remote-control keyboarding is the ability to place the computer and disk drives completely off your work area. This makes a lot of sense if you need the extra desk space (and who doesn't?), but it may not be worth the trouble and expense. Aside from the cost of a replacement keyboard or detachment kit, you'll have to consider the inconvenience of having your disk drives anywhere outside of your immediate reach.

If you decide on a detached keyboard, however, those for the Apple come in two varieties: kits that allow you to remove your existing keyboard and put it in a more portable housing outside the processing unit, and replacement keyboards.

One widely advertised kit for placing your existing keyboard into a detachable unit is called a D-TACH. The D-TACH is nothing more than a lap-sized housing with a cutout that fits your keyboard. To install it, you remove the keyboard from your Apple, unplug its motherboard connection, bolt the keyboard into the D-TACH, and connect the 8-foot extension cord from the D-TACH housing to the keyboard plug inside the Apple. The D-TACH costs $99 and comes in a variety of woods and colored vinyl laminate. Models are available for either the II or IIe keyboard, and the unit also comes with an insert for the Apple to cover up the hole left by the keyboard. The conversion should take less than 20 minutes.

For Apple II or II+ owners, a more popular (though more expensive) way to get a detached keyboard is simply to add a different, external keyboard. The major manufacturer of such keyboards is Key Tronic, whose KB 200 keyboard (illustrated in Figure 2-2) for the Apple II/II+ offers features comparable to those of just about any computer keyboard. You get a standard typewriter layout, complete with working Shift keys and a CAPS LOCK key that lights when it's engaged. To the left of the alphanumeric keys are ten special function keys like those on an IBM PC keyboard, except that they're not user-definable. The functions are preset, and they give you single-key access to frequently used commands, such as booting a disk drive, loading a file, saving a file, deleting a file, deleting a line, and cataloging a diskette.

The right side of the keyboard features a numeric keypad with a standard 10-key layout plus a HOME key and an extra Control key. The left and right arrow keys are in a different location on this keyboard (in the top row) than they are on the normal Apple keyboard, but the 8, 6, 2, and 4 keys of the numeric keypad can also move the cursor up, right, down, and left respectively when used with the Control key. The KB 200 has no effect on the operation of your software or the rest of your hardware, other than making your built-in keyboard inactive.

The bottom line is that, for $298, you get a numeric keypad (which would cost at least $75 separately); a Shift-key modification with auto-repeat capability (another $35 or so); a detached keyboard with a 10-foot cable ($99 for the D-TACH kit); and a more spacious key layout with better keyboard feel, some function keys, and two LED indicators.

While $298 may seem like a lot of money, it's peanuts compared to switching computers. If your major word-processing complaint is the keyboard, this KB 200 is as good a keyboard as you'll find on any machine.

Figure 2-2
The Key Tronic KB 200 keyboard

Installation is clearly explained in the manual, and the process should take less than half an hour. Unfortunately for IIe users, the design of the IIe keyboard makes it highly unlikely that Key Tronic or anyone else will come up with a replacement keyboard for it.

DISPLAY ENHANCEMENT

NOTE: *IIe owners can skip the section on lowercase letters.*

One of the problems with enabling shifted letters on an Apple II is that the normal Apple 40-column display is incapable of showing the lowercase letters you long for. Most word-processing programs written for the 40-column display will show all the letters in capitals, and then differentiate the ones that are really capitals by displaying them in reverse video (dark on light, instead of light on dark). Thus, a normal screen of text will have a bunch of highlighted squares on it that represent capital letters. This can be a disappointing sight after you've gone to the trouble of modifying your Shift keys, but there are several solutions.

Lowercase Letters

If you really don't want an 80-column display, the least expensive way to display lowercase letters on your screen is to install a lowercase display chip. Many companies that produce 80-column display cards (and some that don't) sell such chips for $20 to $30. Installing them, however, brings us back to the question of the Apple II keyboard revisions. If your Apple is a revision 7 or higher, you can simply plug the chip into the keyboard circuit board. If your Apple uses the revision 6 or an earlier motherboard, you'll need an adapter that will cost an extra $20 or so. Installing either of these products is an easy matter that shouldn't take more than five minutes.

Eighty Columns and More

NOTE: *80-column display cards are discussed in considerable detail in Chapter 3; further information is available there.*

If you're doing word processing for business or other formal matters, an 80-column display is a must. You not only see more text on the screen, but with the right software you can see exactly what your text will look like on paper. Other benefits of 80-column displays can include denser, more readable characters and the ability to display lowercase characters (if your Apple II doesn't have a lowercase chip already installed).

Most Apple IIe systems include one of two 80-column Apple display cards. The basic Apple card displays 80 columns of characters, and the Extended 80-column card offers an additional 64K of RAM. These cards also have a built-in "soft switch" that automatically changes the display mode from 40 to 80 columns, depending on the demands of the software you're running.

The technical differences between the character display of the Apple card and competitive 80-column cards will be explained in Chapter 3, but some third-party cards are worth mentioning here, because they offer specific advantages for word processing.

The Videx VideoTerm card, the leader in the field, offers nearly 20 optional character-display sets. These sets include most European languages as well as special characters, such as mathematical symbols, super- and subscripts, underlined characters, and inverse (reverse video) characters. These options cost $29 each, but they're worth it, if you use special characters regularly and want to display them on the screen.

Videx also manufacturers an absolutely top-notch display card called UltraTerm, which can produce up to 128 clearly readable characters across the screen. Because the 128-column display of the UltraTerm is especially great for spreadsheets, we'll save the details for that chapter (Chapter 3). For now, it's enough to say that the UltraTerm has a word-processing mode of 80 columns by 48 lines, which allows you to see about a page and a half of text on the screen at once—very handy if you're moving blocks of text around. In order to fit so many lines on the screen, however, the letters in this mode are necessarily rather squatty. You should take a good look at this display mode in a store before deciding whether or not it's right for you.

If you decide to go with an UltraTerm, make sure your software and your display will support all of its features. Most word-processing software for the Apple now supports an 80 by 24 display, but you'll need special help to take advantage of the UltraTerm's expanded, 48-line mode. Videx offers pre-boot software (an extra disk that you load before you load the actual program) for Apple Writer II, and you can (or will soon be able to) configure PIE: Writer, Word Juggler IIe, Magic Window II, and WordStar (used with a Z-80 coprocessor card) to use the UltraTerm's expanded display features.

BETTER STORAGE

If you do a lot of word processing, particularly with large documents, there inevitably comes a time when you long for better storage. The key issues here are disk capacity and access time: Either you get sick of swapping data diskettes in and out of the Apple's 143K drive, or you wish it didn't take so long to get data to and from disks. This second problem is particularly acute if your word-processing program uses a virtual memory technique, or if its working-text buffer—the holding area it sets aside for work-in-progress—is so small that long documents must span several files, so that you must load and save portions of the document constantly. You'll also notice access times more if the program you use doesn't fit completely into RAM, and has to go out to disk a lot to fetch instructions when you perform various functions.

One solution to this storage problem is free: Slow down a little. We all get used to having things happen so quickly with computers that we grow ever more impatient at even the slightest delay. Once, we were awestruck to see that modifying a file and saving it to disk eliminated hours of retyping. Now, we're in agony because the saving operation takes 20 or 30 seconds. Really, now. Why not take advantage of the break? A growing body of research suggests that such mini-breaks during long bouts of computing actually improve our productivity more than does finding ways to make interaction with a computer faster and more continuous.

But even if you're not having any of this psychological mumbo-jumbo, there are two big, hard-nosed reasons to consider leaving your storage system the way it is. They're spelled M-O-N-E-Y and T-I-M-E. Any improvement in the access time or capacity of your storage is going to cost you—either money for new disk drives or time to adjust to a new operating system, or both. So think before you leap. If you're running a word-processing service, or you're a journalist, or you otherwise have lots of related files you'd like to get at more quickly, maybe the switch is worth it. But getting a new $500 disk drive just because you have to swap floppies once a day, or because you'd like your letter to Uncle Ned to load in 5 seconds instead of 30, is about like using a sledgehammer to hit an elevator button.

ProDOS

One potentially hassle-free way to speed file-loading time greatly is to convert to the ProDOS operating system. This means getting a new word-processing program that runs under ProDOS, but ProDOS loads and saves files an average of six times faster than DOS 3.3. As this newer operating system gains in currency among existing Apple users, most software companies are releasing ProDOS versions of their programs. So, it's quite possible you could go over to ProDOS without having to learn a whole new way of word processing. On the other hand, switching to ProDOS might be just the excuse you need to get a spiffy new program with features you've been longing for.

The other nice thing about ProDOS is that it handles storage devices much more flexibly than DOS 3.3. DOS 3.3 will normally recognize only the 143K Apple Disk II as a disk storage device. ProDOS, on the other hand, recognizes disk drives that hold up to 32 megabytes.

High-Capacity Disk Drives and Diskettes

NOTE: *Hard disks are discussed in detail in Chapters 4 and 5.*

When it comes to extra storage, people usually think "hard disk" exclusively, but I like larger-capacity floppies for word processing. Floppies are easier to back up than hard disks are, and while the average access time with hard disks is only a tenth that of floppy disks, the latter are more rugged and less prone to failure. There's also something to be said for storing information in smaller chunks—it's that much less trouble to replace it, if a diskette dies on you. Besides, with word processing, the amount of information you need on hand at one time is not nearly large enough to require the capacity of a hard disk. Sure, you may get sick of swapping diskettes with 143K drives, because they only hold about 70 double-spaced pages of text, but a double-sided, 80-track floppy drive, such as the Rana Elite Three, will store over 300 similar pages—enough for a whole novel.

Extra-capacity floppy disk drives have been available for the Apple II since about 1979, and now companies such as Rana, Vista, and Microsci offer single- and double-sided floppy disk drives with capacities of up to 2.5 megabytes per diskette. If your word-processing program uses ProDOS, you'll have no problem accessing the extra capacity of a new, larger drive. If you're still using DOS 3.3, you'll have to consider the matter more closely.

Since standard DOS 3.3 only recognizes 143K drives, your DOS has to be modified to take advantage of more disk space. Standard Apple disk drives read and store information on 35 circular tracks on one side of the diskette; high-capacity drives use a 40- or 80-track format on one or both sides of the diskette. To educate DOS 3.3 about this new format, the makers of high-capacity disk drives supply DOS-enhancement programs (or their own complete versions of enhanced DOS). You have to substitute this new version for DOS 3.3 by copying your application program onto a new diskette containing the enhanced DOS.

The problem is that some of the most popular commercial Apple programs that run under DOS 3.3 (including Apple Writer II) are copy protected. You can't copy them, and if you can't copy the programs, you can't install them on disks with the enhanced DOS, so you can't access higher-capacity disk drives. Thanks to this copy-protection tradition among software companies, higher-capacity disk drives will only be of use under DOS 3.3 if you're using unprotected software. PIE: Writer and Format-II are both unprotected, as are some other programs.

The process for modifying DOS 3.3 and installing the program on the new disk is fairly arduous, but once you've done it, you can use the new drives normally from then on. Since the DOS version is the determining factor, the new drives will give extended capacity to modified-DOS programs, and still work like the old Disk II drives when you use protected programs. The only format conflicts you'll have will be when you try to use a high-capacity diskette in your old Disk II drive or if you try to use a program that can't access the greater diskette density—but you know better than that.

If all of this seems daunting, you would do well to consider using a ProDOS application program with new disk drives. The makers of high-capacity disk drives are all redesigning their disk-controller cards to work seamlessly with ProDOS. (Oops! What's a disk-controller card? It's a little circuit board that fits inside your Apple and, as the name implies, controls the disk drive.)

With a new controller and disk drive, your ProDOS application program will automatically determine the capacity of the disk drive and adjust itself accordingly—there's no work to be done on your part. Unfortunately, Apple Computer doesn't make high-capacity disk drives, and therefore isn't reworking its controller. So you'll have to buy a new controller, for about $75, as well as a disk drive. You can't run a new drive off your old Apple controller.

Higher-capacity drives come in several sizes and various prices, but any of them will deliver more kilobytes of storage for your dollar. Apple's new DuoDisk gives you two 143K drives (a total of 286K of storage) for $795. Rana's Elite Three, which is illustrated in Figure 2-3, crams 652K of information onto a double-sided diskette. The Elite Three retails for $649 without a controller and $749 with a controller, but if you shop around, you can frequently find it discounted well below that price. The only thing to watch for in a replacement drive is a drive that seems too cheap. Some Apple-compatible disk drives sell for as little as $125, but if you pay that little, you'll probably regret it.

Along with the higher capacity, you also get advanced drive technology in some third-party drives. One improvement, for example, is the use of metal band positioners (the band positioner controls the location of the disk drive head as it searches across the disk) instead of the plastic one in Apple's Disk II. The use of metal provides greater reliability, longer drive life, and more accurate positioning of the read/write head.

Many replacement drives are also half-height—half the height of standard disk drives—and thus can save some space on your desk. Some drive makers, such as Rana and Indus, offer write-protect switches on their drives, so you can write-protect diskettes with the touch of a button, instead of using those sticky paper tabs.

Figure 2-3
Rana's Elite Three high-capacity disk drive

PRINTING

Printer output is one element of word processing in which a surprisingly small amount of money can make a big difference in performance. One refreshing aspect of the output situation with Apples is that it's really no different from the situation with any other computer—the problems are printing speed and quality, and they apply to microcomputers across the board. Of the two problems, printing speed is more acute, because it applies to any printer on the market. Your Apple ships data to your printer at 9600 bits—about 1200 characters—per second. But the fastest printer you can normally connect to a microcomputer chugs along at no more than 200 characters per second. Since the printer is the slowest part of the output chain, it forces the computer to wait, holding back and feeding the output ever-so-slowly to the printer. Of course, while the computer is waiting, you're waiting.

Buffers

In terms of dollars-spent versus performance-improved, printer buffers are one of the best personal computer buys around these days. A printer buffer is simply some extra RAM, dedicated to the printer, into which your computer dumps its data. Once the computer's RAM is free of the data, you're free for more computing, while the printer takes the slow feed from the buffer's RAM.

Buffers range in price from $125 to about $350, depending on RAM size and other features. Whichever one you choose, a buffer will be a lot cheaper than getting a faster printer, and it will greatly increase the useful computing time your Apple can deliver. There are two kinds of buffer for Apples: internal, which consists of RAM on a card that plugs inside the computer, or external, which is RAM in a box that sits outside the computer. The price is about the same for either kind. You get more data-handling flexibility with an internal buffer, but at the expense of non-transportability.

Internal buffers such as the Buffered Grappler+ from Orange Micro, the Microbuffer II from Practical Peripherals, and the P/S Buffer Card from Prometheus Products, all combine serial (bit-by-bit) or parallel (byte-by-byte) interfaces (or both, in some cases) along with anywhere from 16K to 64K or RAM buffer. This combination gives you a printer interface, plus a printer buffer, on one card in one Apple expansion slot—a nice saving of space.

External buffers, such as the Microbuffer In-Line from Practical Peripherals, illustrated in Figure 2-4, sit outside your computer, between it and the printer. An external buffer doesn't include an interface, but if you should ever switch computers, an external buffer can make the switch with you.

The memory in almost all buffers sold these days is expandable, so you can get into the game fairly cheaply with a 16K buffer and then upgrade it to 32K, 48K, or 64K as your pocketbook permits.

Some other nice features of buffers include their ability to make extra copies of a document, so that you can make multiple printouts while continuing to use your computer for other tasks. Some buffers will also accept incoming, as well as outgoing data, and this lets you receive modem transmissions more quickly, and thus more inexpensively than processing the data through your computer alone (more on this in Chapter 6).

Figure 2-4
The Microbuffer In-Line printer buffer

One unpleasant side effect of buffered printing is that having the printer going while you're trying to do something else can be a nerve-wracking experience. Most printers make so much noise that it's difficult to think at all while they're running, let alone concentrate on another computer project. To solve this problem, you can either buy or build a sound-damping enclosure for your existing printer, or move up to a quieter model.

Printers

Printer technology has improved so much in the past few years that it's a safe bet your printer is no longer state-of-the-art. Chances are, when you bought your system you faced the agonizing decision of either going with a slow daisy-wheel printer for highest print quality (in which case you really need a buffer now), or settling for lower quality on a faster dot-matrix printer. Some striking advances have been made that give you more maneuvering room in this area today.

Dot-matrix printers, oncc thc laughable trademark of personal computer output, now offer far higher quality than they once did. Such products as the Texas Instruments TI-855 and the Toshiba P-1351 offer correspondence-quality printing modes that are practically indistinguishable from daisy-wheel print, and they churn that print out at speeds up to 100 characters per second (cps). These printers give you the dot-matrix technology you need to do graphics or get very fast draft printouts (up to 200 cps), and they offer half-speed, high-quality printing that doesn't embarrass you in front of business contacts.

The Texas Instruments printer retails for just under $1000—considerably more than most other dot-matrix printers, but its quality is really superb. An added feature of the TI-855 is its plug-in typefaces. There are about a dozen different typefaces, each costing $30. These typefaces are stored on ROM cartridges, and three can be on-line in the printer at any time, so you can print documents that contain both roman and italic type without bringing everything to a halt while you change a daisy wheel.

Thermal transfer printers also offer good print quality, excellent speed, and somewhat quieter operation, but so far for a higher cost per printed page. These printers use heated printheads to liquefy the ink on special ribbons. This technique differs from prior thermal technology, in which a heated printhead changed the color of specially coated paper. Thermal transfer printers will print on regular paper. When the ink from the ribbon is liquefied, it soaks into the paper, thereby filling in the dots from the printhead matrix and creating fully formed characters. The single-use ribbons don't last as long as regular ribbons, though, so while they cost about the same as nylon ribbons for regular dot-matrix machines, you have to buy more of them. Apple's Scribe printer is an inexpensive thermal transfer printer. It retails for $299 and will print in either black or multiple colors, depending on the ribbon you use.

Ink-jet printers were once hailed as the saviors of personal computer printing, but while they offer good speed and extremely quiet operation, the quality of their print is still no match for that of daisy wheels or the best dot-matrix printers. The prices of ink-jet printers have come down a lot in the past year, and the quality is improving. Hewlett-Packard's ThinkJet, for example, is $495 and produces print similar to an Epson's correspondence mode. For now, ink-jet printers are good if you're doing a lot of graphics, don't need absolute letter-quality output, and want to be able to carry on a normal conversation while the printer is running. The main advantage of ink-jet printers is their almost noiseless operation, but the print quality should see some dramatic improvements shortly.

Daisy-wheel printers have also dropped quite a bit in price—they're now as low as $500—but I suspect that better dot-matrix and thermal transfer machines will eventually eliminate them from the scene. Daisy-wheel printers are comparatively slow, incapable of producing graphics, and less reliable than dot-matrix printers are. Still, if you already have a dot-matrix printer and want to print letter quality occasionally, you can pick up a 15 cps daisy-wheel printer for about $600 and alternate between the two printers.

SHOWCASE SYSTEMS

I'll leave the choice of word-processing software to you (heaven knows there's plenty of it to choose from), and confine the sample showcase systems for this chapter to hardware enhancements.

APPLE II/II+

Apple II/II+	Currently Owned
Key Tronic KB 200 keyboard	$ 298
Videx UltraTerm	$ 379
Rana Elite Three Plus with controller	$ 749
Microbuffer II+ (16K version)	$ 259
Total Extras	$1685

Added Power: Upgraded, detachable keyboard with upper-/lowercase and numeric keypad; 48-line, 80-column display; 652K floppy disk drive; expandable internal printer buffer with built-in serial (or parallel) port.

APPLE IIe *(including 80-column card)*

Apple IIe	Currently Owned
D-TACH keyboard detacher	$ 99
TI-855 printer	$ 995
Microbuffer/E	$ 159
Total Extras	$1253

Added Power: Detached keyboard; letter-quality, high-speed printer; internal printer buffer.

C H A P T E R

3

SUPERIOR SPREADSHEETS

To anyone whose business involves working with numbers, a spreadsheet program is invaluable. "How much money do I have coming in? How much do I have going out? Where is it all going, and what would happen if . . . ?" Those are the kinds of questions a spreadsheet program helps you answer —quickly, cleanly, and without sheet after sheet of ledger paper and roll upon roll of calculator tape.

VisiCalc was the first spreadsheet program to become available. In fact, it was the fuel in the personal computing rocket, and for nearly a year after VisiCalc's introduction in May, 1979, the only rocket in town was an Apple II. The story goes that Dan Bricklin and Bob Frankston, the creators of VisiCalc, needed a loaner computer upon which to run their program. They borrowed an Apple. And so it came to pass that business people, accountants, educators, financiers, and investors everywhere saw VisiCalc, found it good, and bought Apples.

Until VisiCalc was overtaken by second- and third-generation products (Multiplan in 1982 and Lotus 1-2-3 in 1983), it was the best-selling spreadsheet program. VisiCalc is still in wide use today, and since it is such an important part of the Apple world, it will more or less form the "backbone" of this chapter.

If you are one of the hundreds of thousands of VisiCalc owners, you have a product that was truly revolutionary in its time, but might now be a bit dated. Its standard display, designed for a 40-column Apple II, will show you only four spreadsheet columns at a time. While VisiCalc has a theoretical maximum model (spreadsheet) size of more than 16,000 cells, the actual model size is dictated by the amount of RAM available; on a 64K Apple, that's 34K, or about 1000 cells. Once you become familiar with VisiCalc and begin creating larger and more sophisticated models, that 1000-cell limit can become a problem. For some people, it's like having a four-function calculator on which only the addition function is working. In certain situations, the size limitation can even be embarassing.

1-2-3, IS IT FOR ME?

Say you've happily been using VisiCalc at the office for four years now, but the upstart next door has just gotten herself an IBM PC. She's loaded it up with 512K of RAM, learned Lotus 1-2-3, and is now creating monster spreadsheets that seem to recalculate in nothing flat. When she forgets a command, she has immediate help at the touch of a key, and she can whip out a nicely colored pie chart in a couple of minutes.

Everywhere you turn, it's IBM and Lotus, IBM and Lotus. You recognize a preponderance of Lotus spreadsheets turning up at the departmental meetings. You envy your competitor's IBM keyboard with its numeric keypad. You lust after that IBM display that shows eight columns instead of a measly four. You feel your once-keen analytical edge slipping, slipping....

You wake up from this nightmare in a cold sweat, determined to cashier the old Apple and switch over to the enemy camp. Maybe, you think, you could take out a second mortgage to pay for a new PC. Maybe you could get a leave of absence from work to spend a few weeks learning Lotus and transferring all your files to the IBM format. It all seems so drastic. Isn't there another way out?

Yes. There are lots of ways out. Which one you choose will depend on the kind of spreadsheeting you do.

WHAT DO YOU NEED?

What sort of spreadsheeting do you do, anyway? It's true that an Apple running VisiCalc with the standard 64K of RAM will only accommodate models of about a thousand cells, but maybe that's all you need. Maybe the Lotus-lover in the office next door builds monster worksheets because she's doing the whole division's budget projections for the next five years, and the budget has 700 line items. Imagine trying to remember which part of the spreadsheet contains the paper-clip projection for March, 1987.

And what about the time it takes to load and save files? The bigger the model, the longer this takes. Maybe you see her cranking out the graphics because the marketing people have found out she has Lotus and a three-pen plotter and she's a lot quicker than the art department. This is something you're actually yearning for? The point is that everyone does different things with spreadsheet programs, and everyone doesn't need 1-2-3. Look before you lust, and don't fix things that aren't broken.

On the other hand, maybe your standard Apple really is cramping your style. As you've become a master model-builder, you've come to yearn for more RAM and bigger worksheets. You'd like to see more of the sheet on the screen at once. You'd like things to recalculate faster. You'd rather enter data with a numeric keypad, which you know by touch, than have to look at the number keys atop your Apple keyboard.

SOFTWARE PROBLEMS

The first thing to do is look at your software and how you use it. Are you really making the best use of it? It's amazing how many VisiCalc users are disgusted by the slowness of data entry for years, only to discover one day that they can turn off the program's automatic recalculation mode and speed things up tremendously. People in this boat can clear up a major problem with one little command, but they'll never learn that command unless some angel rides to the rescue or they read the manual more thoroughly. If you have a specific complaint about recalculation speed, data flow, or an apparent lack of other functionality, the best place to start looking is the user's manual.

Improving your skills with a product you already know is infinitely less disruptive (not to mention less expensive) than starting all over again with a new product. The standard VisiCalc manual is an excellent and well-written guide, and there are dozens of tutorial books on the market to provide additional help. Specific problems with VisiCalc or other spreadsheets can also be cleared up by a local expert—doubtless a resident of the nearest computer store, or perhaps as close as the office down the hall.

But suppose you're really up against the limits of the program. You want variable column widths, or the ability to name cells, or other advanced features. If so, you're in the market for new software. The easiest way to handle this is to get another product that runs on your unvarnished Apple, just as your old program did. You'll also want to make sure the new program can read your old spreadsheet files, so you can transfer your data. This is generally not a problem. Beyond this, you should check out products that feature improved capabilities in the areas where you need them.

More Functions, Bigger Models

Microsoft's Multiplan is a cut above VisiCalc in the features department, and it offers a kind of solution to the size problem. Multiplan has better formatting capabilities, with features such as centering numbers in columns, and varying individual column widths. It lets you name cells and then refer to the names instead of the cell locations in formulas. It can also sort entries in columns, and this ability is particularly nice if you use a spreadsheet for keeping personal records. If you use VisiCalc's windowing feature a lot to view different parts of a worksheet, you'll love Multiplan, because you can have up to eight windows on the screen at once instead of VisiCalc's two. Multiplan also gives you an on-line help facility that describes major program commands.

Multiplan's solution to memory limitations is sheet linking. You can create links between cells or areas on an originating spreadsheet and a destination spreadsheet. When you load the destination spreadsheet,

Multiplan automatically goes out to the disk, finds the originating spreadsheet, and copies the values from the linked cells. You can have several supporting worksheets for the final sheet.

With Multiplan, instead of using 1-2-3 to create a monstrous budget, for example, you could create several smaller categorized budgets and transfer the bottom line of each to a consolidated summary sheet that showed only the totals. Because they would be smaller, the individual sheets would be easier to move around in, and through linking, the consolidation sheet would automatically be updated every time you loaded it.

The major difference in Multiplan is that it uses menu-selected commands, instead of VisiCalc's slash commands. If you are used to VisiCalc, Multiplan's row and column designations and formula building are different enough from VisiCalc's to make it a little hard to get used to. The DOS 3.3 version of Multiplan can recognize up to 128K of RAM, so it will take advantage of extra RAM you might add to your Apple, but not as much as other products will.

MAGICALC, from Artsci, is an easier spreadsheet to move up to from VisiCalc, because it has slash commands similar to VisiCalc's, and it uses very similar formula-building techniques. MAGICALC breaks major spreadsheet functions, such as data entry and calculation, file management, and formatting, into separate modules you select from a menu; but since you're doing mostly data entry and calculation, this modularity doesn't slow you down too much.

One plus you'll notice right away with MAGICALC is that it can display up to 70 characters across a normal Apple screen, giving you six spreadsheet columns on the screen at once, instead of VisiCalc's four, without the need for you to buy an 80-column display card. MAGICALC can also access up to 512K of RAM, or twice as much as VisiCalc can handle. Other advantages include variable column widths and individually protected cells.

ProDOS

A software-related solution of another kind is Apple's enhanced ProDOS operating system. Most popular Apple spreadsheet programs are now or soon will be available in ProDOS versions. While the spreadsheet software itself may or may not be the same as it was under DOS 3.3, the way the program uses memory and loads files will be greatly improved. An Apple with ProDOS loads and saves files about six times faster than it does with DOS 3.3, so you'll spend a lot less time waiting to get large models off a disk.

But the best thing about ProDOS is the way it handles memory and storage devices. ProDOS has the ability to detect the amount of RAM available on any given Apple, and to access that RAM accordingly. Software developers will have to modify their programs specifically to take advantage of this feature when they convert their existing software to ProDOS, but since spreadsheets are so memory-intensive, any ProDOS spreadsheet program you buy should give you automatic access to memory expansion cards. VisiCorp's new FlashCalc, for example, is a ProDOS program that will access up to 512K of RAM automatically.

The ability of ProDOS to detect and access extra storage isn't limited to RAM, though. If you buy a high-capacity floppy disk drive or a hard disk that supports it, ProDOS will allow you to take full advantage of the extra storage space automatically. (See Chapters 2 and 4 for more details on high-capacity floppy and hard disk drives.)

Since March of 1984, ProDOS has been the standard operating system shipped with new computers in the Apple II series. If you own an older Apple, you should be able to get ProDOS for a nominal charge.

HOPPED-UP HARDWARE

Despite the fact that most people don't need it, the ability to create larger spreadsheet models is the thing many Apple users crave most. This is such a common complaint that a whole mini-industry has grown up around finding ways to enable people to create larger spreadsheet models on the Apple II. If you really want to build bigger models and have them all in RAM at once, you'll have to add more RAM.

A Little History

VisiCalc was designed to run on a 48K Apple II, which was the biggest standard Apple in 1979. If you bought an extra 16K of RAM on an Apple Language Card, you could bring the total up to 64K, and VisiCalc would use this extra memory, but nobody was really thinking beyond this limit in 1979.

Since many "typical" spreadsheets (say, 20 columns by 50 rows) fit into somewhere between 64K and 128K of RAM, many VisiCalc users were soon bumping up against the 64K limit, and the third-party people began thinking of ways around it. They discovered that the Apple II treated its memory as one 48K chunk and—if you had the optional Language Card—one 16K chunk. VisiCalc fits neatly into the main 48K chunk with room to spare, so it used part of this main bank of memory and most of the 16K bank for storing your data. It was on this second, 16K bank that the developers concentrated.

The Apple's processor can only recognize 64K of RAM at any one time, but that didn't stop developers from figuring out how to swap the first 16K bank with other 16K banks. You could thus have part of a spreadsheet stored in the original 16K bank, and other parts of it stored in other 16K banks, and simply swap the bank containing the part of the model you needed in and out of action when you needed it. Since the switch occurred at electronic speeds, you would never even know it was happening.

Working this magic was simply a matter of teaching the spreadsheet program to look for alternative 16K banks in which to store data, and then building add-in memory (add-RAM) boards that contained the extra RAM. (NOTE: The Apple IIe doesn't have this 48/16K RAM division; it switches RAM in banks of 64K, but otherwise operates in the same way.)

Adding RAM

The following discussion of RAM assumes you have a 64K Apple (either a IIe or a II or II+ with the 16K Language Card installed). If you have a 48K Apple, getting a Language Card will be your first step. The Apple's memory-management system allows for the use of several megabytes of RAM via this bank-switching technique, so any limitations will more likely come from the software you're using and the depth of your pockets.

Different spreadsheet programs use memory in different ways, and some have lower limits on the use of extra RAM than others. Multiplan will normally access models fitting into up to 128K of RAM; VisiCalc will let you build models up to about 220K in size; MAGICALC, FlashCalc, and a product from Videx called UltraPlan, will access up to 512K of RAM. MAGICALC, FlashCalc, and UltraPlan will access additional RAM without modification. If you're using VisiCalc or Multiplan with DOS 3.3 (rather than ProDOS), you have to start up with an additional software disk, called pre-boot software, that "teaches" these programs how to use the extra RAM and lets them know it's there to be used.

Some add-RAM boards come with pre-boot software included. Other manufacturers sell the software separately for as much as $100.

Almost all pre-boot software disks contain the pre-boot "teaching" program, as well as extra, built-in programs that let your Apple use the extra RAM in other ways or that otherwise improve your computer's performance. Some of these extra programs, for example, let you save models larger than 143K (the maximum space on a standard Apple diskette) by watching for the disk to fill up and then prompting you to insert a new data disk before the saving operation continues. Others let you save and load spreadsheet files in as little as 20 seconds.

Some of this latter, fast-loading software, however, only works when you're loading or saving the contents of an entire disk, so you can't have any other files on the disk with your model. Loading a whole disk at a time is faster than finding and reading a specific file off a disk, though, especially when it's done in 20 seconds or less.

In attempts to make all that extra RAM useful for more than spreadsheets, add-RAM manufacturers also include what's called RAM-disk software in their offerings. This software fools DOS 3.3 into treating the extra RAM as another disk drive. When used as a RAM-disk, or psuedodisk, the extra RAM can store one or more data files and give you very fast access to them. Instead of having to go out to the disk drive, spin the disk, find the data, read it, and bring it back, your Apple can find a file and get it from a RAM-disk at electronic speeds—which, to you and me, means almost instantaneously. RAM-disks are very useful for applications that require a lot of sorting or switching from one file to another. Many ProDOS applications have housekeeping programs, called utilities, that let you use a RAM-disk simply by specifying one as a storage option.

Titan Technologies (formerly Saturn Systems), whose 128K RAM board is shown in Figure 3-1, and Legend Industries were the first companies to offer RAM boards and VisiCalc pre-boot software, in 1981. Since then, several other companies have gotten into the business; other major names are Quadram and Omega Microware. Add-RAM cards are available in sizes from 16K to 256K, and range in price from $100 to $700. These cards are frequently discounted up to 50 percent, particularly if purchased by mail order.

Obviously, though, at about $4 per 1000 bytes of storage, you're going to want to think hard about exactly how much RAM you'll need, or whether you really need it at all. Here are the major points in summary:

The Good News: You get the ability to build larger spreadsheet models all in RAM, with the attendant improvements in speed of recalculation and simply in moving from one area of the sheet to another. The

Figure 3-1
The 128K Saturn RAM board

other bonus is being able to use a RAM-disk with other applications. Extra RAM, by itself, won't have any negative effect on your other software or the rest of your computer, except for occupying one or more of the Apple's internal expansion slots (depending on how many additional boards you buy).

The Bad News: Depending on the spreadsheet program you're using (and whether or not it runs with ProDOS), you may need to use pre-boot software. With VisiCalc, for example, you would load the pre-boot software, and then remove that diskette and load your VisiCalc program. With Multiplan, you would actually need to boot *three* diskettes to make use of extra RAM, because Multiplan's copy-protection scheme involves the use of a system diskette that must be loaded before you can load the actual program.

Many hardcore spreadsheeters are happily using pre-boot software and not minding the extra disk-loading. Whether or not you'll mind it depends on how much you use your spreadsheet. If you use the program for long periods of time, the pre-boot procedure won't be too bothersome. But if you switch back and forth between a spreadsheet and other applications all day, the whole process could get old fast. You know your requirements best. You be the judge.

DISPLAY ENHANCEMENTS

In 1979, as business applications such as spreadsheets and word processors became available for the Apple II, people began to want a display that showed more than 40 characters on a line. Radio Shack and

Commodore were expanding the display capabilities of their products, but Apple had its hands full just making enough computers and disk drives to go around. The market was wide open for the first major hardware enhancement product for the Apple II: the 80-column video display card. The first product to fill this golden void was the Sup 'R' Term card from M&R Enterprises in 1980. Sup 'R' Term was followed within weeks by the VideoTerm card from Videx, which has since captured the lion's share of the 80-column card business in a field of perhaps a dozen competitors.

When it introduced the Apple IIe in January 1983, Apple began offering its own 80-column display cards: one with display only, and another with display and an additional 64K of RAM. Most IIe systems have one or the other of the Apple cards, because they are usually bundled in with the systems when they are sold. But the cards fit a special slot that exists only in the IIe—Apple II or II+ owners must go to other vendors for bigger displays.

The 80-Column Derby

These days, third-party manufacturers of 80-column cards either scramble for the remaining II or II+ owners who have yet to upgrade their displays, or they compete with Apple for the IIe business, by offering lower prices or more features. If you don't yet have an 80-column display card, there are a lot of different sources and a lot of different prices to choose from. If you already have an 80-column card, you might want to read on anyway. You may find reasons to make a switch.

The obvious advantage of creating a spreadsheet on an 80-column display is that you can see more on the screen at one time. You not only see more columns across the spreadsheet, you can see more of what you're typing in. The latter is particularly important when you're entering long formulas. It's frustrating to see only part of a formula on the screen, and often, writing the whole formula down on paper is the only way to make sure you haven't made a mistake. If you are using an Apple II or II+, an 80-column card will also enable your computer to display lowercase letters for the first time.

It would be nice if you could simply plug in an 80-column card and get an instant, 80-column display with every software package you use, but this isn't the case. As with RAM cards, your programs must be made aware of the 80-column card and must know how to take advantage of it. In the early 80-column days, no one was writing software that used an 80-column display, because the standard was 40 columns. Now, most software supports both display widths, and generally, when you first run a program, it asks how you'd like everything displayed. You make the choice once, and the program knows from then on how to display itself and your data.

Unfortunately (if you are a VisiCalc owner) VisiCalc is one spreadsheet program that doesn't support an 80-column display. VisiCalc simply assumes you want a 40-column display and leaves it at that. But again, just as with RAM cards, you can use pre-boot software that tells VisiCalc to take advantage of an 80-column display card. In fact, the same pre-boot software sold for RAM cards from Legend, Titan, and Omega Microware enables you to use both the extra RAM and an 80-column display. You can also get combined VisiCalc display/RAM pre-boot software from Videx.

It's nice to have an 80-column display card for most applications, and while there may be some programs—children's educational software, perhaps—with which you'll want to use the Apple's 40-column display, it's better to have a choice. Several different companies offer 80-column display cards, at prices ranging from about $150 to $300. In some cases, you can find these prices discounted by up to 50 percent. What you get for different prices are varying levels of quality, performance, and support.

Videx's VideoTerm card is considered to be the industry standard. When other manufacturers boast about their cards, they say, "It's Videx compatible." Here's what they mean: Not all video cards handle character display in the same way, so software manufacturers must have a certain type of display card in mind when designing their programs. Software companies generally support from three to five different cards, and because Videx's is the best-known card, software manufacturers that offer 80-column display options always support the Videx card. They guarantee that their software will work fine with a VideoTerm. Naturally, you're a lot better off if your card is one of the more popular ones, but you'll probably pay a little more for a popular card than for a lesser-known one.

There's also the question of quality to consider when choosing an 80-column display card. A bad batch of chips or a design flaw could result in intermittent flickering or an inability to display characters as quickly as you'd like. Videx, M&R, Titan, ALS (Advanced Logic Systems), and other major manufacturers (see the Appendix for more) have been around a long time and stand behind their products. Whatever bugs the products once had have long since been ironed out, and you can trust such companies to support you if something does go wrong.

If you own a IIe, there's a special auxiliary slot into which Apple's own 80-column card fits, leaving the other seven expansion slots free. Some manufacturers (Titan's Neptune cards come to mind) make special versions of their cards that also fit the IIe's auxiliary slot, so you can keep all the regular slots available with these cards, as well. Many third-party, 80-column cards, however, will fit only in one of the seven regular slots, in effect making you use two slots to get an 80-column display: The auxiliary slot won't hold anything other than a display card, so you have to use a regular slot to get the display you want.

If you're planning to use a lot of other cards for printers, modem boards, sound synthesizers, graphics boards—the list is quite long—you'll want to consider a display card that helps you economize on your use of the regular slots.

The characters themselves

One consideration in choosing an 80-column card is the size and density of the characters displayed. A computer displays a character by lighting small dots, or pixels, in a certain pattern on the screen. Each character is formed within a predetermined area, or matrix, so many dots high and so many dots wide, as you can see in Figure 3-2. For example, the 80-column card Apple makes for the IIe produces a character within a matrix 5 dots wide by 8 dots high. This matrix size produces characters that appear to be made of alternating rows of green and black horizontal lines. The descenders (tails) on letters such as j, y, and g are short, because the matrix isn't very tall.

Better display cards have 7 by 9, 8 by 9, 9 by 10, or 8 by 11 matrices. The more dots there are in the matrix horizontally, the fatter the characters appear. With more dots in the matrix vertically, the black horizontal lines appear thinner in comparison with the thickened green horizontal lines, and the descenders on certain letters are longer and more natural-looking. If two characters are the same size, the one made with the denser dot matrix is easier to read, so check to see what size the matrix is when you shop for a card.

Yet another feature you can look for in a video card is the ability to change the way characters are displayed. Many cards display only one type of character, but others have three or four different character sizes, densities, or intensities that you can select. Some cards will generate inverse characters, while others won't. If you want any of these special attributes in a card, be sure to look for them.

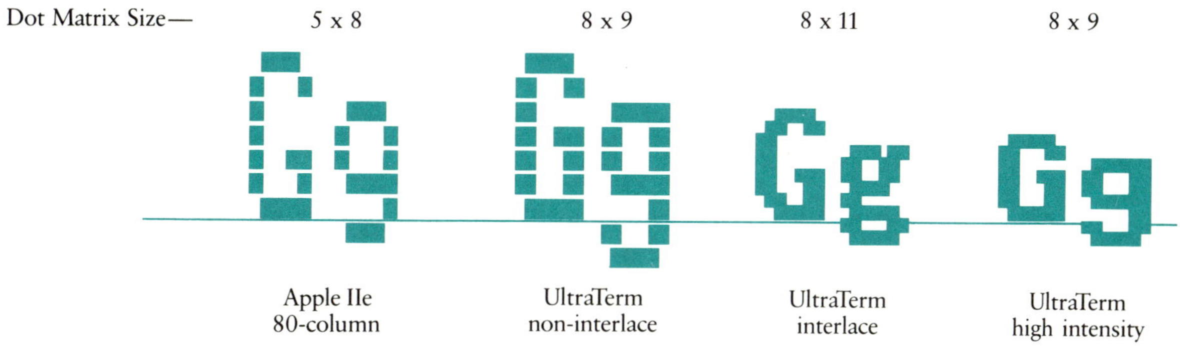

Figure 3-2
Character matrices

Taking advantage of these features may require some skill, and it won't be worth the trouble if your goal is primarily to have a wider display. There are, however, a limited number of application programs that let you control these attributes easily. Videx's UltraPlan spreadsheet, for example, lets you select five different ways to display the intensity of the characters and the background, so you can pick the combination that suits you best.

Beyond Eighty Columns

If you want the absolute best display there is, you should feel especially fortunate in owning an Apple. Videx, which has felt increasing pressure from Apple Computer and third-party manufacturers during the past few years, has overstepped its competition by producing UltraTerm, a display card that positively rewrites the rules for quality and performance.

UltraTerm uses a technique called interlacing to improve the readability of screen characters. Interlacing instructs the screen to display a second set of dots, slightly offset from the first, to fill in the vertical black lines and produce fully formed characters. The difference is striking—it's like looking at text produced on a daisy-wheel printer next to text produced on a cheap dot-matrix printer.

An interlace display is the finest you can have in terms of readability, but it only works if you have a slow-phosphor display monitor. So before rushing off to get an UltraTerm, make sure your monitor will handle it. Videx recommends the Amdek 300A (the A is for amber), or the Apple Monitor III. The Apple Monitor II will also work, as will the USI P3.

Slow-phosphor monitors use a light-emitting phosphor that lingers on the screen a little longer than the phosphor in fast-phosphor monitors, and the lingering is important to the effect of interlacing. What actually happens during interlacing is that the first set of dots is displayed, and then the second set is displayed one-thirtieth of a second later. That doesn't seem like much of a time difference, but if you use a fast-phosphor monitor, the first set of dots will have begun to fade before the second set of dots is displayed. The result will be a flickering image.

The UltraTerm can show you up to 128 characters across the screen. It features nine different display modes, including a standard 80 columns by 24 lines, 80 by 24 interlaced, 128 by 32, 80 by 48, and others. With 128 columns across a 12-inch monitor, the individual characters are pretty small, but UltraTerm's interlace mode produces fully formed, dot-free characters that are easy to read, in spite of the reduced size.

Like any other display-enhancement product, UltraTerm is only as good as your software's ability to recognize and take advantage of it. But, as a product that's almost two years old, UltraTerm is being recognized by a growing number of software developers. Videx sells a pre-boot diskette for VisiCalc that lets the program display up to 128 characters across. UltraPlan, as the Videx spreadsheet program, makes it easy to take advantage of the UltraTerm's capabilities. MAGICALC will also use UltraTerm without a pre-boot diskette if you use its special Videx video-display option. Multiplan is now, or soon will be, available in a version that uses UltraTerm, as well.

The UltraTerm should be fairly trouble free in use. The programs that can handle it will be a delight to use, and the programs that don't support it will still display 40 or 80 columns as they always did. The UltraTerm retails for $379, but you should be able to chop at least $100 off that price if you shop around. You may feel this is a lot to spend on improving a display that you've gotten used to. On the other hand, you may feel it's worth the price, because the larger display would cut down a lot on having to move around your spreadsheets, and because the UltraTerm could also reduce eyestrain.

Two-Fers

If you're in the market for a better display and extra RAM, you could save money by buying a card that offers both. Apple's IIe-only video card is available with or without an extra 64K of RAM; Titan's IIe-only Neptune card comes with 64K, 128K, or 192K of RAM. Generally, you get the 80-column capability for nothing with cards like these—what you're really paying for is the RAM.

COPROCESSORS

Ever since microcomputers were invented, and especially since the advent of 16-bit processors, there has been a growing misconception about the relationship between a computer's processing speed and the type of processor it uses. In the early 8-bit world, the distance between the Zilog Z-80—the processor in such machines as the Kaypro II, the Radio Shack TRS-80 Model III, and the Osborne I—and Apple's Western Design Center 6502 was measured in megahertz (one-million cycles per second). The Z-80 always won: It ran at 2 MHz to the 6502's 1 MHz. Things got worse when the quasi-16-bit 8088 (the one used in the IBM PC) came out: It ran at 5 MHz. Just looking at the numbers, one was tempted to consider the 6502 a total dud compared with its competition.

The 6502's image was further besmirched when it was revealed that Western Design Center had designed its 6500-series microprocessor as a control device for large appliances, such as refrigerators and dishwashers. It was hard to get serious about a computer powered by the brains of a Frigidaire.

The speed, in megahertz, of a microprocessor does indeed determine the rate at which it executes instructions; a 4 MHz Z-80A really does execute instructions at four times the speed of a 6502. But there's more to processing speed than megahertz, and what the Apple's 6502 lacks in muscle, it often makes up for in finesse.

What helps to equalize matters is the chip's instruction set, which is the actual language a processor uses when performing the things it does. No two instruction sets tell their processors to do the same operation in the same way. One might be very direct and efficient, like telling someone, "No." Another might be a little more cumbersome, as in, "Don't do that." And some might be downright clumsy: "I'm really not so sure I'd do that if I were you."

As it happens, the 6502's instruction set is comparatively efficient and compact, and it allows the 6502 to perform roughly the same amount of work as the faster Z-80 in a good deal less time. You might say the Z-80 can go 60 miles per hour to the 6502's 30 miles per hour, but, at the same time, the Z-80's instruction set forces it to go a block and a half out of its way for every block it moves toward the finish line.

Chip architecture, the internal design of the processor, has a lot to do with performance, too. The 6502 uses what's called pipeline architecture, a design borrowed from the processors used in large, mainframe computers. With pipeline architecture, the processor is executing one instruction, and at the same time it's getting ready to execute what it thinks is the next one. Sometimes, as in an "if this, then that" type of situation, a "downstream" instruction depends on the result of the currently executing instruction, and what the processor thinks is the next instruction turns out not to be. Usually, however, that next instruction is the correct one, and a lot of time (as measured by the processor) is saved. The 8088 and Z-80, on the other hand, execute an instruction, finish it, find the next instruction, execute it, and so on, sequentially. This ensures that the processor never goes after an incorrect instruction, but it's a slower way to go.

Another compensating factor is the application software itself. Two programs for the same application working under the same operating system might have very different levels of performance, and the same is true of similar applications running under different operating systems.

What all this means to you is that a 2 MHz Z-80 isn't necessarily faster than a 1 MHz 6502. In fact, the Z-80 is slower in some types of operation. So if you're going after processing speed, you've got to consider a lot more than just the clock speed of the processor.

But just as clock speed isn't the only qualifier in the performance race, it's not the only disqualifier either. Using a different processor or an additional coprocessor in your Apple can provide other benefits. Maybe the operating system that runs on the coprocessor is superior to Apple's DOS in some ways. Maybe a particular program you really want to use only runs on the coprocessor. And, too, maybe that particular coprocessor really is faster overall.

A Faster 6502

The simplest, least disruptive way to get faster spreadsheet recalculations and other processing is to install a faster version of your Apple's own 6502 processor. The standard processor in Apples is the 6502A, but you can buy a card that contains a 6502C processor instead. The 6502C uses the same instruction set as the 6502A, so it will run the same software. But the 6502C has a clock speed of 3.6 MHz, which makes it exactly 3.6 times as fast as the Apple's normal processor. With a 6502C installed, your spreadsheets will be recalculated 3.6 times faster than they were before; your data will be sorted 3.6 times faster; your display will change 3.6 times faster. Your Apple will, in effect, be as fast as a standard IBM PC—even faster, in many cases.

There are a few different companies making these cards, and there are big differences in performance among competing products. Titan Technologies was first with its Accelerator IIE card for the Apple II, and this product is still the best of the bunch. It features a 6502C and its own 64K of RAM.

Having the RAM on the same card makes all the difference in performance because of the way the Accelerator and the Apple work. Without the Accelerator, the program you start up is loaded into the Apple's RAM. The program and your data are then passed to and from the 6502 processor through its input/output pathway, or I/O bus. All of this activity happens at 1 MHz, because the input/output speed is the same as the processor's clock speed. Titan's Accelerator card features its own RAM and I/O bus that run at 3.6 MHz to match the 6502C's speed. The result is that all computing and all input and output occur at 3.6 MHz.

The ease with which you can use the Accelerator card will depend on the type of program you're working with. Spreadsheet programs are usually written in the computer's own machine language, and they can be run on the Accelerator without modification. If a program is written in Applesoft BASIC, you have to use a pre-boot disk to transfer the Applesoft language from the Apple's built-in ROM (where it's inaccessible to the Accelerator) to an area in the Accelerator's own RAM. If you're using a program written in Pascal, you also need to use a pre-boot disk to prepare a special area in the Accelerator's RAM to store the Pascal from your program disk. If you're using a program that simply won't run at 3.6 times normal speed (arcade games, for example), there are pre-boots to slow the Accelerator or to turn it off and return control to your standard processor.

All this potential pre-booting sounds sort of scary, but the chances are your software will use either the Pascal pre-boot or no pre-boot at all. If you're working with spreadsheets and doing any kind of recalculating, the time you spend pre-booting your software (if necessary) will be amply repaid in reduced waiting time. The Titan Accelerator retails for $599, but you can find it for at least $100 less.

There are competing speed-up cards for the Apple that feature 6502C processors. They sell for half of what Titan's card costs, but they don't have their own RAM on the card, so they're forced to use the Apple's standard RAM and I/O bus. Thus, data can be processed at 3.6 MHz, but it can only be moved to and from the processor at 1 MHz. You end up with an Apple that technically processes data 3.6 times faster (as the ads for these cards proudly claim), but that actually delivers much slower overall performance. The moral is that in choosing a fast 6502 coprocessor, make sure it has its own RAM on board.

Z-80 Cards

The nice thing about computers is that their designs are flexible enough to allow us to change or add processors. The beautiful thing about the Apple II is that it makes this sort of thing easy with its expansion slots—just plug in a board and you've got a whole new computer. The Z-80 SoftCard (see Figure 3-3), introduced by Microsoft in 1980, was the first coprocessor for the Apple II. This card made a lot of sense, because the Z-80 had been around at least as long as the 6502, and had become the "standard" processor in 8-bit microcomputers.

The Z-80 ran the CP/M operating system, which predated Apple DOS by a couple of years and had become the favorite operating environment under which to develop serious business programs. In 1979, there were a lot of CP/M-based accounting programs and other business applications to choose from. You could, of course, buy business programs for the Apple's native DOS, but with such software greats as WordStar, dBASE II, and SuperCalc running exclusively under CP/M, Apple-DOS business packages were widely felt to be second-best.

The SoftCard was an almost instant success. It would let an Apple run any CP/M program, provided there was a version of that program available in the Apple's Disk II format. Disk drives on CP/M systems at the time used everything from 100K, 5 ¼-inch diskettes to 500K, 8-inch diskettes, but they definitely didn't use Apple's 143K diskettes. The burden was on software companies to produce special versions of their programs for the Apple's disk format. Most companies were more than happy to oblige, because the Apple had the largest installed base of any computer back then. Having a CP/M card gave Apple owners the best of both worlds: access to thousands of programs in the businesslike CP/M environment, and the best in color graphics under Apple's DOS.

There's no question that having a CP/M card will enhance the capabilities of your Apple. What you should consider is whether it will add functions that you will use often enough to make them worth the expense. Here are the main pros and cons:

The Good News: On top of this wide range of software, you'll be getting some extra capabilities in the CP/M operating system itself. CP/M is much more flexible than DOS 3.3 in terms of its interactions with peripheral equipment. With CP/M, you can specify, via the application

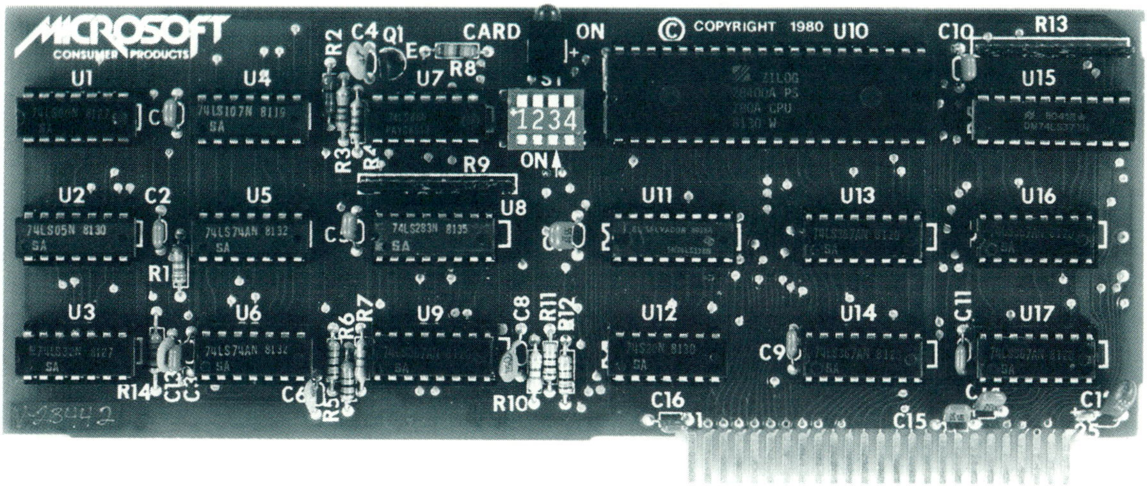

Figure 3-3
The Microsoft SoftCard

program you run, the type of printer, the number of disk drives, the presence of a RAM-disk and its capacity, and the type of video display you're using. Thus, software that can be set up in these ways will take advantage of 80-column cards, the UltraTerm card, and add-RAM cards without pre-boot software. You specify the capabilities of your system once, and then the program is ready to go after that.

CP/M has evolved considerably since it was introduced; newer versions, such as CP/M 3.0, also offer time-and-date labeling of disk files, faster directory searches, an on-line help facility that explains system commands, and automated RAM-disk caching (which will be discussed in Chapter 4). Some Z-80 cards, such as the Premium SoftCard IIe from Microsoft and the CP/M Gold Card from Digital Research, include an 80-column display and up to 192K of RAM on the same card, so they end up saving you slots in your Apple and, generally, money in your pocket. And speaking of saving slots, Microsoft's Premium SoftCard IIe fits in the IIe's auxiliary slot, leaving all seven of the standard slots available for other uses.

The Z-80 processor has also evolved, and is now available as the Z-80A and Z-80B, which run at 4 MHz and 6 MHz, respectively. When used with CP/M 3.0 and the right software, a Z-80B is a very fast processor—certainly faster than a 6502.

The Bad News: You'll have to spend a fair amount of time (several hours, anyway) learning the new operating system and application software, and transferring your spreadsheet files to the new environment.

Upgrades notwithstanding, CP/M is a more complex, less friendly operating system than DOS 3.3 or ProDOS. The ability to describe specific peripherals to the software you use isn't an option—it's a necessity. These configuration, or install, routines can be tiresome and frustrating, as they often require the entry of control-character strings. Compared with DOS 3.3 or ProDOS, CP/M is user-hostile.

You'll also have to spend a minimum of $500—probably more—for the coprocessor and just one decent application program. And while CP/M is a lot more powerful than DOS 3.3 in some areas, many of the inequalities have been reduced by ProDOS, particularly in the areas of speed and access to storage devices.

Lastly, you have to consider software. If you're trying to upgrade spreadsheeting alone, the benefits are questionable. VisiCalc, Multiplan, MAGICALC, FlashCalc, and UltraPlan are all respectable products. SuperCalc and MicroPlan do a few things better, but not better enough in my opinion to justify the upheaval of switching to CP/M. The real breakthroughs in spreadsheet software are in the MS-DOS environment discussed in the next section.

If you need to go with CP/M for another application, or if you're already familiar with CP/M applications and want to run some old favorites on your Apple, a Z-80 coprocessor may well be worth getting. You'll have more flexibility in using peripheral equipment and somewhat faster recalculations of your spreadsheets, too. But if you're only looking for ways to improve your spreadsheet work, you should look elsewhere.

8086/8088 Processors

Since it's a lot of work to change processors and learn a new operating system and application programs, you should expect a lot of improvements in your spreadsheets and other applications.

The most significant strides in software development during the past couple of years have been in products that run on the 8088 and 8086 processors under the MS-DOS operating system. IBM's choice of the 8088 and MS-DOS in its PC have caused just about every other computer and software company to jump on these bandwagons. Lotus Development's 1-2-3 and Symphony, Microsoft's Windows, Framework, Ovation, Open Access, SuperCalc3, VisiCalc Version IV, and Context MBA—all are third-generation products that supposedly leave standard Apple software in the dust.

This generation gap between MS-DOS software and standard Apple software isn't wholly imaginary, but it's not as all-encompassing as it might seem. The ability of 16-bit processors to access more than 64K of memory at a time has enabled software companies to produce larger, more powerful programs. Most software developers find it less time-consuming to put lots of features in large programs than it is to work out ways to improve the functionality of small programs.

But many MS-DOS programs, even today, are basically CP/M or Apple products that have been converted to run under the more recently popular MS-DOS. Examples include WordStar, dBASE II, Microplan (a spreadsheet program from Chang Labs), Home Accountant, and Advanced Version DB Master. Such converted programs may be a little more convenient because they can spread out in a PC's large RAM and not have to access a program disk as often, but they're functionally very similar.

Where the generation gap looms largest is with so-called "integrated" programs that combine spreadsheets, graphics, word processing, or other applications, or that are a good deal more powerful in themselves. A spreadsheet case in point is Lotus 1-2-3, which was the most popular application program in 1983, and which offers a much larger spreadsheet area than, say, VisiCalc, and a number of advanced features.

Unquestioned winners such as 1-2-3 notwithstanding, Apple Computer has publicly ignored the MS-DOS revolution for years, and even now doesn't embrace it explicitly. Nevertheless, the Apple II's tried-and-true flexibility has enabled other geniuses to make MS-DOS coprocessors available, so you can enjoy the same software spoils as the IBM tribe without defecting. Spreadsheet-wise, this means you can now run huge, lightning-fast programs like 1-2-3 on your own little Apple.

Using MS-DOS software on an Apple II involves the processor, extra RAM, and disk-drive formats. An 8088 or 8086 processor will run MS-DOS, but it must have access to enough RAM to store both MS-DOS and the application program you want to run (the minimum for most high-powered applications is 256K). But even if you could stick in an 8088 board and stuff enough RAM into your Apple, you'd still need a way to get MS-DOS and the application software into the computer. Your Apple's standard disk drives use a unique format that allows a maximum of 143K of storage per disk, while MS-DOS-compatible computers use a 320K- or 360K-capacity disk format.

I point out these problems because you can, if you like, go out and buy a plain-vanilla 8088 board for your Apple. You can even get an

Apple-formatted MS-DOS system disk to go with it. But you'll never find any MS-DOS application software in the Apple's 143K format. You will have wasted your money, unless your goal is to develop application programs yourself. If you really want to run MS-DOS programs on your Apple, you will have to change the processor, add RAM, and change your disk drives.

The neatest solution to this problem is the 8086/2 coprocessor and disk drive unit from Rana Systems, which you can see in Figure 3-4. It retails for $1895 and houses an 8086 coprocessor, 256K of RAM (that can be expanded to 512K), and two high-capacity disk drives that will read either Apple or MS-DOS disks. The disk drives and processor automatically sense which kind of disk is being loaded. If it's an Apple disk, the Rana system turns the processing over to your Apple; if it's an MS-DOS disk, the 8086 processor takes over. The Rana unit also generates its own display when running MS-DOS programs, and has the ability to produce either monochrome or color displays if you have the right monitor.

When you're running ProDOS programs on the Apple's processor, you'll also be able to take advantage of the Rana higher-capacity disk drives. Under ProDOS, Apple disks can store 320K of data instead of the old 143K. As an extra bonus, you'll be able to use the Rana system's 256K of RAM as a RAM-disk under ProDOS, which will let you load several Apple files into RAM and have immediate access to them.

MS-DOS computers don't necessarily run the same versions of the same application software, but the 8086/2 has a fairly high degree of compatibility with software that runs on the IBM PC. In the spreadsheet area, the IBM versions of integrated spreadsheet/graphics packages such as SuperCalc3 and Lotus 1-2-3 will run on the Rana system. Major software houses, such as MicroPro (developers of WordStar), Microsoft, Ashton-Tate (developers of dBASE II), and Lotus Development, have also specifically announced their support for the Rana device, so software availability shouldn't be a problem.

In addition, the whole issue of incompatibility among MS-DOS computers should be taken care of by Microsoft Windows, which is a universal machine interface, a kind of link, for which software developers can write their programs. Any program written to the specifications of Microsoft Windows should run on any computer that runs the Microsoft Windows "environment." The Rana 8086/2 is one of three or four dozen systems that run Windows, and most major software developers have announced their support of this standardization idea.

Figure 3-4
The Rana Systems 8086/2 coprocessor and disk drive system

But even if the Rana system lets you run any sort of MS-DOS software on your Apple whenever you want to, will it be worthwhile to have that capability?

On the Plus Side: The Rana 8086/2 has a lot to offer. It lets you run 1-2-3 and other advanced spreadsheet programs. You'll get the ability to make larger models (1-2-3 can theoretically create spreadsheets containing up to 500,000 cells). Thanks to the 8086 processor, which has a 16-bit data bus, as well as a 16-bit processor (as opposed to the IBM PC's 8088, which has an 8-bit data bus), you'll get faster processing speed than you have with a standard Apple or an IBM PC. And because of the high-quality RGB (Red-Green-Blue) color output, you'll be able to use integrated spreadsheet/graphics programs that produce nice, color business graphics from your spreadsheets (this also requires an expensive RGB color monitor, though—see Chapter 7).

To sweeten the deal, the Rana system offers higher-capacity disk storage and 256K of RAM that can work as a RAM-disk under ProDOS, both of which are nice features if you haven't acquired them in other ways already.

On the Minus Side: There's the price, for one thing. $1895 is a lot of change. It's probably more than you paid for your Apple. (But it's a lot less than you'd pay for any other comparably equipped MS-DOS computer.) There's also the question of getting up to speed with MS-DOS and the new software. MS-DOS is almost a direct descendant of CP/M in terms of its system commands and level of friendliness, but Microsoft Windows can (and probably will) be used by software developers to create a far friendlier DOS interface. Another minus is that Lotus 1-2-3 isn't the world's easiest program to learn, either—VisiCalc and Multiplan, both of which you can use without the Rana system, are far easier to learn. Nevertheless, there is all that extra power: instructions you define and then use at the touch of a keystroke, on-line help, graphics, 500,000 cells, and more.

The Rana 8086/2 is certainly not the cheapest solution to improving the spreadsheet capabilities of your Apple. If it's solely spreadsheet improvement you're looking for, this isn't the most cost-effective solution, unless you've decided you can't live without 1-2-3. On the other hand, more and more MS-DOS software offers levels of performance not currently available to users of Apple software, and the chances are that this gap won't narrow for a year or so.

Future Coprocessors

If you can wait awhile, there are a few more coprocessor options for the Apple that will significantly improve your spreadsheet performance. You can probably go out and buy either one of these processors right now, but both of them will have to wait for operating-system and application software before they can do you much good.

The older of the two is the Motorola MC68000, which is a 32-bit processor (with a 16-bit data bus) that Apple uses in its Macintosh and Lisa computers. The MC68000 has plenty of horsepower—its clock speed is 10 MHz—and it will address several million bytes of RAM, compared to the sixty-four thousand bytes a standard Apple will handle. You can find advertisements for MC68000 boards in some Apple magazines, but at this point they're only good for software development.

A newer and more promising processor for the Apple II is the 65816, which was designed by the same company that developed the original 6502. Apple is showing a lot of interest in this processor, because it offers the potential for upgrading the Apple II to a 16-bit computer, while allowing it to continue running its old, 8-bit software. The 65816, like the 8088, uses a 16-bit processor with an 8-bit data bus. It offers a high degree of compatibility with existing Apple software and access to much more RAM . Software developers are now, or soon will be, working on applications for this new processor, and programs, when they appear, should be functionally on the order of anything that's been seen in the MS-DOS world.

A less functional version of the 65816, called the 65802, has the advantage of being pin-compatible with the Apple's 6502—in other words, you could simply unplug your Apple's existing processor and replace it with the newer one. The 65802 has the same limit as the 6502 on the amount of RAM it can address (64K), but it processes data 16 bits at a time and should deliver processing speed similar to that of a true 16-bit computer.

INPUT DEVICES

Serious number-crunchers have long decried the Apple's lack of a numeric keypad for data entry. Many hardcore spreadsheet users know a ten-key numeric pad by touch, and they have to slow down their pace considerably to enter numbers by using the top row of a standard Apple keyboard. The numeric keypad has been deliberately omitted from the Apple II series because it was, and continues to be, Apple Computer's belief that computers with lots of keys are less friendly looking than computers with fewer keys. In keeping with this philosophy, the new Apple IIc, which is aimed at the first-time user, doesn't even have an optional numeric keypad.

Fortunately for business users, though, the Apple II, II+, and IIe all handle an optional numeric keypad with ease. There are several on the market to choose from. Apple itself sells a numeric keypad for $99. Others are available from $75 on up. If you're going to get an external keypad, be sure to get the one that fits your Apple—the II and II+ have a different hookup for a numeric keypad than does the IIe.

If you want to go beyond a simple numeric keypad, a company called Creative Computers produces a line of auxiliary keyboards that (depending on the model) contain either preprogrammed or user-definable

Figure 3-5
The Keywiz VIP keyboard

function keys. The keyboards, called Keywiz, contain from 20 to 32 keys, each of which is or can be programmed with up to eight characters. The keys on the keyboards can be used with a kind of shift key, too, to give you up to 248 different keystroke possibilities. If you do a lot of repetitive, multi-keystroke spreadsheet operations, you could program a few keys and store the keystroke sequences (technically called macros) under one key each. This would give you a keystroke macro capability similar to that of Lotus 1-2-3. The Keywiz keyboards, one of which you can see in Figure 3-5, come in three different models ranging in price from $289 to $369. One model, the Keywiz 83, offers a numeric keypad, along with

30 preprogrammed function keys. The keyboards come with pre-labeled key templates (if the board is preprogrammed) or with blank templates you can label yourself.

SHOWCASE SYSTEMS

There are a lot of different products that enhance spreadsheet work on an Apple II, and they can be combined in many different ways. Here are a few representative systems that will give you some idea of the cost and capabilities of an enhanced system. Note that the prices are suggested retail; you'll probably get from 30 to 50 percent off if you shop around.

CHANGING SOFTWARE

Apple II/II+	Currently Owned
Multiplan	$ 195
Videx VideoTerm display card	$ 279
Titan Accelerator IIE	$ 599
Total Extras	$1073

Added Power: Advanced features of Multiplan; 80-column display; 360 percent increase in processing speed.

ADDING RAM

Apple IIe	Currently Owned
VisiCalc	Currently Owned
Videx UltraTerm	$ 379
Videx VisiCalc pre-boot software	$ 69
Saturn 128K card	$ 499
Apple Numeric Keypad	$ 99
Total Extras	$1046

Added Power: 128-column display; 128K RAM for larger (up to 162K) VisiCalc models; easier data entry.

GOING MS-DOS

Apple II, II+, IIe	Currently Owned
Lotus 1-2-3	$ 495
Rana 8086/2	$1895
Total Extras	$2390

Added Power: Advanced spreadsheet features of 1-2-3; MS-DOS compatibility with added software availability; 256K RAM for MS-DOS programs or (depending on application software) RAM-disk under ProDOS; RGB color display output under MS-DOS; two 320K disk drives for Apple under ProDOS (drives also operate as standard 143K drives under DOS 3.3).

C H A P T E R

4

DYNAMIC DATABASE MANAGEMENT

When you think about how a personal computer stores and manipulates information, it's no surprise that a standard Apple II isn't as well suited for database management as you might want it to be. Think "data base" and you think of a large collection of records—hardly an ideal assignment for a 64K memory or 143K disk drives. Think "database management" and you think of sorting, searching, reporting—you can almost hear your Apple's 8-bit processor huffing and puffing. Small wonder, then, that serious database management has always been considered the stuff of CP/M machines, with their larger disk drives and faster processors. And today's high-powered database applications often find themselves even more at home on 16-bit computers.

Nevertheless, the Apple II stands on a long (in microcomputing terms) and noble history of database applications, and new coprocessors, software, and storage devices keep it viable today.

Most Apple owners come to database management only secondarily—they buy their computers for spreadsheets or word processing, and later want to move into the Data Processing Big Time without changing computers. Perhaps you got your feet wet with Quick File, PFS: File, or VisiFile, and now you want to move beyond their limited record or file sizes. It's a familiar story:

A THRIVING BUSINESS

A small-time entrepreneur chose an Apple II for his worm-farming business because the Apple was easier to learn than the other computers were. He got Apple Writer for creating advertisements and sales letters. He got VisiCalc for budgeting. And just because the computer salesman suggested it, he picked up Quick File for storing customer names and addresses. He set up a simple data base with records for his 75 customers—it was an easy enough task to define data categories such as Name, Address, City, State, Zip Code, Telephone Number, and Favorite Worm. He liked the way he could rearrange the file to suit particular needs. He could sort the list by Zip Code and print mailing labels. He could sort the file by Favorite Worm and make decisions about which varieties of stock to breed. He could sort by City or State when considering where to place ads.

With Quick File's help, business boomed. The targeted advertising brought a 2000 percent increase in sales in one year. The farmer hired four employees to maintain the worm herds, process orders, and keep the books. He tried adding information on new customers to Quick File, but the program was limited to only 600 records, even though he had an extra 64K in his Apple. He was forced to abandon the data base, which wasn't so bad because he didn't have time to maintain it anyway. But then the paperwork got too confusing—he longed for a database management system that his clerks could use, one that the company would never outgrow.

He knew he could get a Z-80 coprocessor and use dBASE II , but he'd heard it was difficult to learn. And besides, it, too, limited a database file to one diskette, so he couldn't increase his file space without getting new disk drives. On the other hand, there seemed to be so many new, friendly, powerful programs for the 16-bit computers that maybe it was time to think about switching. He could get a hard disk, and faster sorting and searching capabilities. He could have all the file space he would ever need, and he could custom-design data entry screens that his clerks would easily understand. After all, he reasoned, the Apple was never intended to be a real business computer, was it?

HOW SOPHISTICATED DO YOU WANT IT?

Well, Steve Wozniak certainly didn't design the Apple with heavy database management applications in mind, but the flexibility of his design will let your computer rise to most data-handling situations. Given the options for faster processors, larger disk storage devices, and better software, your Apple can become a database dream machine. The first item you should look to for enhanced capabilities is software.

Relational or Non-Relational?

In considering a need to upgrade your database software, the first decision you must make is whether or not you really need the relational data management capabilities of really sophisticated database software. A relational database will manage multiple files of information and allow you to relate items in one file to items in another. One file, for example, might contain a customer list, another file might contain sales figures, and a third could contain accounts receivable. A relational database lets you merge, extract, or compare information across files, so it's easy to build relational links between the files and get at specific records in any one. Thus, you might use a customer number in the customer list as a link to outstanding debts from that customer in the accounts-receivable list.

Essentially, a relational capability lets you break your information into smaller, more homogeneous files and yet find specific items by using fields (categories) of information common to more than one file. The good news about these databases is that they give you tremendous flexibility in the way information is organized, sorted, and retrieved. The bad news is that this flexibility generally makes such products more difficult to master.

Non-relational database programs, in contrast, give you broader powers within a single file. While most relational database programs might let you specify 25 or 30 fields of information per record (a record contains all fields for a complete entry), a non-relational database could permit 100 fields per record. So instead of relating four separate files containing 25 data categories each, you would have one file with 100 data categories. Non-relational databases try to get around the one-file limitation by letting you design several windows into a record—you can have fields relating to customer name, address, and so forth, in one window, and fields relating to the customer's account status in another. Single-file programs generally search for and sort data faster, but the individual records are often larger and harder to work with than are the records in a relational database.

NATIVE APPLE SOFTWARE

Compared to the fanfare with which the big CP/M or MS-DOS database management programs are promoted, Apple packages almost qualify as underground favorites. For example, dBASE II, for CP/M and MS-DOS machines, has been heavily promoted since it was introduced several years ago, and it has become an all-time best-seller. R:BASE 4000, an MS-DOS program, has risen to enviable prominence within eighteen months, thanks to a clever and expensive promotional campaign. DB Master, on the other hand, is a lightly promoted product for the Apple that costs $150 less than dBASE II and runs much faster, yet has sold perhaps one-eighth as many copies. VersaForm and Aladin, other fine products for the Apple, suffer from the same situation. It's a pity—each program offers a lot to the Apple user.

DB Master

Having been around since 1979, this is the oldest of the powerful database programs for the Apple. DB Master is not a relational database manager, but offers as much power as anything in its class. Stoneware, the marketers of DB Master, have a delightful policy of soliciting their customers' suggestions and incorporating them into newer versions of the product. As a result, DB Master has been upgraded for the Apple several times, and it gets better and better.

The most exciting thing about DB Master for Apple owners is that it lets you build a very large file (up to 14 megabytes) with a basic, two-disk-drive setup. Nearly alone among comparable programs, DB Master doesn't limit the size of a file to one storage area, or volume. As far as database management programs are concerned, a volume can be as small as one floppy diskette or as large as a hard disk. Since most programs limit files to one volume, they require a hard disk or a high-capacity floppy diskette to be useful. DB Master, however, uses an Indexed Sequential Access Method (ISAM) that places an index of the whole file on each data diskette. When you search for a record that isn't on the data diskette you currently have in the drive, the program tells you which diskette the information is really on. DB Master will report this information within three seconds if you're searching on a key field (a primary field you designate), and then find the record within another three seconds after you load the correct diskette in the disk drive. This ISAM system makes a large, floppy-based data file a workable alternative to the expense of buying a hard disk system. Some DB Master owners maintain files spread across 50 to 75 diskettes; the theoretical limit is over 200. If you have a hard disk, there's also a version of DB Master that works with your drive. If you use diskettes and later change to a hard disk, you can easily upgrade from a floppy-based system with DB Master.

Because DB Master was around well before hard disks were a reality for the Apple II, it has a large following. More than 35,000 copies of DB Master have been sold and, significantly, it is being used (somewhere) in all but three of the companies in the Fortune 500. The program deals with the potentially cumbersome problem of large individual records—it allows up to 100 fields per record—by letting you design up to nine different "screen forms" containing fields. Each screen form can serve as a window allowing you to see a different group of fields in the record. You can redefine these forms at any time.

DB Master also provides conversion programs that work with PFS: File and VisiFile, so you can transfer an existing data base easily from those programs. The product has an excellent tutorial guidebook that introduces you to the wonders and complexities of high-powered file management in a useful and entertaining way. The DB Master package retails for $350.

VersaForm

Another non-relational database program, VersaForm also lets you build a data base by defining screen forms similar to those in DB Master, but in this case, each form represents one complete record. Defining a screen form here is simply a matter of typing each field name and then adding a series of dots to signify the maximum field length. You can copy forms for use in more than one data base, so VersaForm saves you time when setting up new files. Predefined form templates for common tasks, such as invoicing, cash receipts, mailing lists, and purchase orders, are available as options from the manufacturer if you don't want to spend the time defining your own form.

The program has extensive error-checking facilities, so you can check the validity of specific entries according to their length, data type (text or numbers), or format, or by matching an entry with data elsewhere in the file. You can also use a feature that automatically fills in certain fields according to the information in another field you specify—you type in a customer number, for example, and the program finds and fills in the corresponding name, address, and telephone number. These features go a long way toward ensuring the integrity of your data, and this is crucial when you could be dealing with a file several megabytes long.

VersaForm comes in either floppy-based or hard disk versions, but this program really begs for a hard disk. Creating a file that uses more than one floppy is a fairly tedious process that involves copying forms from the first to subsequent diskettes, and this copying must be done before your first diskette is full, because the program creates a temporary file on the source diskette during the copying process. The other drawback to using the floppy-based version of VersaForm is that it comes on five program diskettes and forces you to do a lot of diskette swapping. VersaForm retails for $389.

Aladin

Aladin is the only relational database manager available for the Apple that doesn't require the use of a Z-80 card or some other coprocessor. As with VersaForm, Aladin really shouldn't be considered for serious use unless you have a hard disk system. If you do have one, however, Aladin lets you manage up to five files simultaneously, each of which can contain 65,000 records of more than 4000 characters each. Aladin has powerful sorting and reporting capabilities, but it is correspondingly more difficult to learn than DB Master or VersaForm. If you have a hard disk, this program offers a lot of power without forcing you to the added expense of a coprocessor card. Aladin retails for $595.

On the other hand, the floppy-based version of Aladin won't let you create files longer than one diskette (this can limit you to about 30 large records), and it lacks the ability to perform calculations—necessary for multi-level sorts (on more than one field) and even simple column totals.

HARDWARE

Database management is one of the most taxing applications for a microprocessor. Even with the fastest processor, all that sorting and calculating and formatting can be a long process; with a not-so-fast processor, the work can really drag on. It's not unusual for microcomputers to spend the better part of an hour doing a complex sort on a large data base. Once software solutions to this problem have been exhausted, we must turn to hotter hardware to speed things up.

COPROCESSORS

NOTE: *There is a detailed discussion of coprocessors in Chapter 3.*

Historically, Apple owners have used Z-80 coprocessors for faster data processing, but this is just one of the options available. Switching to a Z-80 or an 8086 coprocessor will require you to learn a new—and less friendly—operating system, and will probably force you to adjust to a completely different software package as well (although there are a few companies that make both Apple and CP/M or MS-DOS versions of what is essentially the same program). There are a lot of added benefits in switching to a totally different processor, but if you're happy with your software and simply wish it ran faster, there's another way.

6502 Coprocessors

Like everything else in computing, the 6502-series processor has been improved since 1977. The 6502 in your Apple is a 6502A, which has a clock speed of 1 MHz. A couple of years ago, Titan Technologies introduced the Accelerator IIE, an Apple coprocessor that contains 64K of RAM and a 6502C processor. The 6502C uses the same instruction set (and therefore runs the same programs) as the 6502A, but it has a clock speed of 3.6 MHz, so any software you run on your Apple's processor under DOS 3.3, Pascal, or ProDOS will run 3.6 times faster on Titan's Accelerator IIE. Your database management program, for example, will search, sort, and calculate 3.6 times faster—imagine the time savings with sorts that formerly took half an hour or more. Although it retails for $599, the Accelerator IIE has been a big hit with Apple owners who do a lot of things, such as database management or spreadsheet work, that put a heavy load on the processor.

Now, there are at least a couple of other companies competing with Titan Technologies for customers. But, beware. The other 6502C coprocessors I've seen sell for about half as much, but they don't contain 64K of RAM on the same board, and this makes a big difference in performance. If a 6502C coprocessor (or a Z-80 coprocessor, for that matter) doesn't have its own RAM, it has to use the Apple's RAM. But the Apple's input/output bus (the pathway to and from its RAM) operates at 1 MHz to correspond to the speed of the Apple's normal processor. This means that a coprocessor, no matter how fast its own speed, must slow down to 1 MHz whenever it goes to the RAM for data or program instructions. It's a lot like owning a Ferrari in a city where the highest speed limit is 35 miles per hour.

Makers of these products may advertise that their coprocessors will speed processing on an Apple by 360 percent, but the actual improvement in performance is far less dramatic. While your processor spends more time working with data during database management than it does on other, less taxing applications, it still spends most of its time getting the data or putting it back, not processing it. A 6502C board with its own RAM will not only process data 360 percent faster, it will also move the data in and out of RAM 360 percent faster—and this is where the real performance improvement lies.

CP/M and MS-DOS Options

The CP/M or MS-DOS worlds are where you'll find the lion's share of powerful database management software. CP/M has a business-oriented history going for it, as well as faster processing and easier access to large storage devices, and MS-DOS lures developers, with its CP/M roots and 16-bit processing (old CP/M programs were easy to translate to MS-DOS, and having access to more RAM lets programmers create bigger, fancier new packages).

The benefits of both CP/M and MS-DOS lie in their use of larger storage devices and their increased processing speed. CP/M and MS-DOS can easily be set up to access multi-megabyte hard disks, and hard disk storage is more important for heavy database management than it is for any other application. In fact, database management is the only application that could be the sole justification for the expense of a hard disk. If you're serious enough about database management to need a hard disk, then going CP/M or MS-DOS will make the drive easier to use.

The Z-80 and the 8086 coprocessors that run CP/M and MS-DOS on the Apple also process data faster. This speed is partly due to these chips' faster clock speeds (5 or 6 MHz compared to the 6502A's 1 MHz), but it's mostly because of their ability to access more RAM. You can't look at higher clock speed as a direct indicator of better performance, because so much depends on the software. R:BASE 4000 is a lot faster than dBASE II on the same 8086 processor, and DB Master is faster than either one, even though it runs on the Apple's 6502.

But many of the CP/M-based Z-80 cards on the market for the Apple have extra RAM that definitely speeds up sorting, and the 16-bit processors that run MS-DOS will access up to a megabyte of RAM directly. The more data a processor has available to it at one time, the less time is spent getting that data to and from disk, and the faster things generally go.

CP/M and the Z-80

Z-80 coprocessors have been around for the Apple for about four years now, and a number of improvements have been made to them, many of which particularly affect database management. Almost every Z-80 board offered today uses the Z-80B chip which, with a clock speed of 6 MHz, is faster than the 16-bit chip used in the IBM PC, even if you take their different instruction sets (described in Chapter 3) into account.

Another improvement is the version of CP/M that is being used. Today, you'll find that CP/M 3.0 is the standard version of this operating system. CP/M 3.0 offers such advanced features as: access to more storage (up to 16 devices of 512 megabytes each); time-and-date labeling of files (so you always know which is the latest version of a file); faster disk access; an advanced filing system that can maintain recently used files in a RAM-disk "cache"; and a vastly improved set of manuals. Of these, the most important improvements for database management are the advanced filing system and the access to more storage.

Normally, a Z-80 card has its own 64K of RAM, but many now come with an additional 128K of RAM, which is used by CP/M 3.0 as a disk cache for recently used files or parts of files. What happens is that the database management software sends the operating system to get data from the disk. CP/M 3.0 gets enough data to fill up the 128K disk cache, and the database program sorts the information. As the program finishes sorting groups of records, the operating system returns them to disk and replaces them with new, unsorted records. Thus, the database program never has to stop and wait for new data from the disk, because CP/M makes certain that some new data are always available in the disk cache. One test of several Z-80B cards conducted in early 1984 showed that a dBASE II sort routine took four and a half minutes on a Z-80 card with a 128K disk cache, and the same routine took two minutes longer on a card without a disk cache. A 45 percent improvement in sorting time isn't too shabby.

Having a 128K disk cache is a bonus, but there are several things to watch for when choosing among individual Z-80 coprocessors. Notice whether the processor is a Z-80, Z-80A, or Z-80B (the A and B versions are faster). Notice which version of CP/M is being used—2.2 or 3.0. If you can, try to find reports on performance comparisons of several cards, based on a test that features the kind of work you have in mind. Often, the plain specifications of a card can be misleading, because performance also depends on how well the card is designed. It's quite possible for a Z-80B card with 64K of RAM and the older CP/M 2.2, for example, to be faster than a Z-80B card with 64K and CP/M 3.0—it depends on how well the card uses the CP/M it works with.

The biggest names in Apple Z-80 coprocessor boards today are Microsoft, ALS (Advanced Logic Systems), and Digital Research. Digital Research is a relative newcomer to the field, but since it supplies CP/M to its competitors, the company may well know a few important things about implementation that give it an edge. There are some inexpensive Z-80 cards on the market that don't have any on-board RAM, or use older and slower versions of CP/M or Z-80 chips, but since high performance is the name of the game, you should go with quality. Good Z-80 cards retail for about $400, but can often be found for less than $300.

MS-DOS and the 8086

In database management under MS-DOS, the current standout is R:BASE 4000 from MicroRIM. This product handles more files faster, with a lot less hassle, than anything that even comes close to its power. R:BASE 4000 will manage up to 40 files, of 2.5 billion records each. Each record can contain up to 400 fields, or a maximum of 1530 characters. This program sorts about five times faster than dBASE II.

R:BASE 4000 has an excellent instruction book and a demonstration disk that will have you using the program extensively within an hour or two, and it features a command mode with extensive prompts that can walk you through every step of the program as a beginner, and then disappear when you're a pro and don't need it anymore. There's also an optional query language that lets you search for records with plain English sentences. Even without this aid, however, the language R:BASE 4000 uses contains only 39 main commands and is easy to master. If you want to go MS-DOS and you want all the software you'll ever need for database management, you can do no better than this program. It retails for $495.

At this writing, the only product worth considering if you want to run R:BASE 4000 or any other MS-DOS software on your Apple is the Rana Systems 8086/2, described in Chapter 3. It retails for $1895, and includes two IBM-compatible or Apple-compatible disk drives (depending on the software you're using), 256K of RAM, an RGB color output, and the MS-DOS 2.1 operating system with the Microsoft Windows interface manager. Rana also throws in ProDOS, GW BASIC (an advanced form of BASIC), and enhancements for using DOS 3.3, Pascal, and CP/M. In relation to MS-DOS and database management, the big advantage of this product is access to software—the Rana 8086/2 will run most IBM PC software without modification.

Once you've entered the MS-DOS world with the Rana 8086/2, you'll get a lot more than a terrific database management program. The Rana 8086/2 contains 256K of RAM that can be expanded to 512K, so you can run the latest, largest, and sexiest of new MS-DOS programs. The system comes with MS-DOS version 2.1 and with Microsoft Windows, which (as software developers take advantage of it) will let you run programs that use a mouse, on-screen symbols or icons for choosing what you want to do, and pull-down command menus.

Pull-down command menus, by the way, are little graphic lists of commands from which you select specific program instructions. Each list is grouped under a heading—file-management commands, for example, might be grouped under the heading FILES, and the list under FILES might contain Catalog, Copy, Rename, Delete, Lock, and Unlock. To gain access to each list, you use the mouse to point to the heading the list is stored under. Then, when you click the button on the mouse, the actual list "pulls down" out of the heading and onto the screen, to reveal the commands. You point the mouse to the command you want, issue the command, and the list disappears back up behind the heading. Pull-down menus make programs easier to use, because they give you almost instant access to all or most of the commands, without having the commands cluttering up your screen when you don't need them.

Microsoft Windows will also improve the transportability of MS-DOS software from one machine to another, because it is a translator between the application program and MS-DOS. As hardware and software manufacturers adopt Windows, any computer running MS-DOS and

Windows will be able to run any software that has been written for the Windows standard.

Supposing software to be equal among native Apple, CP/M, and MS-DOS environments, the 8086/2 also delivers the fastest processing. DB Master for the standard Apple will find a record within three seconds, but Advanced DB Master for MS-DOS will find a record within one second. If you do a lot of database reporting that also includes calculations, you can add an Intel 8087 math coprocessor chip to the 8086/2. The Intel chip will perform such calculations five to ten times faster than the main processor (if the software you're using can take advantage of the increased speed).

Although the Rana system doesn't contain any internal expansion slots, you can still use the Apple's expansion slots to add a hard disk, a mouse, a clock (for automatically keeping track of the time and date), a printer buffer, or other peripherals. Like the Apple, the Rana system can use these devices with ease.

The real problem with the Rana system for database management, as for other applications, is that it's expensive. The unit alone is $1895, and by the time you add new database software and a hard disk for storage, you'll have $3000 to $4000 invested. This is less than you'd have to spend for a new MS-DOS system with comparable features, and it allows you to continue running your collection of Apple software, but it's still a lot of money.

HARD DISK STORAGE

Ideally, we all want storage devices that provide instant access to an endless amount of data. The ultimate disk drive should handle all the data we could ever create, give us any of it within a fraction of a second, and offer total reliability.

A lack of mass storage has always been seen as the Apple II's worst limitation for database management applications. After all, no mass storage, no big data bases. Apple itself only began supporting the use of hard disks with the Apple II when it introduced ProDOS early in 1984. Before then, third-party developers were left to work within the strictures of DOS 3.3. In the interest of selling a lot of hard disks to a lot of Apple users, however, hard disk manufacturers figured out how to make the Apple/hard disk connection.

When you buy a hard disk for the Apple II, you get some software that takes the theoretical storage limits of DOS 3.3 and turns them into reality on the hard disk. DOS 3.3 will only recognize 143K storage devices, but it can recognize up to 254 of them, so each 143K device becomes a separate volume, or "phantom" floppy disk drive on a hard disk. A five-megabyte hard disk, for example, could contain about 35 volumes.

With most application software, you use the phantom floppy drives on a hard disk just as you would if they were real—each volume contains 143K of files, and to locate files you catalog each volume separately. This process is rather a chore, and it is one of the big reasons hard disks never caught on for non-database applications on the Apple II. But developers of Apple database management programs realized it would be much to their benefit to make using a hard disk as easy as possible for their customers, so the popular database programs are all available in either floppy or hard disk versions. The hard disk versions handle the multiple volumes automatically, so that when you look for a particular record, you don't have to know which volume it's on—the program keeps track for you.

This housekeeping makes it worthwhile to own a hard disk if you're doing mostly database management with your Apple II, but it still eliminates a lot of people. Seeing that the world was going hard disk, though, Apple came out with ProDOS, which can access storage devices of up to 32 megabytes without any trickery at all. As far as the user is concerned, there's no difference between using a floppy disk or a hard disk—the hard disk is just bigger. And this improvement promises to make hard disks a popular enhancement for many Apple owners, no matter what application they use most.

The best current solution to the world's yen for data storage is the Winchester-type hard disk drive, which offers many megabytes of storage and accesses data ten times faster than a floppy drive. Other than Winchester hard disks, though, there are a lot of alternatives that offer similar improvements in access time and capacity. Each has its advantages and disadvantages. This section will cover the large-scale storage options for the Apple as they apply to data only. Storage of application programs (and the methods of mounting application programs on hard disks) is discussed in Chapter 5.

Winchester Hard Disks

Originally developed by IBM, Winchester hard disks spin a rigid metal platter at about 3500 rpm, thereby creating a current of air that causes a read/write head to "float" a fraction of an inch above the platter.

This technology allows for very dense recording of data on the surface of the platter and for fast access to the information. But, such devices are extremely susceptible to motion and dust. The head flies so close to the surface of the platter that even a tiny speck of dirt can disrupt the air flow, causing the head to descend upon the surface of the platter and destroy all the data in its path. This occurrence, known as a head crash, invariably means you must reformat the disk and, in doing so, erase any data that managed to survive the crash itself. This is particularly annoying with even the smallest hard disk, because instead of losing 70 pages or so, we're talking about the erasure and destruction of up to 2400 pages. Because the consequences of a head crash can be so awesome, hard disk drives are usually sealed against the outside world to help protect them from dirt, smoke, and moisture.

Because of the clumsiness of using a hard disk with DOS 3.3, there were originally only a few makers of such devices for the Apple II. With the coming of ProDOS, however, the market has blossomed. These days, old-timers in the Apple hard disk market, such as Corvus (whose hard disk you can see in Figure 4-1), Corona, Davong, and Mountain Computer have been joined by Rana Systems, Quark, and even Apple Computer itself, which now makes its five-megabyte ProFile hard disk available for the Apple II line. Prices for a five-megabyte hard disk unit range from about $1000 to $2000, depending on features, performance, and how passionately interested the manufacturer is in selling the product.

One of the most important features to look for in a hard disk is the ability to store files that you've created under different operating systems. Along with your database files, it's quite possible you'll want to store files from your word processor or spreadsheet on the hard disk because the drive is so fast and convenient, and you may well be using programs that run under different operating systems (some DOS 3.3 programs, some ProDOS programs, and perhaps some Pascal or CP/M programs). Davong, Apple, Mountain Computer, and Corvus support at least three co-resident operating systems; Rana's new drive supports five.

A related feature of hard disks is dynamic file allocation, which is the ability to vary the amount of disk space reserved for files running under each operating system. Some hard disks make you specify a certain amount of space for each system and then force you to reformat the disk if you later want to change the amount allocated to each system. Since reformatting erases everything on the disk, that means backing up and reinstalling all your files. Hard disks from Corvus, Davong, Mountain Computer, and Rana all support dynamic file allocation.

Figure 4-1
Corvus hard disk drive

In the performance area, you should remember that one of the big benefits of having a hard disk is quick access time. Manufacturers of hard disks normally provide three specifications for access speed: minimum time, maximum time, and average time. Check the average access time of the units you compare (not the minimum, since this can give you an artificial impression of lightning speed). Corvus hard disks, for example, have an average access time of 68 milliseconds (68 thousandths of a second), while Davong's average 110 milliseconds—the difference might not seem big, but when you look at it another way, the Corvus disk is nearly twice as fast as the Davong product.

Along with access time, look at the peak data transfer rate. Hard disk controllers (the circuit that allows them to interact with the computer) are designed differently for different units, and as a result data are transferred from the disk to your computer at different speeds, depending on whose drive you're using. Corvus claims a peak transfer rate of 687.5

kilobytes per second, while Davong reports 625 kilobytes per second. If you're spending $2000 in either case for a five-megabyte hard disk, you might as well get the highest performance as long as everything else is the way you want it.

Other features that can add to the price or increase the value of a hard disk drive are: the ability to operate more than one hard disk from the same controller; built-in ability to work with a backup device; and built-in support of a file-serving system, which allows more than one Apple or another computer to access the same hard disk. Rana Systems' five- and ten-megabyte hard disks, at $995 and $1495, respectively, are the least expensive, but that's partly because Rana eliminated the circuitry on the controller card that lets you run more than one hard disk. This means that when you want another Rana drive, you have to buy both another drive and another controller. With other units, you would only need to buy the drive, which would cost $300 to $500 less than the original drive-controller combination.

Built-in interaction with a backup device is tremendously useful, because it's a sad fact that most people don't bother to back up their hard disks, and therefore leave themselves wide open to disaster in the event of a head crash (which, unfortunately, is more likely than one would wish). Corvus hard disks feature a built-in interface with an optional backup system, called the Mirror, which is described at the end of this chapter. The Mirror uses a home videotape recorder and standard VHS or Beta recording tapes to store data.

File-serving circuitry will only be important if you plan to share hard disk files among more than one computer. A network of computers sharing a hard disk needs either a file-serving unit or a computer dedicated to the task, to handle the input and output of data flowing between the drive and the various computers on the network. File servers for Apple systems normally cost about $1000, but Corvus includes the file-serving circuitry with its hard disks at a price comparable to that of many other units that don't include the option.

Removable-Cartridge Winchesters

One newer Winchester storage technology that has been in the works for a while is the removable-cartridge Winchester drive. This is a Winchester drive in which the metal platter is encased in a removable plastic cartridge, so when you fill up all the storage space, you can insert a new platter and start over again.

This technology has so far been plagued by problems of head alignment, reliability, and dust-prevention. But a company called Syquest, which is the big supplier of this technology, now says that any performance problems are in the past. Some of these units offer a sealed disk drive in combination with a removable-cartridge drive. If you like this idea, study the current offerings carefully, and watch particularly for warranty and reliability information. A good hard disk drive should have an MTBF (Mean Time Between Failures) of 6000 to 10,000 hours.

Removable Non-Winchester Cartridges

Removable non-Winchester cartridges, currently exemplified by a product called the Infax 101A, use a flexible mylar—instead of metal—disk encased in a cartridge. The flexible disk is spun at 1500 rpm beneath a read/write head, but instead of the air flow from the disk keeping the head flying above it, the air flow pushes the disk up toward the head. This arrangement means that if a dust particle or something else interrupts the air flow (a classic cause of head crashes in Winchesters), the disk drops *away* from the head. Dropping away is a lot better than having the head fall onto the disk, as it doesn't involve the destruction of data.

The Infax data cartridges offer ten megabytes of storage each, and the average access time is a zippy 35 milliseconds. The unit retails for $2595, which is in the same ballpark as most ten-megabyte Winchesters. The makers of the Infax say that their technology prevents head crashes and thus makes the unit far less sensitive to the presence of dust, dirt, and moisture. This is important because removable-cartridge machines can't be protected against these elements as well as sealed units can be. If the technology really is better, you can expect to see a lot more of these devices on the market.

Hard-Disk Backup Devices

This repetition may be getting tiresome, but it's particularly important to back up the data on hard disk systems. Most people don't bother to back up their hard disk data because the procedure is a lot of trouble. It often means you have to transfer data to floppy disks, and with a 35 to 1 size difference between a small hard disk and a standard Apple floppy, backing up data can be a slow process that leaves you with lots of archival floppies hanging around.

The best answer to the backup problem is a system that automatically backs up your hard disk without your intervention—that way, it's impossible for you to neglect this important procedure. Failing this, you should look for a backup system with a storage capacity that at least equals the capacity of your hard disk, so you can keep everything on one piece of storage medium. Preferably, the device should let you back up all your data at the end of a day with just a few keystrokes.

The other way to turn is to use higher-capacity floppy drives for backup. At least then, you don't have to swap floppies so many times. A Rana Elite Three, for example, will back up a five-megabyte hard disk on ten diskettes, whereas an Apple Disk II would require 35 diskettes.

Of the major hard disk manufacturers, Corvus gets my vote in the backup category with its Mirror. This is a controller that connects a Corvus hard disk with a standard home videotape recorder. With the connection made, the Mirror backs up the contents of the hard disk at less than two minutes per megabyte, so the process is a lot quicker than swapping several floppies in and out of a disk drive.

The Mirror can store 18 megabytes of data on a standard 30-minute Beta or VHS videotape. The product sells for $790, which isn't bad when you consider that you can pick up a used VHS video recorder for $200 to $300. With a 120-minute tape, you can store a whopping 73 megabytes of data. There will doubtless be other backup devices for Apple hard disks, now that their use has been legitimized by ProDOS, so keep your eye open for other inexpensive, hassle-free backup alternatives.

SHOWCASE SYSTEMS

FLOPPY-BASED APPLE II+

Apple II+ (with 16K language card)	Currently Owned
DB Master Version 4 Plus software	$ 350
Total Extras	$ 350

Added Power: Powerful, non-relational database management without the expense of extra disk storage or conversion to ProDOS operating system.

HARD DISK APPLE IIe

Apple IIe	Currently Owned
Aladin software	$ 595
Titan Accelerator IIE	$ 599
Rana five-megabyte hard disk	$ 995
Total Extras	$2189

Added Power: Relational database management program; 360 percent improvement in processing speed; hard disk storage that supports five operating systems concurrently, with dynamic file allocation.

MAXIMUM POWER

Apple IIe	Currently Owned
R:BASE 4000 software	$ 495
Rana 8086/2	$1895
Rana ten-megabyte hard disk	$1495
Total Extras	$3885

Added Power: Top-of-the-line relational database management program; MS-DOS 2.1 and 8086 coprocessor with 5 MHz clock speed plus two disk drives, 256K RAM, and RGB color output; hard disk storage that supports five operating systems concurrently, with dynamic file allocation.

CHAPTER

5

INTEGRATED APPLICATIONS

Integrated software is high on the list of personal computer status symbols, and it's likely to remain there for a long time. From the phenomenally successful Lotus 1-2-3 to newer products, such as Lotus' Symphony and Ashton-Tate's Framework, integrated programs have captured the hearts, minds, and pocketbooks of nearly everyone. And since all of these products run on 16-bit computers, they're making 8-bit computers look as though they're headed for the dustbin of history. If you're still using software that performs only one application, you could be having trouble withstanding this apparent tide of modernity.

THE NEW WAVE

You're a marketing manager using an Apple IIe. You've been using it happily for over a year now, switching from VisiCalc spreadsheets to VisiPlot graphs, or from a Quick File vendor list to Word Juggler sales letters. This system works fine for you, but lately the other marketing managers in your group have gotten IBM PCs and are running 1-2-3 or Framework. They *have only one program to deal with, they say, while you're stuck swapping program disks all day long.* They *don't have to worry about using data-interchange programs to put parts of a spreadsheet file into a word-processing document.* They *have loads of on-screen help, command menus, and manuals to prove the sophistication of their software.* They *want to know when you're going to wise up.*

You can hear the quiet snickering as they pass your office door, and you've begun to notice how their conversations end abruptly when you draw near, as if a new fraternity has been established and you're not allowed membership. You try to ignore it all, but it's difficult.

Colleagues sigh and tap their toes noisily as you change software disks and wait for a different program to boot. And you've noticed yourself drumming your fingers impatiently as you wait for programs and data files to load. You've become more and more irritable when interrupted, and for no apparent reason you find it harder to remember the procedures for transferring your unformatted DIF files to Word Juggler documents. As things get worse, you realize that you're actually stopping to look in the window of the local IBM Product Center, and that you linger ever longer over the ads for integrated software in computer magazines.

MYTHS AND REALITIES

As an Apple II owner, it's easy to feel as though life is passing you by in a world of faster processors, flashier applications, and larger RAMs. But it's dangerous and expensive to try keeping up with the Joneses. You could, if you wanted, switch to the latest software every time something newer and better came out, but this would probably force you to spend all your time adapting to new products or earning the money to pay for them. A far better approach is to take a long, critical look at new software or new hardware and to ask yourself honestly whether they will really make *your* computing easier. As long as your current setup does what you want, as well as you like it done, there's no real reason to change.

The first question to ask yourself is, "How many applications do I use regularly?" While some integrated programs will do everything but shine your shoes, it's amazing how few applications a typical user really needs. Word processing, spreadsheets, and database management are still the top three applications, so going through the disruption of learning a new product that offers graphics and communications may not make sense. It's fine to say you've got a package that does everything, but if you don't do "everything," the package will probably be a waste of money.

The only exception to this general rule is an integrated product that performs one application a lot better than any single application program can. Lotus 1-2-3, for example, is the acknowledged king of spreadsheets, so if your Apple is set up to run MS-DOS, it could make sense to buy 1-2-3 just to get the best spreadsheet program, even if you never use the graphics and database functions of the package. But, what you're far more likely to find is that most integrated programs offer a group of applications, none of which is a match for existing stand-alone products. The word processor in Context MBA, for instance, is the slowest thing since hieroglyphics, and neither the spreadsheet nor the database part of the package is at the top of the applications scale, either. Integrated software may require a fast processor or the latest and greatest in "acceptable" quantities of RAM, but as you've seen in the preceding chapters, neither of these is a guarantee of high function. A lot depends on the quality of the software design and the language in which the program is written.

Another thing you'll discover by taking a good, close look at most integrated software is that "integrated" means different things in different products. In a package like Framework, integrated means that you use essentially one software product that has many functions. The commands are very similar, whether you're using the spreadsheet or the word processor, and moving from one application to the next is an almost seamless operation. This is really the goal of integrated software: to allow users to move quickly and effortlessly from one application to another. And ideally, all applications in such a product have the same type of data structure, so that files created for one application can be used in other applications without requiring any modification or special transfer routines.

The problem with packages integrated in this way is that they often use unique file formats or modified versions of DOS, so it is difficult for them to work with data or programs from other vendors. If, as with 1-2-3, such an integrated program is extremely popular, third-party software developers often create utility (housekeeping) programs to enable data interchange between the dissimilar programs. But you won't be so lucky if you're not using one of the top products.

Other integrated programs are really just collections of several applications. In a product such as Software Products International's Open Access, moving from one application to another requires that you "exit" one application and "enter" another via a menu. Sets of commands and data structures are not completely compatible between applications, so a mailing list created with the address-book program can't be merged with a form letter created with the word processor. Integration in this sense is really just a fancy name for having a lot of products, all accessible through one main menu, on the same set of disks from the same manufacturer. Like the more completely integrated packages, these collections of applications may have trouble interacting easily with other products, and for the same reasons.

A third type of integration is the environment concept exemplified by Apple's Lisa, VisiCorp's VisiON, DesQ, and Microsoft Windows. The environment is either an operating system itself (as in Lisa) or it is a software overlay for the operating system (as in Microsoft Windows) that unifies the workings of different application programs for the user. Such environments allow you to combine different application programs from different manufacturers by using them with a common interface that tends to make products from different manufacturers work alike. All programs written for VisiON, for example, use mouse command selection and pull-down menus—anything else would seem out of place, not to mention unfriendly.

The ultimate effectiveness of environments will depend heavily on how much support they get from third-party software developers, because environments require software written to their specifications. One of Lisa's early failures was the lack of support (and therefore lack of software) for its environment. VisiCorp and Microsoft are now both avidly seeking support from software developers for VisiON and Microsoft Windows. In the end, there will certainly be a shakeout—software houses simply don't have the resources to rewrite their products for more than one or two different environments. When the shakeout comes, you could be out on a limb if you've made the wrong choice.

If you've decided that integrated software is really for you and you don't particularly want to give up your Apple, you're in luck, as usual. You can have any of these kinds of integration on an Apple II: You can have an all-in-one program that runs on your current, unmodified Apple; you can use a family of programs that share the same data structure and general operating style; or you can move to an operating environment.

ALL-IN-ONE PROGRAMS

There are now several products for the standard Apple II or IIe that combine two or three applications on one disk. Because the Apple can't access more than 64K of RAM at once, the functionality of all-in-one programs written for standard Apples is generally lower than it would be in the same type of program written for 16-bit computers. It makes sense. Any program that can stretch out in a luxurious 256K of RAM can have more bells and whistles on it than can one that must fit inside 64K of RAM. Nevertheless, clever designers have produced some remarkable multi-function products for the native Apple. While they are not as capable as Framework or Symphony, these programs offer surprising function and convenience for far less money than their 16-bit counterparts.

The Incredible Jack

The first all-in-one program for the Apple II was The Incredible Jack, which combines word processing, file management, and a spreadsheet on a single diskette for $179. The program runs under DOS 3.3 in any 64K Apple II, II+, or IIe. Integration in this case means that the programs all reside on one disk, that they can exchange data easily, and that the commands are similar in all three applications. The Incredible Jack is essentially a database program that lets you perform calculations in certain fields, create database files that are actually letters or memos, and merge records or calculations from a database file into a form letter. It's a matter of creating similar files with different formats, and of merging files to exchange data.

A file you create with The Incredible Jack can be a data base (of records you've entered on self-designed screen forms), a group of calculations, or a short letter or memo. Database files can hold up to 1000 records, each with up to 100 fields or 2000 characters. You work on one type of project at a time: When you want to go from one application to another, this program works no differently from single-application products, except that you don't have to switch program disks.

Each program has four modes, which are selected from a main menu. The Disk mode is used for copying, deleting, loading, saving, and creating files or records within files. The File mode is used to modify files or to add new records to database files. The Select mode is used in searching for records, or in merging them with other files. The Print mode is for output.

The Incredible Jack is less expensive than many single-function products for the Apple, but while the database portion is more powerful than products such as Quick File and VisiFile, the word processor and spreadsheet are rather limited. Still, if your word processing consists mostly of short or form letters, this package might not be a bad way to turn. The makers of The Incredible Jack have recently announced Jack2 for the Apple IIe, which adds graphics capabilities to a more powerful word processor and spreadsheet, and costs $259.

AppleWorks

Apple's entry in the all-in-one software sweepstakes is AppleWorks, a ProDOS program that combines a database manager very much like Quick File, a full-function spreadsheet comparable to VisiCalc, and a fairly powerful word processor. AppleWorks uses the IIe's Open Apple and Closed Apple function keys extensively, so you can't use this program on a II or II+. While the program will run on a 64K IIe, an additional 64K gives you about four times as much file space, so it's useful to have an Extended 80-column card (with its built-in 64K of RAM) or some other source of additional RAM. AppleWorks retails for $250. (The word-processing capabilities of AppleWorks were discussed in Chapter 2; this section will focus on its integrated applications.)

AppleWorks treats the Apple's available RAM space as a "desktop" on which you can keep up to 12 files (depending on how much RAM you have). A "Desktop Index" keeps track of these files, so you can refer to them quickly and easily. You could be working on a word-processing file, for example, call up the Desktop Index, choose a spreadsheet file, and move into the new file automatically. You don't have to worry about saving the previous file or loading a different kind of application software—the files are all in RAM anyway, and AppleWorks automatically goes out to the program disk and gets the application software you need, depending on which type of file you choose to work on.

AppleWorks features a somewhat higher level of integration than The Incredible Jack in a number of other ways, too. Files created with its spreadsheet, database, or word-processor programs can easily exchange data, and you can move between different applications very quickly.

The data-handling structure and commands in different AppleWorks applications are very similar, regardless of which one you're using. And certain features are the same in all programs—spreadsheet, database, or word processor. You use ESC to toggle between the main program menu and the file you're currently working on, and use the Open Apple and Q keys in combination to bring up the Desktop Index. Obviously, you won't need to search for characters in a spreadsheet or recalculate fields in a data base, so some commands are different, but an effort has been made to make as many commands as like one another as possible. Each of the three applications is displayed in a similar way, with a status line at the top of the screen and a comment line (where you're prompted about your options at any point in the program) at the bottom.

You can exchange data between programs by copying the information into a buffer called the Clipboard, switching files on the screen with the Desktop Index, and then "pasting" the information from the Clipboard to the file location you've specified with your cursor. Thus, it's easy to move part of a spreadsheet or a data base into a word-processing document.

AppleWorks files aren't the same as regular ProDOS files, but they're very similar, so the program is not only capable of exchanging data between AppleWorks applications, it can also load data from DIF (Data Interchange Format—in other words, unformatted ASCII) files or standard ProDOS text files. This makes it more likely that other programs will come along to enhance the function of AppleWorks. Already, Apple has announced a program that lets you generate form letters by merging an address list from an AppleWorks data base with a letter created with the word processor. A spelling checker that works with AppleWorks documents has also been released by Sensible Software.

The major benefit of AppleWorks is the ease with which you can switch from one of the three applications to another. You can be typing away at a report with the word processor, and then call up a customer record from a data base within a couple of seconds. The AppleWorks database manager isn't as powerful as the one in The Incredible Jack, but the overall level of functionality across the three applications is higher. AppleWorks is an excellent product for first-time Apple users, and because it's so easy to learn and use, it makes sense for experienced owners as well. If you're an experienced user, you'll want to compare AppleWorks with the capabilities of your existing word-processing program, and with your database manager, in particular, before deciding whether AppleWorks offers the functionality you need. If it does, work on your Apple will be a lot more convenient.

Jane

Jane is a word-processing, spreadsheet, and database package from Arktronics Corporation, and its most noticeable feature is its use of a mouse and screen icons to control what the program does. It's tempting to say that Jane works like the Macintosh or the Lisa. Program functions appear as graphic symbols, or icons, at the top and bottom of the screen, and you select the one you want by highlighting your choice with the aid of a mouse. The Apple's high-resolution graphics are used in Jane to let you display three different sizes of text on the screen, as well as underlined and boldfaced characters.

Jane is sold with its own mouse for $295 or without a mouse for $179, and is compatible with the AppleMouse II from Apple, which retails for $149. Apple II and II+ owners will be delighted to learn that Jane will work with any Apple II computer, as long as it has 64K of RAM.

Jane comes with a 230-page manual, but you won't have to refer to it much, because the icons at the top of the screen are used to identify program options and are pretty much self-explanatory, as you can see in Figure 5-1. You create word-processing files by selecting the typewriter icon, spreadsheet files by selecting the calculator, or database files by selecting the file cabinet. Along with these, you use a pair of scissors for cutting out and putting data into a temporary buffer; a paste jar for pasting buffered data into another file; a camera for copying a file or parts of a file; a printer for selecting print options; a diskette for cataloging or copying disks; a stop sign for exiting the program; a computer terminal for adjusting display attributes, such as the size of text on the screen; and a question mark for getting help.

In addition, you use the symbols at the bottom of the screen to select specific program capabilities. Since these capabilities are unique to the program being used, this row of symbols changes to reflect the functions currently available to you. The spreadsheet, for example, shows calculating symbols for adding, subtracting, dividing, and so on, as well as for such functions as averaging, and retrieving minimum and maximum values. For the word processor, this row changes to offer justification options, search functions, and text printing attributes such as boldfacing, underlining, sub- and superscripts, and foreign-language accent marks.

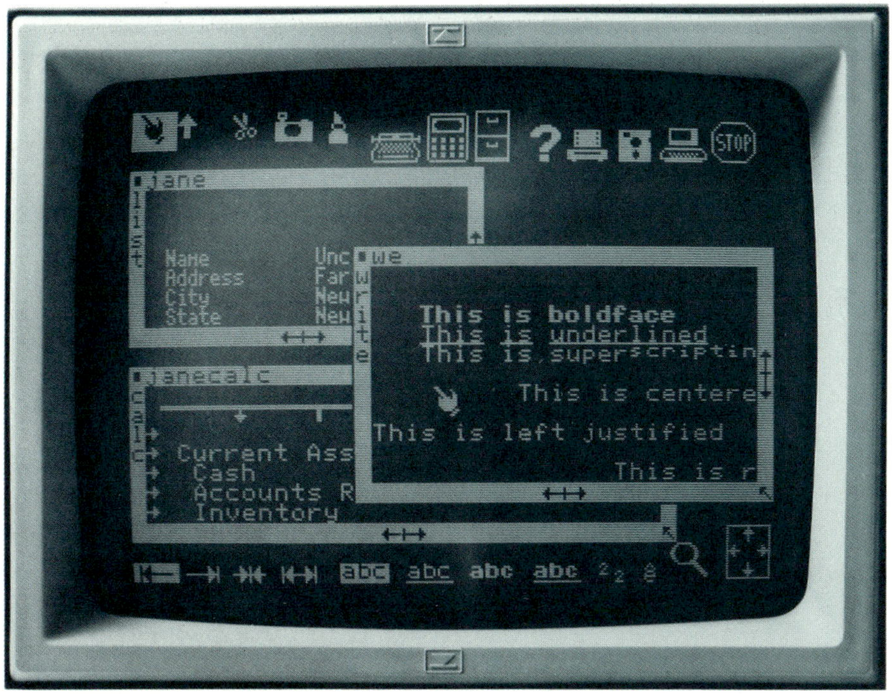

Figure 5-1
A sample Jane screen display

While the icons make Jane incredibly easy to learn and use, the program uses graphics extensively in other areas, too. You can display up to four different "windows" on the screen at once, each of which can contain a different file. Windows can be made bigger or smaller, or moved about the screen, and you can scroll in any direction within a window to see different parts of your file.

Only one window can be "active" at any one time, but you can copy material (with the camera icon) from one window to another, simply by highlighting the information in one window, activating another window, and then copying the information to the place you indicate with the cursor.

It doesn't matter whether you copy spreadsheet data into a word-processing document, database information into a spreadsheet, or word-processed text into a data base—all data look the same to Jane.

Of the three all-in-one programs mentioned in this chapter, Jane has the most consistent command structure across different applications and is by far the easiest program to learn. Because of the extensive use of the mouse and icons, though, you may find Jane slower to use, since you're constantly moving one hand between the keyboard and mouse. It lacks advanced capabilities, such as file-chaining in the word processor or sheet-linking in the spreadsheet application, but this program will meet the needs of a large percentage of Apple users. Jane doesn't create standard ProDOS files, however, so it isn't likely that anyone except Arktronics will come up with other products (communications or spelling software, for example) that work with Jane.

INTEGRATING SEPARATE PROGRAMS

Data interchange between one program and another is a particular problem with the Apple, because this ever-flexible computer can currently run any of five different operating systems (if you count MS-DOS), and each operating system has its own unique way of structuring files. On top of this, some developers modify file structures for better performance (as in the case of AppleWorks) or they use an operating system of their own (as with Jane). So, in many ways, it can be a relief to know that all the programs you use will exchange data with no problems.

Word Juggler/Lexicheck/Terminus

If word processing and communications are your main concerns and you own a IIe, you should definitely check out Word Juggler IIe for better product integration. As mentioned in Chapter 2, Word Juggler is very powerful and fairly easy to use as a word processor, and it integrates very well with a spelling checker called Lexicheck. Word Juggler loads completely into RAM, so you can load it and replace its program disk with the Lexicheck program disk. And, once you've done this, you can get to the speller from Word Juggler at any time. You can have Lexicheck guess at alternate spellings of any word you indicate in the document you're working on, or you can have the whole document checked for errors. Either of these operations is a matter of two keystrokes, and the response time is as fast as your disk drive can spin.

Quark, Inc., maker of Word Juggler, also makes a communications program called Terminus, which interacts with Word Juggler files as easily as Lexicheck does. With a couple of keystrokes, you can transmit a document you've loaded into memory or you can send a file or group of files from disk. You can receive files directly onto disk from any computer (regardless of the communications software being used) without disturbing a document in your Apple's memory, and if the computer you're sending to is also using Terminus, you can also send disk files without disturbing the document in your computer's memory. The Terminus program will send both DOS 3.3 and ProDOS files, and it will work with an add-in clock card that allows your Apple to send and receive electronic mail without attention from you (see Chapter 6).

The only problem with using Word Juggler and Terminus on a floppy-based system is that you have to have the Terminus program disk in the program drive for instant access to it. Since this same requirement applies to Lexicheck, you have to decide which program you want to have available for immediate use. If you have Word Juggler and these programs on a hard disk, however, there's no problem—you can have both the speller and communications programs at your beck and call. Either way, though, the ability to use a spelling checker or communications program and then to return automatically to your word processor is extremely convenient, if communications and word processing are your two main applications. Word Juggler and Lexicheck together retail for $189, and Terminus costs an extra $89.

FAMILIES OF PRODUCTS

Another way to get a fair amount of integration from separate applications is to use a family of programs, so that you can buy individual products and add new applications as your needs grow. Companies such as Software Publishing, VisiCorp, and MicroPro offer product lines of individual programs that all work in much the same way and that can easily exchange data with one another. On a floppy disk system, you'll still have to do some swapping of program disks to move from one application to another, but your program family will be able to share the files on a common data disk, so at least you'll be saving one step.

The PFS: Family

The most famous family of products for Apple computers is the PFS: series from Software Publishing. The first product was PFS: File, introduced in September 1980. PFS originally stood for Personal Filing System, but the three-letter acronym became a trademark as the software's popularity soared, and it now appears at the beginning of each of Software Publishing's product names. Today, the family consists of PFS: File, PFS: Report, PFS: Graph, PFS: Write, PFS: Proof, and PFS: Access.

Individually or in groups, these products have graced the upper levels of more software best-seller lists, and for longer periods of time, than has any other family of personal computer software—and with good reason.

PFS: products are inexpensive ($125 to $170 each), easy to learn, simple to use, fairly powerful, and similarly structured. Once you've used one PFS: program, you have little trouble learning the others. And any of the programs you buy will share data easily with the others in the family.

As a user of the PFS: series, you could handle a project in this way: After updating the records of a customer base in PFS: File, you could print a summary from the same file with PFS: Report. The summary would total sales, average the size of individual orders, and perhaps sort the entries by date. You could send this report to your boss (who understands the nuts and bolts), but you'd want a more polished version for the home office. So, using PFS: Graph, you could take the same PFS: File data and create a nice pie chart that showed a breakdown of sales in different product areas. After storing the chart, you could write a sales report for the home office with PFS: Write, and then insert the chart into the report as an illustration. To check the final version before you sent it off, you could use PFS: Proof. After this, you could use PFS: Access to transmit the file to the main office. During this process, you would have to change your program disk six times, but there would be no hassles with converting files from one type to another, because you could use all six programs with the same sets of data.

If you use a lot of different applications, a family of programs, such as the PFS: series, can be a blessing. Otherwise, the best level of integration you can hope for is to use a group of programs that have utilities they can use for exchanging information. One problem for Apple II or II+ owners, however, is that PFS: Write uses the IIe's function keys extensively, and won't run on older Apple models.

HELP FROM A HARD DISK

NOTE: *Further technical information about hard disks and the use of multiple operating systems with them can be found in Chapter 4.*

Aside from the ability to use similar sets of commands and to exchange information freely between applications, the advantage people seem to like most about integrated software is fast access—the convenience of having a variety of applications at their fingertips.

In floppy disk systems, however, this kind of convenience demands a tradeoff. Either you have a single-disk program that lets you move quickly between programs, but doesn't have as much power as individual products you've been using; or you have a family of products that make you swap program disks to change applications; or you have a group of powerful products that share common data types or have conversion utilities for each other's data, but force you to swap program floppies *and* data disks. Somehow, it should be possible to have your favorite applications at your fingertips, and avoid both loss of function and the need for floppy-swapping.

Obviously, there is a solution: Store all your application programs and data on a hard disk. With everything in one place, floppy-swapping will become a thing of the past. But if hard disks offer the storage capacity and quick access you crave, getting your favorite programs onto them can be a problem, because most Pascal, DOS 3.3, and ProDOS application programs are copy protected. If you use a Z-80 coprocessor with CP/M programs, you'll have few problems copying your software onto a hard disk. And if you use certain kinds of protected DOS 3.3, ProDOS, or Pascal software (database programs are the most likely), you may be able to buy versions made specifically for installation on a hard disk. But if your software collection contains disk-based software for DOS 3.3, ProDOS, or Pascal, you'll probably have some problems copying your programs onto a hard disk.

The whole subject of copying protected software, of course, is a well-known and often hotly debated topic. There are hardware and software products available that can, with varying degrees of success, copy protected programs either from diskette or from your computer's RAM. If you want to try using a copy-cracking product, the choice is yours. Remember, though, these products don't always work. Beyond that, since you are no doubt already aware of the arguments for and against copying protected software, let your conscience be your guide.

Catalyst

One good approach to getting some protected software onto a hard disk, however, is a program called Catalyst from Quark, Inc. Originally developed for the Apple III, for which it remains one of the software bestsellers, Catalyst is now available for any Apple computer in the II series at a retail price of $149. Catalyst runs under the ProDOS operating system, and it works best with ProDOS products. It lets you move up to 48 protected ProDOS programs onto a hard disk, and then places each program on a menu, so that you can select different applications easily from one place.

Quark president Tim Gill has done something remarkable with Catalyst. Gill recognized the need for software developers to protect their software, but he also wanted Apple owners to get more use out of hard-disk storage. He found a way for Catalyst to copy a protected program onto the hard disk *without disturbing the developer's protection scheme.* Programs are protected on diskette, and they're protected on the hard disk, too. Catalyst lifts the protection scheme of a program just long enough to move it onto a hard disk.

In order for this setup to work, the Catalyst program has to know in advance what sort of protection scheme a protected program is using. This means that software companies must furnish Quark with their protection schemes so that Catalyst can copy their software. Getting software companies to reveal their protection schemes, even to a fellow software manufacturer, doesn't seem easy, but Quark has already enlisted the support of Apple Computer, BPI Systems, and Microsoft, among others. Unlike asking a company to modify its software to run under a different operating system, Catalyst only asks a manufacturer to divulge the protection scheme of an existing product. Since "support" in this case is so simple, other software companies are sure to support the Catalyst scheme as hard disks grow in popularity.

Although it works best with ProDOS software, Catalyst will also support CP/M programs to some extent. In these cases, Catalyst sets aside a special area of the hard disk for the operating system, then treats CP/M as a ProDOS file. The Catalyst menu displays CP/M as a menu item, so once you select CP/M from the menu, you have access, through the activated operating-system "file," to the CP/M programs you've stored.

Ideally, using Catalyst should mean you can store all your ProDOS or CP/M programs on a hard disk and easily get to them all via one menu. But, of course, it's not as simple as that (it never is). ProDOS programs that support the Catalyst system will work as easily as described, but CP/M programs have their limitations where Catalyst is involved.

Most CP/M programs can be copied, and you can get these onto a hard disk without Catalyst. But here's the rub: At this time, Catalyst will only give you menu access to programs running under CP/M Plus on an Advanced Logic Systems (ALS) CP/M Card. Thus, if you're not using the ALS CP/M Card, you can put your CP/M programs on the hard disk, but you can't use Catalyst to put them there. And because Catalyst only recognizes CP/M Plus with the ALS card, the CP/M area of your hard disk won't show up on the Catalyst menu. So, to get at CP/M programs without an ALC CP/M Card, you'll have to retrieve them in the same way you would without Catalyst.

My feeling about the complications of CP/M is similar to my feeling about makers of ProDOS programs supporting Catalyst: Eventually, market pressures will prevail. Sooner or later, makers of other CP/M cards will support the Catalyst system under CP/M Plus. Within a few years, failure to have done so will severely limit any CP/M program's marketability to Apple users, and software companies are, after all, in business to sell products.

One final note: If you use a lot of Pascal software, you can rule out using it under the Catalyst system. You can mount Pascal programs on a hard disk, but not under ProDOS. ProDOS takes up too much of the Apple's memory by itself to permit Pascal to co-reside there, so there won't be a ProDOS version of Pascal. And since Catalyst can only deal with programs as ProDOS files, this means it can't recognize Pascal-based products. Unfortunately, this means there'll never be a hard disk version of the current PFS: family for the Apple.

The Bottom Line

As a potential hard disk user looking for more convenient access to software on your Apple, you can draw the following conclusions: You can use some programs very conveniently with Catalyst; you can use some programs less conveniently without Catalyst; and you can use some (non-copyable) programs not at all. If your software meets the Catalyst requirements, switching from one product to another on a hard disk will simply be a matter of choosing products from a menu (or of selecting CP/M from the menu and then loading the specific program you want). If the products also share the same file structures, or have data interchange utilities, you'll have a high degree of integration among applications, with the ability to access programs quickly and swap data among them.

If you're not using Catalyst, you can access unprotected ProDOS or CP/M programs directly from a hard disk by using file names (called path names under ProDOS); or you can access unprotected, standard DOS 3.3 programs by specifying the volume name—the "phantom" floppy disk drive—as discussed in Chapter 4. You can still move between programs, although you'll have to remember specific file names or volume designations instead of simply choosing them from a menu. Data exchange between programs will be as easy as your various programs allow it to be. If you use a bunch of different programs and you have to figure out whether they have utilities for exchanging data with one another, take heart in knowing that you'd have exactly the same problem on a 16-bit computer.

With each passing month, the number of Apple programs that won't work on a hard disk is diminishing. Renegade versions of DOS 3.3 will gradually retire from the field of battle. Makers of Z-80 coprocessors are moving up to CP/M Plus and will likely support Catalyst, and makers of ProDOS programs will find that supporting Catalyst is so simple that it won't make sense not to do so. All in all, the future of applications integration via a hard disk looks brighter for the Apple II all the time.

OPERATING ENVIRONMENTS

If the native Apple solutions to integration seem too complex or creative to you, or you can't sleep at night knowing that you and your IBM-based cohorts are taking different approaches to integration, you can always take the MS-DOS option. Using the Rana 8086/2 coprocessor, you can convert your Apple to a 16-bit computer and run the high-powered, integrated programs your friends are running on their IBM PCs.

The Rana system has been described in Chapters 3 and 4 so, briefly: It is a box containing two IBM-compatible disk drives, an 8086 processor (faster than the IBM PC's 8088), 256K of RAM (expandable to 512K), and an RGB color output port, all for $1895. The disk drives will read either IBM-type or Apple-type diskettes, so you can run 16-bit programs some of the time and then run your favorite Apple programs at other times. Since the Rana unit is supplied with MS-DOS and Microsoft Windows, you can even have a Lisa-like operating environment.

Depending on how successfully Microsoft gains the support of software developers for Windows, you should be able to use any software with the Rana system that you can with another 16-bit computer with up to 512K of RAM.

So far, the Rana system without Microsoft Windows has proven to be about 85 percent compatible with IBM programs. It imitates the IBM PC's input/output system, so the Rana system only has trouble with software that interacts directly with specific locations in the IBM hardware. For example, developers sometimes bypass the IBM PC's input/output system so their programs manipulate the display or whatever directly from RAM and thus gain execution speed, particularly with graphics. This is the reason Flight Simulator (a simulation of flying that includes a full-color instrument panel and views from the cockpit of an airplane) doesn't run on most IBM clones, including the Rana system. Nevertheless, if the 8086/2 sells well to the large number of Apple users, most MS-DOS software companies are sure to go after this lucrative market with versions of their products that will work on the Rana system.

SHOWCASE SYSTEMS

The following systems reflect the three approaches to integration on an Apple: using an all-in-one program on a standard Apple; using a hard disk to get fast and convenient access to more than one program; and using a 16-bit coprocessor to run more functional all-in-one programs.

UNADORNED APPLE

Apple II, II+, or IIe (with 64K)	Currently Owned
Jane software with mouse	$ 295
Total Extras	$ 295

Added Power: Highly integrated, mouse-driven software with windowing capabilities and easy-to-use, graphics-oriented command structure.

HARD DISK INTEGRATION

Apple IIe	Currently Owned
Catalyst software	$ 149
Word Juggler IIe software	$ 189
Terminus software	$ 89
VisiCalc software	$ 250
Apple ProFile five-megabyte hard disk	$1295
Total Extras	$1972

Added Power: Instant access to spelling checker or communications from within word processor, menu access to spreadsheet, data exchange capability from spreadsheet to word processor, hard disk storage.

GOING 16-BIT

Apple II, II+, or IIe	Currently Owned
Rana 8086/2	$1895
Lotus 1-2-3	$ 495
Total Extras	$2390

Added Power: 16-bit processing, MS-DOS compatibility, two 360K disk drives, RGB color output, integrated spreadsheet, database, and graphics applications.

C H A P T E R

6

COMMUNICATING WITH CLASS

The ability to use an Apple to communicate has less to do with the Apple's own powers than it does with the type of modem you use and the condition of the phone lines. Processing power and RAM size are comparatively insignificant in communications, so the Apple continues to perform this application as well as any other personal computer.

To a certain extent, the quality of communications software affects the ease and flexibility with which a computer can transmit information, but here again, the rest of the industry has nothing on Apple. While some IBM versions of programs may initially have had more features, these features have been transferred to Apple software as well. Now, there are more communications programs available for the Apple than there are for any other personal computer, and these programs can do anything from checking transmissions for errors, to sending and receiving electronic mail, to making your Apple pretend it's a terminal attached to a mainframe computer. In fact, most of the companies that make communications software or hardware for the IBM PC started out making their products for the Apple II.

As for other applications, current advertising tends to make the Apple look like a second-rate communicator compared with 16-bit computers, but this is an illusion. If you see a lot of ads for options that join IBM PCs in networks, it's because most IBM PCs are used in situations in which networking is more likely, not because you can't set up a network for Apples. Apples have been successfully linked in networks in schools and businesses for longer than 16-bit computers have been on the market, and today Apples can be placed on the same network with other models of 8- and 16-bit computers, as well.

In individual communications, the same fallacy about Apples being limited is again fueled by Madison Avenue. Advertisements rave about using IBM function keys to make communicating easy, or they boast about menu-driven operation, or on-line help. But when it comes to basic functions, there's no real difference. What is being promoted as a difference is really just a higher degree of automation and hand-holding for the user, and this can actually be a two-edged sword.

Because of their larger amount of RAM, 16-bit computers can run bigger communications programs that feature more bells and whistles. But the more bells and whistles, the less flexible the program is. A Dow Jones communications program that lets you ask for stock quotes in your own language (as in, "List yesterday's closing price of Apple Computer's stock," instead of something like "//Quotes AAPL,") may require less learning time, but you won't have a clue when something goes wrong (and believe me, something will). All you learn with such a program is how to start it, how to log on to the system, and how to begin typing queries in your own words. You might not even be aware of the complex interrelationships among your computer, the software, the modem, the phone system, and the host computer and its software.

No one would argue that it's anything but a good idea to make word processing or spreadsheet programs more "transparent," or automated, for the user, but when it comes to communications, there's a potential danger. At best, communications is a frustrating and unreliable application. Once upon a time you had to be a mechanic to operate a car successfully; while you don't have to be a telecommunications engineer to use a modem and software, it sure helps to know the fundamentals. You shouldn't even try to approach telecommunications without biting this particular educational bullet.

As an Apple owner, you can take comfort in knowing that this situation is no different for you than it is for any other computer owner, whether the other computer happens to be a personal computer, a minicomputer, or a mainframe. Much of the frustration in telecommunicating comes from the chasm between what is theoretically possible and what is actually possible. An ad shows a sales representative sending a memo to fifteen different cities at the touch of a button, and you wonder why you can't even get your modem to dial out. You no sooner begin trying to telecommunicate than you become ensnared in a mass of parameters (specific settings), protocols (sets of procedures), and hardware and software instructions. What seems so simple in the ads ends up being very complicated on your desk.

WHY IS IT SO COMPLICATED?

There are three central problems that make communications such a difficult application. First, communications is a multi-faceted process that involves more levels of hardware, software, and human interaction than does any other application. Second, different brands of computers use different sets of rules, called communications protocols, for sending and receiving data. And finally, the key medium of computer communications happens to be a voice-grade telephone network that was never designed for the transmission of computer data. Let's look at these problems one at a time.

As a multi-level process, computer communications offers more opportunities for trouble than any other application. With other applications, you have software, through which you talk to the computer. If the software and the hardware work, and you understand how they work, you're in business. With communications, on the other hand, you generally have software, through which you talk to your computer, through which you talk to your modem, through which you talk to the telephone system (and then, perhaps, a switching network, such as Tymnet), through which you talk to the receiving modem and computer and, perhaps, to another computer user. It's a precarious system in which success depends upon everything pulling together at the same time, and upon your understanding of the interrelationships. Communications is also a system in which one of the elements inevitably isn't playing along.

There are certain parts of this process over which you have a lot of control. You can, with some diligence, figure out how to get both your hardware and software working together flawlessly, and your telecommunications partner can do the same. But all that work still only gets you over the first of the three hurdles.

The second hurdle is getting your two computers to talk together flawlessly. If you both use Apples and the same communications software, matters are a lot easier. You only have to make sure that you're using the same transmission speed, or baud rate, and that you're observing the same communications parameters. But if you are using different computers with different communications software, you also have to worry about matching protocols. One set of software may offer setup options that don't even exist on the other, and you may have to do a lot of guessing to get your computers to talk to one another. This often results in the absurd situation in which you and your intended telecommunications partner must talk on the phone, trying to figure out how to enable your two computers to talk on the phone. Usually, by the time you figure things out, you could have *told* each other whatever it was you wanted to transmit via the computer-modem link. And, if you're transferring files instead of merely communicating via keyboard, then you also have to make sure that the files you're transmitting have similar structures, or you could end up receiving a file that your computer's software is incapable of deciphering.

But assuming you get over these two hurdles, the big one—the one you really can't control at all—still awaits: the telephone system. Telephone lines were made for transmission of voices, not data. If you're listening to someone on the phone, you can tolerate a lot of static or other "noise" on the line and still understand what the other person is saying. But computers talk to one another with a very precise set of sounds and are quite intolerant of such noise. On a noisy line, the tone that signifies the number "0" might sound like "1" to a computer. As a result, the data you send over a noisy telephone line sometimes gets to the other end as unreadable nonsense.

Sometimes, telephone lines are clear and everything works as advertised, but making a phone call is really a crapshoot, because you can call the same place two different times and have your call routed a totally different way each time. As modem technology improves, all computer owners will be able to communicate at higher speeds, with less worry about the condition of the phone lines, but these advances are still a few years off.

The telephone network is the weakest link in the whole setup, but a lot of the complexity of communications would evaporate if everyone who made communications hardware and software agreed to use the same set of protocols, to play by the same rules. Of course, this sort of cooperation goes against the grain of the entrepreneurial computer industry, in which all manufacturers think their ways of doing things are better. Nevertheless, manufacturers are aware of the need to make communications seem less complicated, and their solution is to make the process more automated. And some automation can be a good thing.

THE OLD DAYS

If you're still living with 1977-era communications technology, making connections can be a real ordeal. You've probably got a serial card inside the Apple, and an old, acoustic-coupler modem next to your telephone. Imagine the joy of communicating: The Apple screen shows only the BASIC prompt. You "wake up" the modem by entering IN #2 (because your serial card is in slot 2), and a light glows on the antique wooden case of your acoustic coupler. You type in a few more control characters to set the communications parameters (the number of data bits being sent, the bit parity, the addition of a line feed after each carriage return, and other items), and then you flip a couple of switches on the modem to set the baud rate and the duplex.

Ready at last, you lift the telephone handset and dial the number you want. You listen anxiously for the answer, and the high-pitched tone that tells you a computer has answered your call. Soon, an ear-splitting tone comes over the receiver. Now, you are ready to put your handset in the modem's acoustic cups to complete the connection. As you lower the handset toward the cups, an ambulance screams by your window, sending its siren song into your office, and into your telephone's mouthpiece. The computer at the other end, appalled by the sound it's getting, decides to hang up.

This sort of thing doesn't happen too frequently, but even when you complete the connection successfully, you must send a few keystrokes to make your computer acknowledge the other computer before you can really begin communicating. The whole process takes a few minutes each time, and you feel like you've earned a degree in telecommunications just getting the system to work. And of course, whenever you want to call someone new, you have to study a different set of communications parameters and figure out how to make your computer tell your modem about them. When you were young and irrepressible, it seemed like little enough to do, to actually communicate via computer, but now you look at the whole procedure, compare it with the simplicity of making a phone call or mailing a letter, and you ask yourself, "Why me?"

Who's running the show—you or the computer?

THE NEW DAYS

Fortunately, all this hacking, which was simply to establish the communications link before transmitting anything, is handled automatically by today's modems and software. Most of today's Apple software comes with several predefined sets of parameters that allow you to connect with major information utilities, such as THE SOURCE or Dow Jones, without knowing what parameters those utilities require. (Of course, when a utility changes its method of access, as THE SOURCE did in early 1984, you have to reset the log-on routine yourself, so it still pays to know the ropes anyway.)

Beyond this, many of today's programs have keyboard macro functions that let you store a set of keystrokes (the commands to a specific stock quote, for example, or to search for news stories by key word) under one or two keys. Using macros, you only have to go through the agony of learning and storing the actual set of commands once. Thereafter, you can rely on a simple one- or two-key combination to carry out the commands for you.

The software base for Apple communications was established in 1978, when a cassette-based program for logging on to the Dow Jones information service became available. That base has expanded, and it is going strong today with upgraded versions of old favorites such as United Software's ASCII Express, and with new software, such as Era 2 from Microcom. In the hardware arena, the old acoustic couplers have been replaced by intelligent modems, which come either on internal cards or as separate units. Much of the newer hardware and software will also work with clock cards that enable your computer to send or receive information when you're not around. You can still run into trouble with the telephone lines, but today's Apple products can help by dialing alternate numbers, re-dialing the same number until the connection is made, or verifying the accuracy of data transmitted.

COMMUNICATIONS SOFTWARE

The most important features of a communications program are its compatibility with the modem you're using, the variety of ways it can transfer or receive data, and the ease with which it makes these things possible. Like software in general, communications software for the Apple varies widely in complexity, price, and power, partly because different manufacturers use entirely different approaches to solving the same problems. A lot of communications software is sold by modem manufacturers. Hayes, Microcom, Novation, Transend, and Apple all supply software as well as hardware, and buying a hardware/software combination from a single vendor will ensure compatibility. Otherwise, you have to make sure the software supports the modem you're using.

Hayes is the largest seller of modems in the country, and these days most makers of communications software for personal computers make their programs Hayes-compatible, because they expect most of their market to be using such Hayes products as the Micromodem IIe or the Smartmodem 1200. Hardware has led software in this case, and now modem manufacturers are making sure that their products, too, are Hayes-compatible and will work with all the Hayes-compatible software that's out and around.

Modem interface cards, which contain the circuitry that enables your computer to interact smoothly with your modem, must also be checked for compatibility with your software. Some programs easily support a wider variety of interface cards than others do. You can probably set up a program to support a card that it or its documentation doesn't specifically list as an option, but it's a lot easier to use a program with which you simply choose your interface card from a menu.

Because of the different protocols and the variety of communications modes, the process of computer communications can be complex. Software companies are constantly striving to make the routine easier for us to use. The chief ease-of-use tactic right now is menus. Some software, in fact, lets you do everything from setting parameters to storing log-on routines, from defining keystroke macros to making a connection, all by selecting options from menus. Menu-driven programs require more RAM than other types of programs do, and they often have smaller data buffers, or they load themselves in from disk in overlaid sections, so that you're slowed down by repeated disk accessing.

Menu-driven programs, however, are much easier to use than are programs with few or no menus. In that respect, they're helpful for beginners who aren't familiar with the details of communicating, but they can really slow you down once you know the ropes. If you know you want to go directly to, say, terminal mode and place a call to a certain person, it's a shame to have to step through four menus to do it.

Once the compatibility and ease-of-use issues are resolved, your own needs will determine the sort of file-transferring capabilities you need. Most communications programs transfer individual files to other computers from a memory buffer they create in your computer's RAM. The file is first loaded from disk into memory, and then it is sent directly from memory to the modem.

The difference in capability from one program to the next lies in the size of the program's buffer for transferring files in this way. Since the same RAM used for file storage also has to store the program itself, fancier communications programs can take up more space in RAM, leaving less room for the data. The buffer on Transend 2, for example, holds only about 14K, while the more workaday ASCII Express Professional has a data buffer of 26K on the Apple IIe and 32K on the Apple II+.

One way programs get around buffer limitations in this transfer mode is by having a capability called auto buffer save that lets them automatically save the buffer contents on disk when the buffer gets full. If your program has this feature, you can theoretically receive a whole diskful of information at one sitting. Buffered data exchange has the disadvantage, however, of requiring a lot of attention. If you want to send a selected group of files from disk or you want to receive more than one file and save them to disk separately, you have to send or save each file manually.

Advanced programs get around this file-sitting requirement on your part by offering disk-to-disk transfer, which allows you to send some or all of the files on a disk, one after another, automatically. In order to ensure that multiple files are transmitted accurately when you're not around, software that features multiple-file transmission uses error-checking routines, or protocols. A word of warning about these protocols, however: Some manufacturers subscribe to a common protocol, such as the ones known as the Christensen protocol or Microcom's MNP, but other manufacturers use their own protocols. Software that uses a proprietary error-checking protocol requires both the sender and the recipient of the data to use the same program to communicate.

Another important data-transmission issue is the variety of file types a program will handle. Most programs will only send files created on the same operating system under which they run. Thus, you can't use a communications package that runs under DOS 3.3 to send a word-processed file created under ProDOS or Pascal. Some manufacturers, however, make more than one version of a package to handle other file types. The makers of ASCII Express, for example, also make a CP/M package called Z-Term and a Pascal package called P-Term. Other companies, such as Transend, are beginning to get around this limitation on file types by permitting the transfer of non-native files if an entire disk is sent. Transend 2, version 5.0, for example, is a DOS 3.3 program that permits full-disk transfers of Pascal, CP/M, or ProDOS files. While it can be inconvenient to send a whole disk just to transfer one short Pascal file with a DOS 3.3 communications program, it's cheaper to go through the hassle than it is to buy a separate Pascal communications program. But, if you know you want to send a variety of file types, you should either find a program capable of sending files created under different operating systems or you should buy more than one communications program.

Two other methods of file transfer are the unattended and the electronic mail modes. These modes both require the communications software to support a clock card, and require you to install such a card in your Apple. The unattended mode is simply the automatic transfer of files at a preset time, and electronic mail is the transfer of files to or from several predetermined locations at a preset time.

Electronic mail programs let you create individual "mailboxes" on a diskette for storage of mail from several different sources, and they also let you create lists of correspondents' names and telephone numbers, and the procedures you use for communicating with each. This kind of fancy footwork requires the use of error-checking protocols, however, and can be accomplished only if all the participants are using the same software, or at least the same protocol.

ASCII Express Professional

One of the old favorites among Apple users, United Software's ASCII Express Professional, has been upgraded several times since it was first introduced in 1980. There is a less expensive version of the program called ASCII Express, but the higher-end, Professional version is definitely worth having, especially if you plan on using your computer a great deal for communications. This program's main claims to fame are its extensive macro capabilities, its large data buffer, and its remote-operation mode.

ASCII Express Professional allows you to create up to 26 macro library files, each of which can contain its own telephone number, log-on routine, and keystroke macros for specific data searches or data-transfer procedures. Individual macros can be up to 500 characters long. Several macros can also be linked together, so the possibilities for simplifying and automating the program's interactions with up to 26 different computers are extensive.

ASCII Express Professional also has one of the largest data buffers around (26K for the IIe and 32K for the II+). This buffer size lets you communicate longer via the keyboard and handle larger individual files than you can with most other programs. When you're receiving in the buffered mode, the program has an auto buffer save feature that lets you capture files larger than buffer size. For error-checking, ASCII Express Professional uses the Christensen protocol, which, as the oldest and most widely used error-checking scheme, is as close as this segment of the industry comes to a standard. Because it is something of a standard, the Christensen protocol enables you to communicate more easily with a wider variety of programs than any other protocol allows, although this supremacy is now being challenged by the MNP protocol used in Microcom's Era 2 (discussed in a later section).

The remote operating mode of this program will be particularly useful if you or someone else wants to access your computer's files while you're away. Instead of having to set up a schedule ahead of time, you can leave your computer running and awaiting a call, and then you or someone else can call into it from another computer. Once you make the connection, you can retrieve files from disk or send files to disk and then break the connection when you're through. This feature could, for example, be handy for salespeople who want access to a lot of product information without having to carry it around.

The manual for ASCII Express Professional isn't terribly clear, and the program isn't as easy to use as other, more menu-driven products, but the program is a very solid and powerful piece of work. What it lacks in polish, it more than makes up for in power, speed, and flexibility. ASCII Express Professional costs $129 and is currently available in a DOS 3.3 version, although a ProDOS version is doubtless in the works. The DOS 3.3 version isn't copy protected.

Transend

Transend is really a family of three programs, Transend 1, 2, and 3. Transend 1, a fairly simple program that now sells for $79, was introduced in late 1981, and it was followed six months later by Transend 2, which added file-transfer abilities with error-checking, without making the program significantly harder to use. Transend 3 adds an electronic mail function to Transend 2. The key feature of these products is ease of use.

Transend 1 is a buffered transfer program that lets you send or receive files by means of a 14K data buffer. Although 14K is fairly small for a data buffer, the program has an auto buffer save feature that sends the buffer contents to disk when the buffer is full. You can specify and store communications parameters for up to eight different computers, and then store up to 22 macros for each of the eight sets of parameters. The program also features an auto log-on capability that lets you define a log-on procedure for another computer and then run the procedure automatically when you boot the program disk. Several empty lines that you can define in the auto log-on sequence allow you to enter enough information to get well into specific areas of information utilities.

Transend 2 is identical to Transend 1, except that it adds an error-checking transmission mode and sells for $119. The program uses a proprietary error-checking protocol. Until recently, you had to be sending to another Transend 2 user to take advantage of the error-checking mode, but the new ProDOS versions of Transend packages give you a choice of either the Transend or the Christensen error-checking protocols. Newer versions (5.0 or greater) also let you send ProDOS, SOS (the Apple III's Sophisticated Operating System), CP/M, or Pascal files in addition to DOS 3.3 files. You have to send the contents of a whole disk (instead of individual files off the disk), and the receiver's disk has to be blank, but nevertheless, these newer versions save the cost of buying a separate program to transmit files created under another operating system.

Transend 3, which sells for $220, works like Transend 2, with the addition of an electronic mail feature. Transend 3 lets you create individual mailboxes for dozens of people, and lets you send and receive mail from the mailboxes under the control of a clock card. The program supports all the major Apple clock cards, but you have to be communicating with other Transend 3 users to make it work.

All of these Transend programs are completely menu driven—to the point that some might say the use of menus is excessive, as there are more than 100 in the program. A selection from one menu brings up another menu, and a selection from that one usually brings up yet another menu. The menus make the program easy for beginners to use, but since you often have to go through three or four menus to place a call, they are also cumbersome. For experts, however, Transend features an Expert mode, in which you can enter, at one time, all the menu selections you'll need to make in order to get where you want to go. From the main menu, for example, you can enter ABBA as the selections for the next four menus, and the program will take you directly to the point following the fourth menu. This shortcut saves a little disk-access and menu-display time, but you can't use it unless (or until) you know enough about the menus to be able to specify the choices in advance.

Nevertheless, because Transend is price competitive, easy to learn, and well advertised, and because it packs most of the features of other programs into one of its three versions, this program is a popular choice among Apple owners. It has been made more popular by its inclusion in combination packages called Transpacks, which include one of the Transend software products, as well as the necessary Transend hardware (a Transend serial interface card, and either a Transend 300-baud modem card or a Transend 300/1200-baud external modem). The modem is as good as anyone else's, but you can do better in an interface card, as you'll see in the hardware section toward the end of this chapter.

Era 2

Like Transend and others, Microcom, of Norwood, Mass., manufactures modems as well as software. The company's Micro-COURIER software has long been popular, but Microcom recently began selling a hardware/software package called Era 2. With Era 2, Microcom is trying to establish its own error-checking protocol, called MNP (Microcom Networking Protocol), as the industry standard. If Microcom is successful, MNP could well make error-checking transmissions possible between any two personal computers, regardless of brand, but of course you could say the same thing for Christensen or any other protocol that became the industry standard.

With Era 2, Microcom packs just about every conceivable communications feature into one package, and then charges you $499 for it. What you get is error-checking software that permits disk-to-disk transfer with any other computer using MNP software, auto log-on capabilities, keyboard macros, storage of a theoretically unlimited number of telephone numbers (the real limit is disk space), terminal emulation that lets your Apple imitate major mainframe computer terminals (which include the

DEC VT-100 and the IBM 3101), electronic mail features, and the ability to send or receive data files in unattended mode without requiring a clock card for control. You also get an internal, 300/1200-baud intelligent modem. The software is menu-driven and easy to learn, and when you add its long list of features to the inclusion of a modem, the package deal looks like a good one, whether or not Microcom succeeds in getting MNP standard off the ground.

MODEMS

When it comes to modems, you can choose anything from a very inexpensive dumb modem to a highly sophisticated intelligent modem. Most of these products are external, and will work with any computer, but because the Apple has internal expansion slots, you have the option of saving some money and desk space by installing an internal modem. Generally, the more intelligent the modem, the easier it is to use. Such "intelligent" features as automatic dialing, automatic answering, and automatic redialing of busy numbers really take the burden out of communicating, and they're well worth having for a few extra dollars.

In terms of price, you can get a plain, dumb, 300-baud Anchor Signalman Mark I or Novation J-Cat for $150 or less. Or, you can get an intelligent modem, such as the Microcom PCS 2000, which has a 64K data buffer and a built-in clock and software, for about $1000. Or, of course, you can get something in between.

Transmission speed marks the real dividing line in price as far as the modem market is concerned. A top-of-the-line 300-baud modem, such as the Hayes Smartmodem 300, will retail for less than $300, while an average 300/1200-baud modem will cost close to $500. If you're planning on doing a lot of communicating, particularly if it's long-distance communicating, it will be worth your while to go with the more expensive, 1200-baud modem, because its faster transmission speed will save you at least 60 percent on your telephone bill. Over the life of the modem, your phone bill will undoubtedly exceed the modem's original cost anyway, so it pays to minimize your phone charges, if you can.

Modem prices have also been dropping steadily over the past few years, and the extra speed should soon be within everyone's financial reach as technological improvements continue. For example, one big cost saving for manufacturers, that has since been passed on to consumers, was the development of a single chip that could handle the tasks of a 300-baud modem. This chip reduced assembly costs and increased reliability, as well. A faster 1200-baud modem-on-a-chip should also be available soon.

Another issue, other than price, that you must consider in choosing a modem for the Apple is whether you want an internal or external model. An internal modem will save you money and desk space, but you can't move it if you ever buy a different type of computer. With an internal modem, you have both the modem and the necessary modem/computer interface on one card that fills one slot in your Apple. Often, you also get some software which, depending on the modem, can be anything from limited to very flexible. An external modem takes up desk space, and it requires an interface card in a slot, anyway. An internal modem costs roughly what an external modem costs, but with an external modem, you have to spend an added $100 to $150 on an interface card.

Compatibility with Hayes products is also something to consider. Hayes is the granddaddy of microcomputer modem manufacturers, and virtually all the good communications software is designed to work with Hayes or Hayes-compatible modems. It's actually pretty hard to find a modem that's not Hayes-compatible, but if you do, think carefully before buying it.

The last major consideration is the level of sophistication you want in a modem: dumb, smart, or fancy. Dumb modems are the cheapest, the smallest, and the least trouble. They force you to dial your own phone, select the mode that either originates or answers a call, and set half or full duplex (transmission out, in, or both) manually. They're not pretty, but they deliver basic performance. Intelligent, or smart modems make life easier. They work with your software to dial numbers, answer the phone, and hang up by themselves. They usually have built-in speakers so you can monitor the progress of a call when you are making a connection. Most smart modems also let you select either pulse or tone dialing, which is important if you're using alternative telephone services, such as MCI or Sprint, with which only tone-dialed calls are allowed.

Modems at the third level of sophistication could be called fancy modems. They are smart modems that offer added features, such as their own data buffers, their own built-in software, and internal clock/calendar features. These modems cost a few hundred dollars more than smart modems, but they don't require any extra software. Because they have their own data buffers, power supplies, and software, fancy modems can operate independently of your computer, so you can leave such a modem on at night to receive files without having to leave your entire computer running, too.

Dumb Modems

These days, it really doesn't make sense to buy a dumb modem for an Apple II, unless you have a IIc. The IIc has a built-in interface, so you don't have this extra expense, and a dumb modem is worth considering for price alone. With any other II-series Apple, however, by the time you buy the modem, the software, and an interface, you'll have spent as much as you would have on a smart internal modem with software. Still, there are some inherent advantages, such as simplicity, to dumb modems, so if you want to consider them, here are a few choices.

The Anchor Signalman Mark I and the Novation J-Cat are battery operated and, as mentioned earlier, they are inexpensive ($150 or less). With both models, you plug the modem into your computer and phone line, push the originate switch if you're calling out (or the answer switch if you're receiving), and then you take the telephone handset off the hook and dial out or receive the call. There are no DIP switches to be set, no indicator lights to dazzle you, no baud rates for you to select.

Dumb modems are usually 300 baud or 110/300 baud, and they range in price, at retail, from $75 to $150. If you don't do much communicating, or only communicate with one person all the time, you may not miss the frills of a smart or a fancy modem.

Smart Modems

Smart modems range in price from a low of $129 to as much as $700, at retail. The cheapest are the internal modems, such as the Zoom Telephonics Networker, the Transend Modemcard, the Hayes Micromodem IIe, or the Novation Apple Cat II. These products are priced between $129 (Networker) and $389 (Apple Cat II), and are all 110/300 baud only. They are all sold with some software, ranging from limited in the case of the Networker to very nice in the case of the Micromodem, which comes with Hayes' Smartcom program.

Internal smart modems are simple, yet sophisticated products because they are designed to work effortlessly with the programs with which they are sold. You simply plug the modem card into an expansion slot in your Apple, boot the software (which is sometimes already set up especially for the modem), and communicate to your heart's delight. There are some functional differences between products, such as better software or the ability to dial both tone and pulse calls. Of all the internal Apple modems, the Hayes Micromodem IIe is the best known and, like all Hayes modems, has always been a best-seller in its class.

You can also have 1200-baud speed on an internal modem. Novation's 212 Apple-Cat II and Microcom's Era 2 modem are both 1200-baud internal smart modems. The Microcom product is $499 with software, a good value.

The external smart modems are exemplified by the Hayes Smartmodem 1200—the product the rest of the industry tries mightily to compete with. This isn't the cheapest modem on the block at $699 retail (other 1200-baud modems retail for as little as $400) but, like the Micromodem IIe, the Smartmodem 1200 has an impeccable reputation and is compatible with any sort of software you might need. The Smartmodem 1200 is also widely discounted, and it can easily be bought for a more reasonable $500 or so.

The Smartmodem 1200 was introduced in June, 1982, and has topped sales charts for this type of modem ever since. Although another company, called Bizcomp, had an intelligent external modem out about six months earlier, Hayes had superior marketing, and today you'll find that the Smartmodem design has been widely imitated.

Software is extra with the Hayes Smartmodem, but if you're not determined to own a Hayes product, you can find other 1200-baud hardware/software package deals and save some money. U.S. Robotics, for example, sells its Password 300/1200-baud modem and Telpac software for $449. With any external modem, you'll have to invest an extra $100 to $150 on a serial interface card, but you'll end up with a modem you can take anywhere.

Fancy Modems

I place fancy modems in a category by themselves. They deliver a lot more function than smart modems do, but at a generally higher price. Fancy modems have built-in data buffers, which start as small as 16K and go up to 64K; they have built-in clock/calendars; and they have their own software and power supplies. The best-known of the fancy modems is the Microcom PCS-2000, which you can see in Figure 6-1 and which, at $1195, comes with built-in software, a clock/calendar, and a 64K data buffer. Other fancy modems range in price from the Prometheus Pro-Modem 1200, with its Options Processor, for $750, to the Visionary 1200, from Visionary Electronics, for about $1200.

Without the need for extra software, fancy modems can send or receive electronic mail when you're not around, dial up a data base and download (collect) information, or receive data when your computer is

Figure 6-1
The Microcom PCS-2000

turned off. Changing the duplex or baud rate, changing the date, storing phone numbers, setting the time, or creating log-on files for different data bases are all easy tasks with fancy modems.

Some of these products have friendlier software than others, but generally they're all quite easy to use. Most of them have LED or LCD character displays that tell you when you have messages waiting, or indicate how long you've been connected. The buffers on fancy modems can be used for both outgoing and incoming data, so you can send a file out to your modem's buffer for transmission and then continue working with your computer on something else at the same time, or you can receive a file without dropping whatever else you're doing.

All in all, fancy modems give you a lot of convenience, and if you do a lot of communicating, the buffer and the modem's capacity for unattended operation will be worth the extra money. If your needs are less complex, you can get away with a cheaper system.

The best course is to think of the software first, and consider your needs in light of its capabilities. Once you've done that, you'll have a wide choice of modems on which to implement it. You can send electronic mail at 1200 baud with an Era 2 setup and a clock card, for example, but by the time you spend that much money you might find yourself within shooting distance of a fancy modem with those features, plus a buffer.

MODEM INTERFACE CARDS

If you go with an external modem, make sure you get a convenient interface for it. Any modem needs a serial interface card, but there are two basic kinds of serial cards, and choosing the right one can save you a lot of hassle. One type of interface card has a programmable processor chip that controls the baud rate of the card; the other kind of interface does not. For communications, this one factor means the difference between being able to use a simple software command to switch between 300 and 1200 baud, or manually having to flip a switch or move a jumper on the interface board itself.

Imagine the inconvenience of the latter: You call somebody to transmit a file, but once you make contact you learn that the other person has only a 300-baud modem, while yours is set to transmit at 1200 baud. If you have a non-programmable interface card, you have to hang up, turn the computer off, remove the computer's lid, move the jumper or flip a DIP switch on the card, put the lid back on, turn the computer back on, reboot the software, and reselect the file you want to send. Then, you have to call back and make contact again. With a programmable card, on the other hand, you could simply change the speed through a software command without the need to shut the computer off and reboot. Having a software-selectable baud rate seems like a small thing, until you get into a situation like this one.

It was mentioned earlier that the interface card in the Transpack package was not the best available, and this is the reason. The Transend ASIO card supplied with that company's Transpack 1200 uses a non-programmable processor, and you have to move a jumper on the card whenever you switch baud rates on the modem.

Beyond determining the type of interface card you prefer, you could go for extra goodies on the card itself, such as two communications ports instead of one (many cards have both a serial and a parallel port on the same card) or a clock (as on the Mountain CPS card). A basic serial interface card, such as the ALS Dispatcher, will cost you from $100 to $150; extras will cost you extra.

MAINFRAME INTERFACES

A lot of people think that you need an IBM PC in order to talk to an IBM mainframe computer, and certainly the magazines are filled with IBM PC interface boards that make this communication possible. But you can also buy such an interface for your Apple II. The Apple Communications Protocol Card endows your Apple II with the synchronous communications ability it needs to converse with an IBM 370 mainframe (in other words, the card puts your Apple on the same internal timing as the mainframe). The card will let your Apple emulate, or imitate, an IBM 3278 or 3780 terminal and let it talk to a 370 as if it were a member of the IBM family. The card sells for about $1000, and opens up yet another "serious" business application widely thought to be the exclusive turf of the IBM PC and other 16-bit computers.

If you use the Communications Protocol Card, you'll also want terminal-emulation software, so the display on your Apple looks just like it would on the terminal it's pretending to be. Such communications programs as ASCII Express Professional and Era 2 include this capability. The display on actual terminals is 80 columns across, so if you don't already have an 80-column display card, you'll need one for this particular application.

CLOCK CARDS

Unless you buy a fancy modem, you'll have to install a clock card in your Apple to perform electronic mail functions. Clock cards cost from $100 to $150 and may seem like a shocking waste of money in most situations, but they're required for unattended transmission or receipt of data. If you use a clock to transmit files automatically during low-rate calling periods, the reduced phone bills will more than offset the cost of the clock in the long run.

For example, suppose you want to call THE SOURCE or send a file to a friend. You could do it in the middle of the day, when connect time is the most expensive, or you could wait until the middle of the night and have your computer do it automatically. You can save 60 percent on your phone bill by sending during the off-hours, and you have the added benefit (when dealing with information utilities) of using the system when very few others are. If you're sending electronic mail, you have the benefit of the dollar savings of calling during off hours, as well as that of using the phone network when the lines are likely to be freer of the kind of noise that can disrupt or even prevent an error-checked transmission.

Clock cards for the Apple usually come with a software diskette that lets you set the time, display it in different ways, and verify the clock's accuracy or the adequacy of its batteries. All clocks run on batteries, which usually last four or five years. Once you plug in a clock and verify that it is producing the correct time and date, you will probably be able to forget about it completely for a long time. Unless the software you're running is looking for it, a clock is invisible to your Apple.

For maximum usefulness from a clock, you should buy one that is supported by major software manufacturers. The most popular clocks are the Mountain Hardware Clock from Mountain Computer and the Thunderclock. The people at Thunderware have managed to finagle Apple into naming the Thunderclock the "Official ProDOS Clock," so it might be wise to go with that brand. On the other hand, the Thunderclock is at the high end of the price range, so you might want to substitute a lesser-known brand that offers Thunderclock compatibility. As with modems, clock-card makers realize that the Thunderclock has the lion's share of the market and that all the good software is written to support its particular design, so they make sure their clocks will act like a Thunderclock and thus be supported by the software, too.

Some clocks are also sold with calendar or appointment software, but often such clocks are not compatible with the Thunderclock, and they will force you to choose which application you really want the clock for. If you're going to use software for electronic mail or you want to transmit files automatically in the wee hours of the morning, check the software you're using to see which clocks it will support. A lot of clock-using software comes with discount coupons that get you 20 to 30 percent off the price of a Thunderclock, so this might be the way to go. Otherwise, you can find clocks discounted to about $100 from mail-order houses.

Communications is probably the best excuse to buy a clock card, but once you have one, you can use it for more than communicating. A clock supported by ProDOS will label files with the date and time you create or modify them, so you can tell which is the latest version of a file simply by looking at the times listed next to the files in the disk catalog. Clock cards also work with some database management programs to date reports you generate automatically, and some word processors can access a clock to date form letters automatically. And if you are truly adventurous, some clocks, such as the Thunderclock from Thunderware, can be used to drive the BSR X-10 home control system, which turns lights, alarms, and appliances on and off at preselected times. Factory-installed clocks in computers are becoming more and more common (as in the IBM PC XT and the Apple Macintosh), and as they spread, software that makes good use of them will doubtless follow.

NETWORKING

If you own a small business or you work in a department where there are several computers, networking can help unite your electronic resources. With your computers linked in a network, you have both computing power on your desktop and a lot more power via the network. Large hard disks, laser printers, large plotters, and other expensive peripheral equipment can be shared easily by dozens of Apples or other computers. From your Apple, you can send electronic mail to other computers, exchange files, or access disk storage far larger than your individual computer could handle. Networks are excellent for uniting several computers that are being used for common applications, such as accounting. They are also an efficient way for a group of otherwise incompatible computers to communicate with each other.

Network options for the Apple II have been available since 1980. Corvus Systems, for example, had an early system called the Multiplexer that linked up to five Apple II computers. Today, Corvus sells its Omninet network, which allows Apple II, Apple III, IBM PC, Texas Instruments Professional, DEC Rainbow, Zenith Z-100, and Corvus Concept computers to communicate and share data as if they were all the same make and model.

This type of teamwork is the goal of most newer network systems, and such systems offer you a way to make your Apple II part of a group of newer computers, instead of having to upgrade to a newer computer of your own for the sake of compatibility. The new networks, such as the Corvus Omninet, allow you to link 32, 64, or even more "nodes," or individual devices (computers, printers, hard disks, and so forth), so a network can handle the needs of a fairly large business or office.

Network systems always include at least one hard disk, two or more computers, network interfaces for each computer, network software, and cables and connectors that hook the computers to each other and to the hard disk. Unless the hard disk has built-in file-serving circuitry, as the Corvus Omnidrives do, you'll also need a separate file server to direct the incoming and outgoing traffic from various computers, and to make certain the right computer gets the file it asked for. If you want to share printers, you'll need a printer server, which is a control box that directs traffic to one or more printers.

If your needs demand it, a network can become quite large and powerful. On a 32-node network, for example, you might have twenty different personal computers, ten 20-megabyte hard disks, and two printers. With the right software, any individual computer would have access to the 200 megabytes of storage, or it could send messages to any other computer on the network. Because the system uses cables instead of telephone lines, it is far more reliable than phone-based networks.

The installation of a network is fairly complex, and definitely shouldn't be undertaken without professional advice, but there are some basic considerations you should keep in mind. If you are planning to operate several different kinds of computers, make sure the network system will accommodate all the equipment you want. The system must be compatible with the different computers, and that means that the network cable must work with all your computers, and the hard disk must support all the different operating systems the computers use (for more on this, see the section on hard disks in Chapter 4).

Beyond this, you must consider that networking software can vary from one supplier to another. Software is available from network hardware companies, such as Corvus, Davong, and Apple, as well as from independent vendors. Some manufacturer-supplied software only takes care of the basic data interchange between the computers and the hardware. Fancier software allows for electronic mail among computers or file-management extras, such as password protection of certain hard-disk volumes. Whatever your needs, choose the software that gets *your* job done.

And one last item to consider in a network installation is a backup device for your hard disk. This device can simply be another hard disk that contains the same information as the primary one, or it can be a dedicated backup unit, such as the Corvus Bank. Network software should provide a means to back up the hard disk easily (and preferably automatically) with either type of backup device.

Any way you slice it, a network installation adds up to a lot of money, even if you assume that the computers have already been purchased. Hard disks large enough (20 megabytes or more) to be useful in a network cost about $3000 on up. External file servers cost about $1000 more. Printer servers are another $1000. The cost for cables and connectors is nominal in comparison, usually less than $400 for a five-computer system. And for each computer in the network, the interface will run anywhere from $300 to $500. For a five-computer system with a 20-megabyte hard disk and a printer server, you're looking at about $7500, plus installation.

Networks are becoming more and more popular, however, particularly in large businesses that have bought several different kinds of personal computers over the years, and the prices of network components are dropping steadily. Within a few years, network interfaces for individual computers should drop to less than $100 each, and the prices of hard disks should decrease at least 30 percent. As networking technology becomes more popular, it will probably become simpler as well, eventually making it possible for anyone with a pair of pliers to install a network.

And as far as you and your Apple II are concerned, perhaps the most important thing to remember is that you won't be left out of the action as networking and other communications technologies move ahead.

SHOWCASE SYSTEMS

These three systems will give you an idea of the different classes and varying capabilities of communications equipment for the Apple. Networked systems can contain different components, at widely varying prices, so it's difficult to present a system that represents a typical installation.

BARGAIN BASEMENT

Apple II, II+, or IIe	Currently Owned
Zoom Telephonics Networker modem	$ 129
Transend 1 software	$ 79
Total Extras	$ 208

Added Power: Auto-dial, auto-answer, 110/300-baud internal modem; easy-to-use software with basic buffer transfer mode.

MIDDLE OF THE ROAD

Apple II, II+, or IIe	Currently Owned
Microcom Era 2 hardware/software package	$ 499
Thunderclock	$ 150
Total Extras	$ 649

Added Power: Auto-dial, auto-answer, 300/1200-baud internal modem; full-featured software with error-checking, multiple file transmission, and electronic mail features; clock for electronic mail and unattended operation.

TOP DRAWER

Apple II, II+, IIe	Currently Owned
Microcom PCS-2000 modem with 64K buffer	$1195
Practical Peripherals SeriALL interface	$ 159
Total Extras	$1354

Added Power: Auto-dial, auto-answer, 300/1200-baud external modem; electronic mail and error-checking transmission capability; clock/calendar; 64K data buffer; software-switchable interface card.

C H A P T E R

7

GORGEOUS GRAPHICS

Apple was the company that brought graphics to the personal computer, and Apple has remained a leader in this field ever since. Before the Apple II was introduced, most computer manufacturers treated the display of text or graphics as something unimportant. The memory that handled the display was separate from the rest of the computer's memory, so the interactions among the processor, the memory, and the display were fairly slow.

Apple's breakthrough was in combining the text and graphics display memory with the regular memory. Thus, Apple's display of a graphics demonstration program at the 1977 West Coast Computer Faire marked the introduction of flexible, interactive graphics and text displays on personal computers. Apple changed the display screen from something that merely told you what the computer was doing to an easel on which you could manipulate words or pictures, for pleasure or profit. Since then, all personal computer manufacturers have followed Apple's lead and have given their machines built-in display memory.

In the early days, creating graphics on the Apple II was difficult. You had to know the memory addresses (information-storage locations) that corresponded to each pixel, or dot of light, on the screen. The Apple high-resolution screen contains over 53,000 individual pixels, and since one memory address can control only seven of them, it's easy to see that people wanting to use graphics in those days had to keep tabs on a lot of addresses. To manipulate pixel groups to produce graphics, early users had to write programs that would turn different screen pixels on and off and would make the Apple's processor produce different colors. This programming was an extremely slow process, however, and it was frustrating to developers who wanted to be able to concentrate on the *kinds* of images they produced for games and educational programs, rather than on getting the Apple to produce the images in the first place.

To make life easier for would-be graphics wizards, graphics utility programs began to appear by the dozen. Some of these programs provided an interface ("translation") between the screen-display codes and the user, and they allowed developers to "draw" objects in different colors, locate the objects on the screen, and duplicate or save them to disk by using the keyboard or a joystick. Other utility programs simply added graphics commands to the Applesoft BASIC set of commands, so that people could control graphics more easily by programming in a higher-level, more English-like language, instead of having to address the hardware directly via assembly or machine language.

As utility programs became easier to use, developers created an ever-widening array of programs for various applications. Artists awoke to the potential of computer graphics. Architects began substituting the Apple for expensive CAD (computer-aided design) systems. Television producers started creating storyboards on Apples and saving them to disk so they could be replayed later. Analysts began generating charts from spreadsheet data. New applications begat new programs, and new programs begat new applications, and soon hundreds of Apple graphics programs were being used by thousands of people.

When the IBM PC was introduced, it was hailed as an advance in graphics hardware because of its 16-bit processor and higher-capacity disk drives. The larger amount of RAM possible on the IBM PC was also a blessing. For example, one Apple high-resolution screen image (roughly comparable to the IBM's four-color, medium-resolution mode) uses up over 8K of storage. So the IBM's potential 256K or 512K of RAM provided that machine with a decided advantage over a 48K or 64K Apple II. Similarly, at 8K apiece, it was possible to store only about twelve high-resolution pictures on a 140K Apple II diskette, while a 320K IBM diskette would store nearly three times as many pictures. (Developers were already using picture-packing techniques to compress graphics data files and increase the graphics storage of Apple disks by then, but it was still nice to have more diskette space to work with.) Finally, the IBM's larger amount of RAM made it a lot easier for business software developers to combine graphics with spreadsheet or database programs. Graphics were a more visible application in the 16-bit world, and graphics software developers began to concentrate on products for the IBM PC as its market share grew.

Meanwhile, other personal computers, from the NEC Advanced Personal Computer to the Commodore 64, promised either more colors or higher resolution than the Apple II. Game developers began to prefer the Commodore or Atari machines to the Apple, because they had a wider following among game-players. And even Apple's own Lisa and Macintosh featured easier input and better graphics software than did the Apple II. All these factors make the Apple II look as antiquated as it might very well be, if your graphics hardware and software haven't kept up with the times.

AN EYE OPENER

For example, suppose you're a commercial artist in the art department of a large company. You've used an Apple II with a color television and an early graphics package for a couple of years. Mostly, you use your Apple to create graphics for use in the video department's programs, or to produce special, three-color drawings for board meetings. But having to "draw" with a joystick feels so unnatural that you often do things by hand, anyway.

At a recent meeting of your professional society, someone demonstrated an IBM PC with an RGB monitor and that funny little pointing device everyone calls a mouse, and you went wild. This equipment let you draw just as you would on paper, and it reproduced your images accurately on the screen. The resolution on the monitor was so good that you could barely see the individual dots in the screen images, and the dots barely showed when the images were printed out with the ink-jet printer that was hooked to the system. With such a system, you thought, you could do all your work more easily. Tools like these would really let you concentrate on your drawing, instead of on the software that you used to do it.

On the other hand, maybe you're not an artist at all. Maybe you've been smitten by the new graphics-oriented interfaces now being offered on the Macintosh and the Lisa, and by windowing environments such as VisiON and Microsoft Windows. Maybe you think screen icons, mice, and pull-down menus are the wave of the future, and you're afraid you'll be left behind with your Apple II or IIe.

THE IIe WATERSHED

As far as the trend toward higher-resolution screens goes, the Revision B of the IIe represents the dividing line between levels of function on your Apple. Here's why:

A few months before the IIe was released (but after the final design of the IIe had been approved), someone at Apple figured out that the extended memory card being produced for the IIe could be used to double the horizontal resolution of the IIe's normal high-resolution graphics display. The scheme, essentially, involved using part of the extra memory on the Extended 80-column card to store a second high-resolution screen image that was separate from the image stored in the computer's RAM. The regular high-resolution screen and the auxiliary high-resolution screen that resided on the Extended 80-column card could then be combined to deliver twice the horizontal resolution (in other words, twice as many pixels across the screen).

The design involved a change in the motherboard, and unfortunately, Apple had already made some 70,000 IIe units by the time it decided to go ahead with the revision. If you own a IIe, you can tell which version you have by looking at the serial number at the back edge of the motherboard, next to the cutouts for interface cables. If the number is followed by an A, you're out of luck—no double high-resolution graphics for you, unfortunately. If the number is followed by a B and you have an

Apple Extended 80-column card (not someone else's display/memory card), you're in business. To produce double high-resolution graphics, all you have to do is install a jumper on your Extended 80-column card. You can find instructions either at an Apple dealership or in some of the software packages that use this added power. If you own a Revision A IIe, your best bet is to change your motherboard. Apple has been offering free exchange motherboards to Revision A owners, as long as the owner has also bought an Extended 80-column card. The double high-resolution graphics don't work without the extra memory, so Apple requires that you own the card to get the free exchange. You should be able to have the board exchanged in a few minutes at any Apple dealer, but call first to be sure the dealer has a replacement Revision B board in stock before you pack up your system and head over there.

The enhanced graphics capability of the newer IIe was pretty much ignored during the computer's first two years on the market, but now Apple and others are putting it to work. And if you're wowed by the Macintosh display, which has a monochrome resolution of 512 by 342 pixels, you'll be pleasantly surprised by a double high-resolution Apple IIe, which has a monochrome resolution of 560 by 192 pixels (as opposed to the normal high-resolution display of 280 by 192 pixels). Vertical lines will still have dots in them, because the vertical resolution doesn't change, but horizontal lines will be even sharper than they are on the Macintosh, and that's saying something. Eventually, this clarity will be translated into Macintosh-like devices for using software, such as pull-down menus and screen icons that are controlled by a mouse. Apple has already prepared for this change with its release of the AppleMouse II, and more and more programs are appearing to support a mouse all the time.

But while it's true that an Apple IIe can give you twice the resolution of an Apple II, there is a lot of graphics power available for the owner of either machine. Developers of graphics software are increasingly taking advantage of double high-resolution graphics power, but they're also continuing to support the regular high-resolution mode of the early IIe and the II/II+ line. So whether you're a frustrated artist or a non-artist who wants to keep up with general trends in software technology, you can upgrade your Apple II to satisfy almost any need in this area.

GRAPHICS SOFTWARE

Any personal computer graphics system depends on compatibility among software, hardware, the input device, and peripherals. Graphics on the Apple is no exception. Different software developers support different input and output devices, so you will have to match your needs to both the graphics software and the devices it supports. If you are new to graphics, for example, and you want to try drawing with a mouse, you'll have to find a program that accepts mouse-generated input, and that will print your pictures on your printer. Likewise, if you want to draw pie charts with a plotter, you'll have to be sure the software you choose matches the plotter you want. If you're using a dot-matrix printer for output, you'll have to make sure the program you use will transfer graphics to the printer. And if you want to transfer graphics files via modem, you'll have to be sure the program creates files that can be sent this way.

Once you satisfy these requirements, you'll find there's a wider selection of graphics software for the Apple than there is for any other personal computer. Prices range from about $30 to as much as $2000 for a complete CAD system, but most of the consumer-oriented programs sell for less than $150.

Choosing a package is really a matter of deciding what you want to do. Here are some examples of the types of programs available for different graphics applications, but this sampling only scratches the surface of graphics software for the Apple II. The chances are that whatever your need, you can find a program to fill it, whether you want to generate charts from dBASE II files, produce graphic displays of audio frequencies, create quality video animation, graph the results of scientific experiments, develop your own video games, or just doodle.

Drawing Programs

Just about the easiest way to explore the graphics capabilities of the Apple II or IIe is with MousePaint, a program being sold with the AppleMouse II for $149. If you buy the AppleMouse II for use with another application, getting MousePaint, too, is a nice bonus indeed.

MousePaint was meant to be a demonstration program that showed off the AppleMouse's capabilities, but it is a very sophisticated product in its own right. The program was written by Bill Budge, one of the kings of Apple graphics, so perhaps it isn't so surprising that MousePaint is a simple, yet exceedingly powerful product. Inspired by the MacPaint program sold for the Macintosh, MousePaint looks very much like its relative, except that it's in color, instead of black and white.

The standard MousePaint display screen shows a drawing area with a group of shapes and drawing options on the left side and a selection of patterns to fill in your artwork at the bottom. You use the mouse to choose one of five different brush sizes, a pencil, or a spray can to draw with, and you draw shapes by holding down the button on the mouse and by moving the mouse pointer in the drawing area. If you choose the option for drawing a square or a circle, a "rubber-band" effect lets you preview the size of a shape before it's drawn: As long as you hold the mouse button down, the circle or square grows or shrinks as you move the mouse pointer away from or toward your original starting point, and when you release the mouse button, the shape is permanently drawn at the size shown.

Once your shape is drawn, you can fill it in with any of 30 different, colored patterns. In addition, you can use a utility called FatBits to enlarge a section of the screen or a fill pattern so you can change individual pixels to modify the existing patterns or to create new ones. And if you make a mistake, no problem. You can use the mouse to choose an eraser icon and rub out all or part of a drawing. You can copy all or part of an object, or you can move it to a different part of the drawing area. And, there's a text mode that lets you add text to your drawings in any of several type styles.

MousePaint is addictive: Once you begin playing with it, you lose all track of time. MacPaint is causing a sensation with the Macintosh, and MousePaint delivers nearly the same capability (you trade a little execution speed and lose a few drawing functions in favor of color) for $149. If you're going to want to print your MousePaint creations, though, be forewarned that the program only supports Apple's own Scribe and Imagewriter printers at this time.

MousePaint was the first graphics program to use the AppleMouse II, but several other products now available also use this small device, and you can expect to see more mouse-compatible drawing programs in the future. Dazzle Draw from Broderbund Software and The Graphics Magician from Penguin Software, for example, are just two other examples of powerful, inexpensive products that let you produce eye-popping graphics without knowing a thing about programming or pixel addresses. Dazzle Draw, for example, offers double high-resolution quality and offers on-line help from a pull-down menu. Although Dazzle Draw's double high-resolution graphics make the program off-limits to anyone who doesn't own a IIc or a Revision B IIe with 128K of RAM, the program supports several dot-matrix printers and sells for only $49.95. A separate program, called Dazzle Dance, that sells for the same price, lets you store several Dazzle Draw pictures and display them quickly for an animation effect.

The Graphics Magician, on the other hand, will run on any Apple. It doesn't offer as many drawing options as Dazzle Draw does, but it uses a file compression technique that lets your Apple store hundreds of graphics on the same disk and then play them back in rapid succession for a kind of animation.

Business Graphics

Since screen resolution isn't nearly as critical with business graphics programs as it is with drawing programs, most business graphics software will work on any Apple. So, if you've got business on the brain, Apple graphics programs can help jazz up your presentations or reports, or their results can even take the place of slide shows. For example, there are a lot of programs that translate spreadsheet data into pie, line, or bar charts. PFS: Graph, a popular Apple-compatible product, can create several different kinds of graphs from VisiCalc spreadsheet data. If you're also using PFS: Write, you can even insert graphs created with PFS: Graph into written reports or letters. PFS: Graph retails for $125 and supports a variety of printers and plotters.

Along with reading spreadsheet data, some programs also offer a wider variety of graphics functions. Graphics Department, from Sensible Software, produces pie, line, scatter, and bar charts from VisiCalc files, but it also contains a lettering kit, so you can produce different titles on the charts in any of twenty different type styles. Further features of this $125 package include a tool kit that lets you rearrange charts, change the display colors, or combine charts on one screen, and a slide projection option that lets you arrange several charts and then display them in sequence. Unlike PFS: Graph, however, this program is primarily for slide shows; it doesn't have built-in facilities for printing the data you create on the screen.

One of the best-selling programs for creating monochrome drawings and printing them out is Fontrix, a product of Data Transforms. Fontrix lets you create large pictures—up to sixteen times the size of the Apple's display area—and then print them out on any of more than two dozen different brands of dot-matrix printers. Along with graphics, the package comes with eleven predefined fonts, or typefaces, as well as an editor that lets you make up your own character sets. Data Transforms also sells separate diskettes containing additional fonts. The program runs on any Apple II computer and sells for $75.

Another easy-to-use program for a different set of needs is The Print Shop from Broderbund Software. This is a limited-function program specifically designed to make it easy to create and print signs, greeting cards, stationery, and letterheads. You can choose type styles, background patterns, objects and borders and then place them on a greeting card, sign, or letterhead with the text you enter. The program comes with eight different type styles and sixty pre-drawn objects, and there's a graphics editor that lets you create your own shapes or objects. The Print Shop retails for $49 and supports seven different brands of dot-matrix printers.

GRAPHICS COPROCESSORS

The Commodore and Atari machines have superior graphics abilities to the Apple II because each of these machines contains a separate chip that does nothing but produce graphics on the computer's screen. Since the Apple's 6502 processor must handle graphics along with data processing and other functions, it can't perform as well. One way to dramatically improve the Apple's capabilities is to give it an extra graphics display chip. The chip comes on a plug-in circuit board, much like a RAM board or a video display board, and significantly enhances the Apple's graphics display powers.

The major graphics coprocessor boards are the Sprite boards from Synetix, Inc. The Sprite boards come in three models: Sprite 1, Sprite 2, and SuperSprite, which cost $149, $249, and $395, respectively. Each of these boards lets you create up to 32 "sprites," or graphics objects, on the screen at once. These objects can be moved over a fixed background, and can be displayed in up to sixteen different colors.

Sprite boards make it easier for you to animate objects and move them about the Apple's screen, but it takes some effort to use them. The boards are supplied with a programming language called Ampersprite, but using it requires a programmer's diligence. (Sprite boards are discussed in further detail in Chapter 8.)

INPUT DEVICES

In graphics applications, how the graphics get into the computer can be just as important as what you can do with them once they're there. While it would be senseless to switch from the keyboard just for the sake of using newer technology, an alternative input device can deliver better speed and accuracy in graphics applications when it is used with the right software. The keyboard, for example, is a less than ideal input device for drawing applications, in particular; mice or light pens can be much simpler alternatives for anyone.

Because most alternative input devices depend on pointing, you usually use programs that support such devices by pointing to commands that are already on the screen. Pointing is far easier than having to remember a sequence of keys, so alternative input devices are being taken up everywhere as a way to make computers simpler for everyone to use.

Because of its strong following in the home and education markets, the Apple II is often the proving ground for new input devices. Some of these devices (trackballs and joysticks) have been around for years on scientific or military instruments. Some, like light pens, have failed to live up to their initial promise, while others (touch tablets) are still in the process of getting off the ground.

The Light Touch

A light pen can be the cheapest alternative input option. Some models sell for less than $50. Others, such as Koala Technologies' Gibson Light Pen, which is shown in Figure 7-1, cost about $250. The difference between the two extremes is sensitivity. A light pen works by reading the light emitted by the screen, and some pens are far more accurate at pinpointing the light source than others are.

Unlike an off-screen pointing device, such as a mouse, a light pen has two major drawbacks. First, you have to hold it up to the screen's surface to draw, and that can become tiring after a short while. Second, television and monitor screens give off static electricity that can cause the light pen (especially one of the lower-priced models) to misread the optical information it's getting. When the pen becomes confused by static, it may put unwanted lines into a drawing or select the wrong option from a menu. The nice thing about a light pen, however, is that it plugs directly into the Apple's game port and saves you the hassle of installing a separate interface card.

For the most accuracy and the most natural drawing "feel," digitizing tablets are the choice of many game developers and commercial artists. The surface of the tablet represents the screen, and a pen connected to the tablet is used to move the screen cursor. Since the tablet surface mirrors the screen, the relative location of the pen on the tablet surface is an accurate reflection of the relative location of the cursor on the screen. Digitizing tablets are the most accurate pointing devices, but they are also

Figure 7-1
The Gibson Light Pen

the most expensive. Apple, Summagraphics, and Houston Instruments sell digitizing tablets for the Apple II, with prices running from $395 (for the Summagraphics product) on up.

Touch tablets are a relatively new wrinkle in this market. Instead of moving a pen on a digitizing tablet, you point with your finger or a wooden stylus on a plastic membrane that detects the pressure and translates your touch into directions for the screen cursor. A touch tablet isn't a mirror of the screen, however—it knows how to turn your finger movements into cursor movements, but it doesn't know where the cursor is in relation to the edges of the screen. Thus, instead of moving your finger from one side of the tablet to another to move the cursor from side to side on the screen, you may have to repeat this process a couple of times.

Touch tablets aren't as accurate as digitizing tablets or mice are, but they don't cost nearly as much, either. They might succeed as an alternative input device for business and productivity programs, as well as low-end drawing packages, because none of these applications requires extreme accuracy. Like light pens, touch tablets plug directly into your Apple's game port.

The first touch tablet for the Apple was the KoalaPad shown in Figure 7-2, which retails for $125 but can be found for closer to $100. The drawing surface is a 4-inch by 4-inch square, so this pad is small enough to hold in one hand while you work. The makers of the KoalaPad are now offering an increasing amount of business and graphics software, including a drawing program called Graphics Exhibitor for $40.

Another popular touch tablet, called the PowerPad, costs $100, but offers an 11-inch by 11-inch drawing surface. The makers of the PowerPad have so far concentrated on the home and educational markets, with software for art, music, and games of logic.

Picture Perfect

One novel, but relatively expensive way to get pictorial images on your Apple's screen is to use a digitizer like the ones used in specialty shops to print portraits on T-shirts, aprons, and calendars. A digitizer is an interface that takes a video image from a black-and-white camera and breaks the picture down into digital (binary) information that can then be displayed on the screen. Since the camera doesn't care what it's looking at, you can digitize complex pictures, faces, objects, or drawings simply by pointing the camera at them.

Digitizers produce several dozen different levels of gray for shading, and they can generate in seconds an image that might otherwise take hours to create by hand. One digitizer, the MicronEye Bullet, consists of software, an interface, and a tiny video camera for $295. Another example is the Computech digitizer, which produces high-resolution pictures on

Figure 7-2
The KoalaPad

an Apple screen for $295, without the camera. A fancier version of the Computech product that takes advantage of the double high-resolution graphics on the newer IIe is also available.

Mouse Mania

Of all the alternative input devices to come along, the mouse is undoubtedly the most popular. There are two kinds of mice, optical and mechanical. Optical mice have been used for years in computer-aided design (CAD) and other applications that require a high degree of accuracy. An optical mouse emits beams of light that are reflected by a grid etched into a special tablet. The tablet corresponds to the size or dimensions of the computer screen, and when you move the mouse on the tablet, its movements are translated into movements of the cursor on the screen. Although optical mice are more accurate than mechanical mice, they're more expensive. One widely sold optical mouse is the Summagraphics SummaMouse, which sells for about $300.

It is mechanical mice, however, that seem to be gaining support throughout the personal-computer industry as the input device of the future. Two big reasons for this support are their price (mechanical mice are cheaper than optical mice), and the fact that they don't require a special mouse tablet.

A mechanical mouse is a little palm-sized box with a ball bearing underneath it. The ball bearing is connected to motion sensors, and when the mouse is rolled around a desktop or other hard surface, the sensors read the distance and direction of the movement and move the cursor on the screen accordingly. The sensors remember where they left the cursor, and they know which direction to move it in as the ball bearing moves, but they have no way of knowing where the cursor is in relation to the whole screen. Thus, you have to watch the screen as you move the mouse to get the cursor where you want it, just as you do with a touch tablet.

There are now a couple of mechanical mice available for the Apple. The AppleMouse II from Apple is packaged with MousePaint, and since you get both for $149 you essentially get the excellent software for nothing. WICO Corporation, maker of best-selling joysticks and track-balls (control devices consisting of a rotating sphere mounted in a box) for the Apple and other computers, is now selling its WICO Computer Command Mouse, shown in Figure 7-3, for $59, but you have to buy a $199 interface card for it. It costs more than the AppleMouse, but the WICO mouse and interface offer more flexibility. The interface, called the SmartCard, translates the mouse input into instructions that can be understood by most application programs. The SmartCard comes with software that pre-sets it to work with popular programs, such as VisiCalc, so you can have a mouse option with programs that don't specifically support a mouse. The SmartCard can also be set to work with programs it does not specifically support. Because it's the only mouse/interface combination that lets you use a mouse with any program, the WICO system could easily be worth the extra expense.

You can also get a mouse when you buy the Jane integrated software package discussed in Chapter 5, but you have to spend about $120 on software that you may or may not want.

Figure 7-3
The WICO mouse

DISPLAY DEVICES

All this easy input and graphics software virtuosity may not mean much if you have to look at your work on a black-and-white television or a monochrome monitor. On the other hand, color displays are nice, but to be fair, I have to admit they're probably a lot more important for use with a drawing program than they are with a business graphics package. A lot of users of business graphics never see their charts or graphs until they're printed on paper. Often, color and titling options in these programs are limited anyway, so it's not worth the expense of a color monitor to preview graphics of this type.

But drawing programs are another matter. With them, a large array of shapes, colors, and freehand magic is at your command, and you will definitely benefit from seeing what your work looks like, instead of trying to imagine it. The cheapest way to display color with an Apple is to get a $20 to $30 RF (radio frequency) modulator that will enable you to hook up your computer to a color television. If you don't like the idea of tying your Apple to the family television in the den, you can pick up a decent used color set for less than $200—not much more than what you'd pay for a good-quality monochrome monitor.

The problem with using a color television, however, is that your graphics won't be anywhere near as sharp as they would be on a color monitor. Television sets are designed to show large images at a distance, not small ones close up. If you get close to your TV and look closely at the lines it displays, you'll see just how blurry the display really is. Furthermore, to display your graphics on a color TV, your standard Apple display output (which is called composite video) must be converted to an RF video signal, and must then be decoded and displayed by the television. You have to convert the signal to RF because most color televisions don't accept a computer's composite video signal. So, on top of the relatively inferior television display, you also have a signal that's been further processed through the RF modulator.

If you buy a composite color monitor, your display signal goes directly from your Apple's video output to the monitor. Even here, though, the display won't be as crisp as it can be, because composite video treats all color information as a unit—the colors are displayed in combination, rather than individually, so the colors you see are not distinct. And since the colors are in a jumble, the display has no way to separate them completely. If you look closely at a white area on a composite color display, for example, you'll see pixels of color mixed in with the white. A typical composite color monitor has a resolution of 260 by 300 pixels, so it's also quite possible (in the IIe's double high-resolution mode) that you could create a very crisp drawing, only to have the monitor's resolution limits make it fuzzy.

Nevertheless, composite color monitors, such as those sold by Sanyo, Amdek, SONY, Quadram, Taxan, and other companies, are an improvement over a color television. They display more pixels on the screen, and they offer fairly sharp pictures. The cost of a composite color monitor should be comparable to, or less than, the price of a similarly sized color television because, although the resolution is higher, there's no television receiver inside the monitor. Amdek's Color-I is a popular, 13-inch monitor priced at $379 retail.

If you want the finest in graphics displays, however, you really have to go with an RGB (Red-Green-Blue) monitor. The RGB method tells your computer to break colors down into separate red, green, and blue signals and transmit them to the monitor that way. When the monitor receives these signals, it can assemble the basic color elements in virtually limitless combinations. Since the color signal isn't a jumble to begin with, the colors displayed aren't a jumble at the end: Blue objects are solid blue; light blue is decidedly different from medium or dark blue; and white areas are pure white.

RGB monitors also offer higher resolution than composite color monitors do. A typical model, such as the Amdek Color II Plus, has a resolution of 640 by 200 pixels, so the clarity of your graphics will be limited by the Apple's capabilities, rather than by the monitor's. The Color II Plus, which is a 13-inch monitor, retails for $529; other RGB monitors range fairly widely in price from a low of about $400 to a high of more than $800. The manufacturer's reputation, length of the warranty, and screen size can all affect the price.

You can plug a composite color display directly into your Apple, but you'll need a special interface card to enable your computer to produce RGB output. These interfaces are sold by the makers of RGB monitors, and they vary in capability. Some of the more adaptable cards let you change displays from 40 to 80 columns, and they offer several different levels of resolution and varieties of color. A card should be able to produce sixteen colors in RGB mode, and it should also be able to drive a monochrome monitor or a composite color monitor. One such card is Amdek's DVM-80E video card, which sells for $195.

Your eyes and the application you use should determine whether you need to spend extra money on an RGB monitor. If you're just looking for a color display for personal use or for displaying the graphics equivalent of slide shows, you may not need the extra quality. But if you're going to be making color slides from photographs of the screen, or if you're trying to create quality graphics for video use, then you'll want all the display quality—RGB quality—you can afford.

OUTPUT DEVICES

Getting the graphics out of your Apple (or any other computer, for that matter) is without a doubt the most frustrating aspect of this particular application. You can buy software to create just about any type of graphic you want, and then you can display your work beautifully on the right monitor, but getting an output device that can reproduce your graphics on paper or transparencies can be very difficult. For example, while dot-matrix printers can reproduce the Apple's high-resolution screen in all its detail, few of them will print in color, and few of those color printers work with drawing software (although there are ways around that, as you'll soon see).

The trouble is that different graphics programs produce screen images in different ways, and different output devices produce output in different ways. There are some "standards," but they are limited to a narrow range of products. Black-and-white graphic output produced on dot-matrix printers, for example, tends to center around the Epson "standard," so that any dot-matrix printer that is Epson-compatible will work with any graphics program for Epson printers. In the same way that

Epson dominates the dot-matrix market, Hewlett-Packard dominates the color-plotter market; since software tends to support HP plotters, it forces competing hardware to be HP-compatible.

The worst compatibility problems occur with drawing programs, and this problem will likely get worse before it gets better. As such drawing products as Dazzle Draw or MousePaint entice far greater numbers of people down artistic paths, the demand will grow for accurate color reproduction of the drawings on paper. But reproducing the bit-mapped graphics (pixel-by-pixel instead of in larger blocks) produced by these programs is far more difficult than printing simple business charts or graphs. While dot-matrix printers are now rising to the challenge, the promise of sharp, rich color output still beckons somewhere in the future.

Dot-Matrix Printers

Epson is the king of dot-matrix printing, no question about it. Epson invented this technology so that judges could have quick printouts of athletes' times at the 1964 Summer Olympics in Japan, and the company has dominated the field ever since. Epson makes good, solid printers. A lot of manufacturers have imitated its designs, and Epson-compatible printers can be purchased for as little as $200 these days—less than a third of what the original Epson MX-70 cost in 1981.

Epson has improved its printers since the MX-70, and now offers better letter-quality modes and more graphics features. But since the company sells to the entire personal computer market, it hasn't been able to support any individual program or group of graphics programs particularly well.

Graphics programs, like other application programs that produce hard copy, have different ways of making printers do their bidding. This situation is even further complicated because different printers have different capabilities. One word-processing program, for example, might tell a printer to underline a word by backspacing after each letter and then adding the underline. Another program might tell the printer to underline the entire word at one time. A third might have the printer underline the letters as it prints them. The same differences exist with graphics printing.

This whole, complex situation forces software developers to write their programs for a low common denominator, or else risk limiting their market. If a developer wants a program to support most printers, then the program has to use printout instructions that can be executed by most printers, even if that means ignoring some of the technical improvements offered by the more capable machines in the group. For example, if some of the printers can print complex graphics in a single pass of the printhead, while others require two passes of the printhead, a program striving for wide printer support must opt for the slower, double-pass method.

Some graphics software developers, however, have refused to compromise their products' performance or potential output speed by catering to the masses in this way, and consequently they are forced to support fewer printers. The main thing about dot-matrix printers and graphics is to be sure the hardware is as compatible as possible with the software. Your printer should be explicitly supported by your graphics program. If, in addition, your printer is one of a small group of supported devices, chances are that the performance will be quite good. The larger the group of supported devices, the lower the common denominator.

But even if dot-matrix graphics is still a can of worms, dot-matrix printers are the most economical alternative. These printers let you print fair-to-good quality text, and then switch to graphics a moment later. Besides, the constant improvements in this technology keep resulting in better quality at lower prices.

If you're shopping for a graphics system and are also prepared to buy a new printer, you can match your software to some printers that offer a lot of graphics improvements over conventional technology. Apple's Imagewriter and Scribe printers, for example, have been designed to print optimum graphics output from programs such as LisaDraw, MacPaint, and MousePaint. These programs talk to printers in similar ways, and the new Apple printers are set up to receive and translate the input to finished graphics as efficiently as possible. This doesn't mean that you can't use an Epson to print out MousePaint graphics; it just means that you'll have more trouble getting the Epson to perform, and when you do, it will more than likely be a lot slower than an Apple printer would be. Of course, if you're using software written for the Epson standard, then the shoe is on the other foot.

The Imagewriter is $599, and features a large, dense dot matrix that provides exceptional resolution in a single pass. Apple's Scribe printer is only $299, and while its output isn't as nice as the Imagewriter's, its thermal-transfer technology allows it to print on transparencies. The thermal-transfer method uses a heated printhead to liquefy the ink in a special ribbon. The ink is transferred through contact between the printhead and the paper or transparency. Because the ink liquefies and then dries, it can adhere to smooth surfaces, such as plastic or clay-coated paper. The ribbons are expensive (about $7 each), however, and unlike the fabric ribbons used on most dot-matrix printers, they can be used only once. Nevertheless, thermal-transfer printers have fewer parts, are quieter, and are cheaper to manufacture, so you can expect to see more of them in the future.

If you're looking for color in a dot-matrix printer, you can find it, but compatibility is an even greater problem here. Integral Data Systems has made its Prism-series printers for years, but a lot of the newer software isn't compatible with these printers. The Prism printers use special three-color fabric ribbons to print in up to eight colors. These printers aren't cheap, at $1200 or so, but they have a fairly nice letter-quality mode and can be substituted for a daisy-wheel printer, to allow you to combine presentation-quality charts or drawings and text.

"Dumping" the screen

One alternative to finding compatible software is to use a printer and a printer interface that allow screen dumps. A screen dump is just that—the "dumping" of whatever is on your Apple's screen to the printer. Special graphics printer interfaces, such as the Orange Micro Grappler, the Apple Dumpling and the Graphicard are made for screen dumping. Once you have such an interface, you can issue printer control commands to reproduce screen graphics, regardless of the software you use to create them. Even if you have a graphics program that doesn't support printers at all, or you have a printer that isn't among those supported by your program, screen dumping solves your problem. Screen-dump cards don't care how an image got to your screen; their mission in life is to take whatever is on the screen and reproduce it faithfully on a printer. Of course, if you're using software that has a built-in, screen-dump utility, it's even easier.

Before you buy a screen-dump card, though, you'll have to make sure your printer is capable of reproducing the images dumped. Some printers simply don't have the right-sized dot matrix or the right printing abilities to reproduce some images faithfully. If this is the case, you'll still get a screen dump but, for example, where the image on the screen is an unbroken vertical line, you might end up with a row of exclamation points as a substitute. One printer, shown in Figure 7-4, that faithfully produces graphics in color and has its own screen-dump button is the Transtar 315 from Transtar/Vivitar. When used with Transtar's 315 PICS interface card, this printer gives you a printout of your Apple's screen at the push of a button.

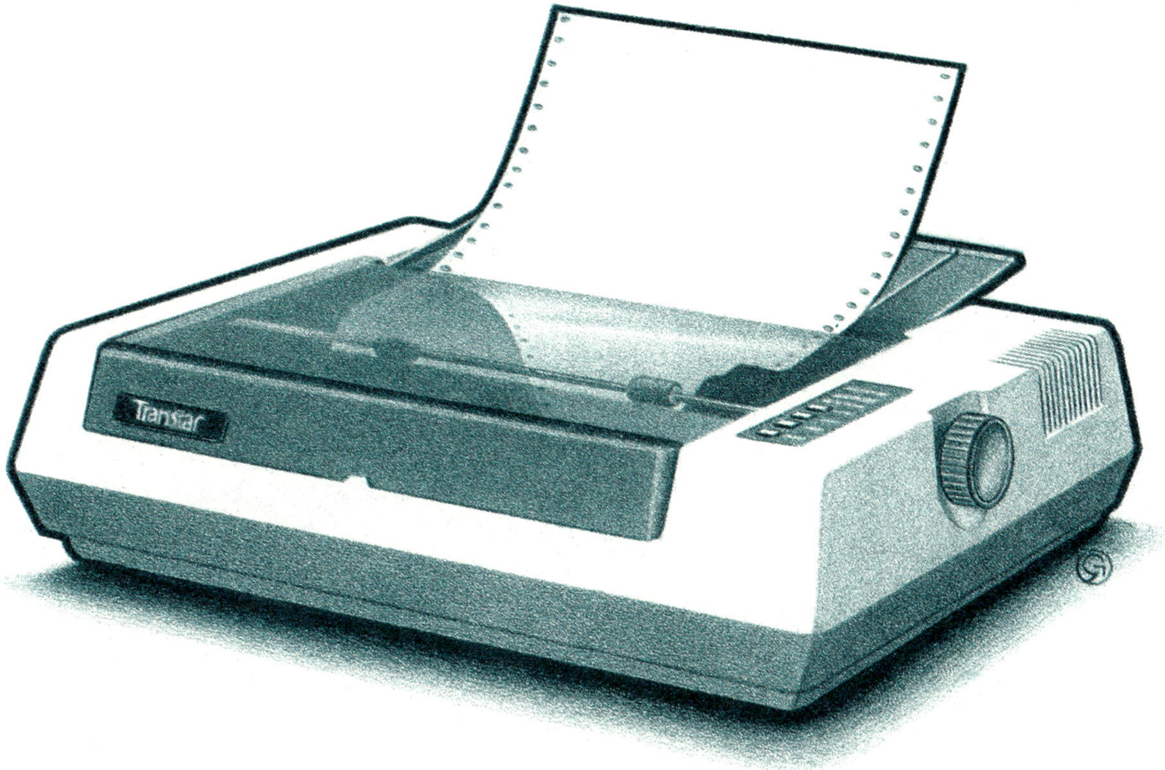

Figure 7-4
The Transtar 315 printer

Some programs have modes that let you display just the picture while the rest of the options disappear, but one problem with screen dumps is that many graphics programs display the drawing options as well as the drawing. If you dump the display from a program such as MousePaint, for example, you'll get the drawing you made, but the screen dump will also reproduce the options at the top, side, and bottom of the screen.

Ink-Jet Printers

A quieter and newer printing technology that is related to dot-matrix printing is ink-jet printing. Here, ink is sprayed onto the paper in any of a variety of colors. The ink patterns are formed into characters or graphics by a magnetic field in the printhead so ink-jet output looks like dot-matrix printing. The advantages of these printers are that they will easily print on transparencies, and they are far quieter than dot-matrix printers are. A unit such as the Diablo Series C printer produces up to seven colors and sells for $1295. Other ink-jet printers sell for as little as $500 or as much as $7000, with speed, resolution, and reliability making the difference.

One big problem with ink-jet printers has been clogging of the tubes that carry the ink to the printhead. If the printer isn't used for a few days, the ink in the tubes dries up. Also, adding ink to such printers can be a messy affair. Still, several major manufacturers (including Quadram, Siemens, and Hewlett-Packard) produce these printers, and ongoing improvements may bring them more into the printing limelight as quiet alternatives to more traditional printing methods.

Plotters

If you are producing business graphics, such as pie or bar charts for presentations, a plotter is the best equipment for you. With a plotter you get crisp, dot-free lines, a variety of colors, fairly noiseless operation, and reasonable prices. Most plotters will draw on either paper or transparencies, in either 8½- by 11-inch or 11- by 17-inch sizes. Hewlett-Packard has long been the leader in this field, but a lot of smaller companies are challenging its dominance with less expensive products.

The major change in plotters in the past few years has been the inclusion of more colored pens for less money in a smaller package. In the old days, plotters had only one pen to draw with, so producing a three-color chart involved stopping the plotter twice to insert new pens. Today's plotters offer anywhere from two to eight pens, either in a rack or a carousel at the side of the plotting area, and the plotter arm changes colors automatically.

Hewlett-Packard's fairly new 7475 plotter, for example, sells for $1895 and features six pens in a carousel. As usual for an HP plotter, it is supported by most business-graphics programs. Enter Computer, which is headed by a former employee of Hewlett-Packard's plotter division, sells its Six Shooter plotter for $1095. Enter says its plotter is compatible with Hewlett-Packard machines and performs almost identically. The Six Shooter weighs about 30 percent less than the HP 7475 and takes up less desk space. Enter Computer's first plotter, the Sweet-P, was long sold as a portable device, because it fit inside a standard briefcase.

Other makers of plotters in the $750 to $1300 range include Amdek (whose six-pen plotter is shown in Figure 7-5), Mannesmann Tally, Apple, and Roland. After compatibility with the graphics software you're using, look for plotter speed, mechanical accuracy (0.001 inch is a nice benchmark), and repeatability—the ability of the plotter arm to return to the same point (this helps when you're drawing circles and want the line to end where it began).

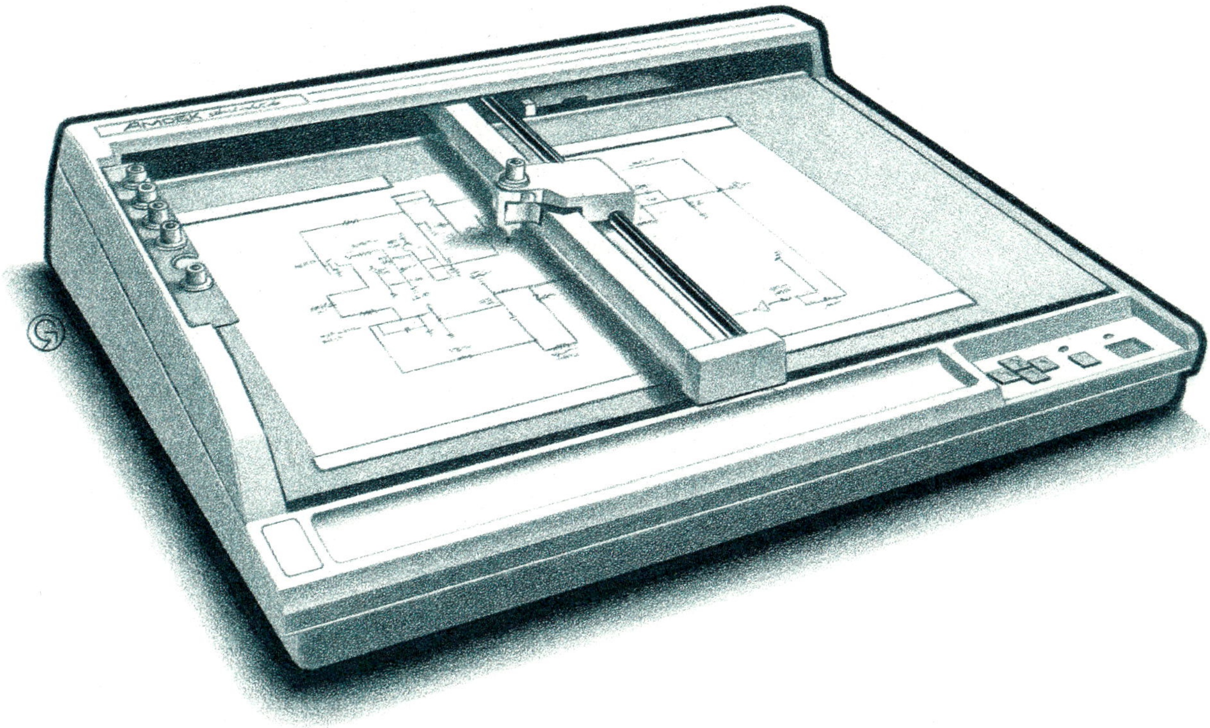

Figure 7-5
The Amdek six-pen plotter

Slide Makers

Another kind of output you can get from your Apple is 35mm slides. Instead of making color transparencies with a plotter or an ink-jet printer, you can quickly produce color slides for use in a normal slide projector. The simplest and least scientific way to produce slides is to darken the room and point a 35mm camera at the screen. You'll have to be sure to use slow film (ASA 64 or less) and take the pictures with a shutter speed of no more than 1/60 of a second.

If you're going to make slides regularly, though, you'll probably find it worthwhile to buy a slide maker, or at least some camera hardware that simplifies the screen-shooting process. If you don't want the expense of a slide maker, Polaroid and Kodak make hoods for your camera that fit over a 12- or 13-inch screen and that seal out external light while they hold the camera at the optimum distance from the surface of the display. Hoods like these cost $100 to $200 and require no modification of your camera or computer, although you'll get the best results from an RGB monitor. You can also buy a camera and hood together, for about $500, from a company called Datacam. If you use Polaroid slide film and a Polaroid AutoProcessor with any of these options, you can have finished slides within an hour of taking the pictures.

Several other companies make slide-making devices that are considerably more expensive, but are also surer and more convenient. A slide maker is a long, sealed box that contains a tiny RGB display at one end and a camera at the other. You load film into the camera end and connect the slide maker to the Apple with an RGB interface card. Most exposure settings are automatic, so once you're hooked up, you can make slides simply by pushing a button on the slide maker. Unfortunately, you have to spend between $1300 and $7000 for this kind of convenience, but if you make a lot of slides and want the best 35mm quality, the expense could be worth it.

SHOWCASE SYSTEMS

As an Apple owner, you have more graphics hardware and software options than you do with any other computer. You can start out small and upgrade as your graphics skills and needs develop, or you can plunge right in with a sophisticated, high-end system. Here are a few relatively inexpensive examples for the beginner.

LOW-END DRAWING POWER

Apple II, II+, IIe	Currently Owned
Amdek Color-I composite monitor	$ 379
AppleMouse II with MousePaint	$ 149
Transtar 315 PICS interface	$ 120
Transtar 315 color dot-matrix printer	$ 599
Total Extras	$1247

Added Power: Composite color display, mouse and mouse-driven drawing program, color dot-matrix printer and interface.

BUDGET BUSINESS GRAPHICS

Apple II, II+, IIe	Currently Owned
Graphics Department software	$ 125
Apple four-pen plotter	$ 779
Total Extras	$ 904

Added Power: Flexible chart-making software with custom title generator, four-pen plotter for drawing on paper or transparencies.

C H A P T E R

8

FOOLING AROUND

Everyone has to relax sometime. Your Apple II's abilities as an entertainer underscore the company's commitment to the philosophy that a truly personal computer should be more than a glorified office machine. Apple was the first computer company to recognize the importance of fun as a means of bringing people and computers closer together. While competing CP/M and MS-DOS machines either came late to this realization or ignored the subject entirely, Apple and several dozen software developers, as well as thousands of users, were having the times of their lives. And today, the game-software industry's major players—Broderbund, Sierra On-Line, Datasoft, Electronic Arts, Sir-Tech, Infocom, and Penguin, to name a few—still focus much of their fun on Apples.

To be fair, we all have to admit that the Apple II's natural sound and graphics capabilities aren't equal to those of the lower-priced Commodore 64 or Atari 800. That's because those machines use separate chips to produce graphics and sound, while the Apple's 6502 processor handles everything itself. The Apple can generate fewer sounds, and it produces only 16 colors, as opposed to the Commodore's 256.

Nevertheless, the Apple is still a friendlier machine than some. When you want to use a program, game or not, you want to get it loaded and onto your screen as quickly as possible. Since Apple programs come with the operating system already on them, you can insert one diskette, start up, and be on your way. With the Commodore 64, on the other hand, you must type a BASIC command and wait two or three minutes for the program to load from disk. Comparatively speaking, in this respect, the Apple tries to stay out of your way as much as possible.

Flexibility, as you've seen throughout this book, is another Apple advantage. Unlike a primarily games-oriented computer, the Apple—especially with all its available software and its many hardware enhancements—lets you turn from writing the Great American Novel to battering the bad guys, as fast as you can switch disks. So the best thing about entertainment on the Apple is that, as with other applications, you have so many options. Apple's history of support for games (game paddles were one of the first peripherals the company offered) and its large, enthusiastic user base have encouraged the development of more programs, input devices, sound generators, audio amplifiers, and graphics enhancers than you'll find for any other computer around. Of course, if you have taken too much advantage of this wealth of products, you could be in a sorry state....

A CLEAN SWEEP?

Suppose you've been playing games on your Apple since 1979. The only games out then used game-paddle controllers, and you have a vintage set of them from Apple. But along about 1980, you decided you wanted the flexibility of a joystick for playing maze-type games. This meant you had to open up your computer and switch controllers at the internal 16-pin connector, but that wasn't such a big deal because you only had two of them. Of course, that was only the beginning.

Game software has come a long way since the days of Breakout and Pong, and in your misguided attempts to keep up, you've created a kludge: Your game paddles, joystick, touch tablet, and trackball all fight for space on your desktop, and you have to wade through a mass of wires to unplug one set of controllers and connect another whenever you switch games. Your original 9-inch green monitor is making you miss all those gorgeous colors in today's games, and your Apple's tiny speaker makes the most outrageous galactic confrontations sound like the beeps from a digital watch.

Software got better (while your Apple stayed the same) so gradually that you didn't notice the growing inconvenience or lack of function until the eight-year-old next door got a Commodore 64 for his birthday. He invited you over to see his computer, and you indulged the little nipper by accepting. But your condescending smile soon changed to a grimace of outrage as you realized this kid's toy, this merchandise from K-Mart, was creating enough sounds, colors, and animated graphics to make your Apple look silly. And you were supposed to be the neighborhood computer expert.

You made a quick excuse about leaving a program compiling on your Apple and headed home, one step ahead of humiliation. In the computer room, your old standby sprawled on the desktop, a Stone-Age mass of wires and switches that, for all their technological impressiveness, couldn't hold a candle to the neighbor kid's Commodore. You cringed in terror at the possibility of the kid bringing his Commodore over to your house for a comparison.

You certainly don't want to admit you're licked by rushing off to get a Commodore to run games, but you wonder if it's worth the effort—or if it's even possible—to upgrade your Apple to a level of gaming respectability. How can you show off the Apple in its best light, and get more playing pleasure in the bargain?

SOFTWARE

One big problem with computer games is that many have tended to be of the arcade variety. On land or sea, in the air or in outer space, there's been one shoot-'em-up, maze, or obstacle course after another. Of course, they're fun to play at first, but when the newness wears off, it's time for another challenge.

As usual with the Apple II, you're in luck. Not only is there an enormous number of games available, but as far back as 1979, some developers saw the writing on the wall about arcade games and began to use four different approaches—complexity, variety, player involvement, and education—to make games more interesting, for a longer period of time. Some of these tactics are also being used by developers of games for other computers, but the Apple environment is still the main fount of inspiration.

And just how did developers use Apples to make games more complex? Text-only adventure games had been around before, but these developers added graphics to the adventure and created a new wrinkle that continues to inspire software authors today. Instead of letting you simply shoot at moving targets, adventure games invite you into a specific world where you become a specific character. Often, you choose the character's makeup by selecting attributes, such as strength, intelligence, and stamina. From early products, such as Epyx's Temple of Apshai, this approach to gaming has progressed to levels of complexity that can test even veteran game-players for months.

One current example is Ultima III, the third in a series by games-master Lord British. At $54.95 it isn't the cheapest game around, but it will hold your interest a *long* time—one fan I know has played Ultima III for over 100 hours without completing it successfully.

In this game, you control four different players, which you choose from eleven possible professions and to which you assign a combination of several characteristics in varying degrees. There are various enemies, and a number of different "worlds" in which to travel and fight as you search for treasure. You can, of course, store the state of your game, because you will doubtless spend dozens of hours playing it.

Ultima III (as well as Ultima II and the original Ultima) have been at the top of game best-seller lists as long as any other programs have. If you like a protracted involvement and a lot of mental challenge in a game, such products as the Ultima series, the Wizardry series, and Castle Wolfenstein are well worth a look. There's a lot more to these games than there is to a shoot-'em-up, so be prepared to pay from $30 to $70 for one.

A simpler approach to producing games with staying power is to offer more and more variety in what are essentially arcade-type games. Early efforts, such as Space Invaders, placed your game piece on one playing field, with one or two kinds of enemies, but today's incarnations of these products offer 10, 50, or even 100 different playing fields to choose from. The most popular of these products at the moment is Broderbund's Lode Runner, which offers 150 different levels of play. The action on each level is the same (you evade pursuers while gathering treasure), but the various levels are different enough to maintain your interest for a long time. When, and if, you finally master all 150 levels, or find the challenge wearing thin, the fun can still continue: You can use a built-in game generator to design your own game screens.

Game generation is really a third approach to entertainment, since it goes beyond mere variety by allowing you to be creative (instead of reactive) within the game. Much of Lode Runner's popularity probably depends on its game-generating feature, and there are a number of other products that offer the same potential. One all-time favorite in this category is Bill Budge's Pinball Construction Set, which lets you position familiar pinball-machine elements, such as flippers, bumpers, and chutes, on a playing area. When you've created a design you like, you can then play the game. Much of the fun in a game like this comes from the challenge of creating games that no one can score well on, or from creating levels (as in Lode Runner) that few can successfully master. The entertainment becomes a mental exercise, rather than simply a matter of good hand-eye coordination. Another game in this category is Broderbund's Arcade Machine, for which the company actually held a contest among customers for the best design.

Educational value is the last, and perhaps the most promising avenue for game developers wanting to prolong the shelf life of their products. Educational games differ from educational programs in that their play value is greater than their educational benefit. This ratio of play to learning may very well be subjective, but there's still a general category of products that are like this. One that comes particularly to mind is Flight Simulator II from SubLogic. By the way, the earlier version of this game, Flight Simulator, is the subject of some misunderstanding in the marketplace, so let's clear things up a little: Just about everyone knows that Microsoft sells a version of this game for the IBM PC, but most people don't know that Flight Simulator for the Apple has also been available, from SubLogic, since 1979.

Flight Simulator II, which retails for $49.95, is Bruce Artwick's newest rendition of this classic game. It puts you in the cockpit of a Piper Cherokee, complete with standard airplane instruments and electronic navigation equipment. Through the window, above the instrument panel, you see a realistic simulation of airfields in Chicago, New York, Los Angeles, and other cities. As you fly around, you see aerial views of these metropolitan areas, but the real excitement is in flying the plane. There are adjustable variables, such as weather, wind speed, and temperature, but they are only the beginning of this game. Flight Simulator II strives to recreate the experience of actually flying the Piper Cherokee as faithfully as possible, so you must control the engine speed, the stick, the fuel mixture, and other real-life variables. And along with realistic flying, you can also select a mode that puts you in a World War I aerial battle, but you'd better know your way around the airplane first, because skill definitely counts.

Flight Simulator II will soon be available in a multi-user version, too. This version will require either an Apple IIc or a IIe, with an 80-column card, a serial interface, and 128K of memory, but the game will come with the hardware needed to allow several of these Apples to run the program together as a network. The game provides a simulation of several airplanes in the same airspace, with the attendant possibilities of crashes and traffic when you are landing or taking off. Incredibly, the simulation is so real that you can actually see the planes of other players out of your window when they're close to you. Naturally, the World War I dogfight becomes far more complex as well, because it involves more than two planes, and all of them are user-controlled.

GAME CONTROLLERS

As game software has become more sophisticated, so has controller hardware. When the only games around were Pong descendants, such as the Breakout game Apple demonstrated at the first West Coast Computer Faire, the only kind of controller a player needed was a game paddle that could move an object up and down or from side to side along one axis. Apple offered game paddles for the Apple II from the beginning, but soon a simple paddle wasn't flexible enough for the software. Once the player-controlled objects in games (planes, cannons, or characters) could move all over the screen, more sophisticated control devices were called for.

Today, you can choose from a variety of joysticks, touch tablets, trackballs, and mice for game control. Most of these controllers are also compatible with at least some other kinds of software for graphics, word processing, and other productivity applications. The compatibility between your particular game controller and application software, however, will probably depend on whether the software supports the device, because most software has to support different input devices specifically, no matter whether the devices are keyboards, touch tablets, or mice.

If you use a WICO controller, however, the WICO Corporation sells an interface board for the Apple that enables any software you're using to accept input from the WICO joystick, trackball, and mouse. The interface is called the SmartCard, and it costs either $199 for the Apple II/II+ version or $249 for the Apple IIe version. (The price difference is due to the different keyboard designs of these two computers.)

The SmartCard comes with a setup disk that contains pre-stored configurations for popular software, including VisiCalc, Bank Street Writer, Apple Writer, and AppleWorks. To configure any of these programs for use with a WICO controller, simply select the appropriate menu option. For unlisted software packages, there's a manual that shows you how to create and store configurations on the setup disk. Although it's expensive, the SmartCard is an important product, because it lets you use alternative input devices with existing Apple programs instead of having to wait for newer versions of software that specifically support these products.

Joysticks and paddles were the first game controllers. Both are descended from full-sized arcade equipment and some of the personal computer versions are supplied by the same companies that make such devices for coin-operated games. Apple itself has sold joysticks and hand controllers since 1977, but some other companies that have come along can offer more features, lower prices, or higher technology than the Apple products offer. The biggest of these companies is the WICO Corp. The world's largest maker of parts and accessories for arcade games, WICO established a consumer-products division in 1982, and has since sold over a million joysticks for personal computers. WICO's Apple joystick sells for $49.95. Apple's own product costs $59.95. Joysticks from other companies, such as Hayes Products, Kraft Systems, and Mimco Inc., cost about $50.

Some people complain about the relative price of joysticks for the Apple compared with those for Commodore or Atari computers, but they don't realize they're getting a much better product. The $15 or $20 joysticks sold for less expensive computers use digital technology: When you move the stick in any direction, the stick toggles an internal switch that then sends on/off signals to the computer. Since many of the motions in games are matters of distance or degree, the on/off signal must be translated by the software (often by counting the duration of the signal) into the distance or degree of movement. The software has to go through some extra steps to do this.

Figure 8-1
The Hayes MACH III joystick

On the other hand, Apple joysticks, such as the two models shown in Figures 8-1 and 8-2, are analog devices. They use potentiometers—variable switches, like household dimmer switches—that register not merely the presence, but also the relative degree, of joystick movement in any direction. Potentiometers relieve the software of the translation burden, and make for quicker and more precise responses. When you move the stick, the potentiometer senses the difference between a slight motion and a dramatic one, and it sends the appropriate signal to the Apple, where an analog/digital converter translates the relative analog signal into a digital data signal the software can understand. Potentiometers are more expensive than simple on/off switches are, so the greater accuracy is what you get for your money when you buy an analog device. Analog/digital converters are also expensive, and this is just one of the many reasons why Apples are more expensive—and better—computers than are Commodore 64s.

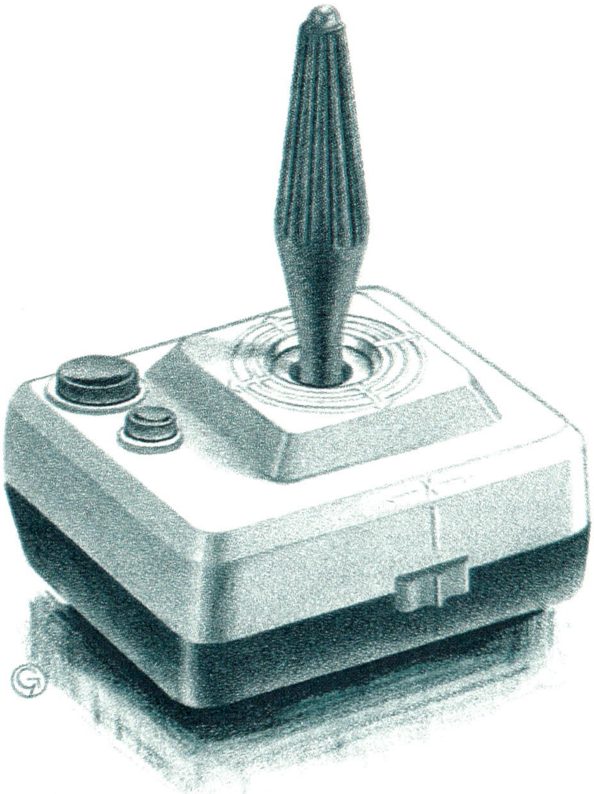

Figure 8-2
The WICO joystick

Joystick styles vary from fairly large units, with hand-sized sticks (that may or may not have a fire button at the top), to smaller models, with finger-controlled sticks. The position and number of fire buttons also varies. Along with the style of the stick and the location and number of fire buttons, joysticks differ in the number of adjustments and convenience features they offer. Most joysticks are self-centering, so the stick always returns to the middle of both the horizontal and vertical axes, but some products let you choose between a self-centering or a "floating" stick that stays where you put it with the flip of a switch. Trim controls are another nice feature; they are used to fine-tune the potentiometers, so you can adjust the relationship between stick position and cursor position more closely. Apple's joysticks have trim controls inside the case (you remove the bottom of the joystick to get at them), but most third-party products offer external trim controls for easier adjustments. And for convenience, the Mimco Stick also offers a built-in, 9-pin port of its own, so you can connect an alternate controller (a paddle or trackball) and you can easily toggle between the Mimco Stick and the device connected to this port.

Joysticks are by far the favorite control device of game-players, but they're not nearly as effective as trackballs or mice (which we'll get to next) in games in which you must move an object quickly, over a fairly long distance, in any direction. Joysticks are best for limited-movement games, such as Lode Runner or Miner 2049er.

Other Controllers

NOTE: *Mice and touch tablets are covered in detail in Chapter 7.*

In games where the motion is strictly side-to-side or up-and-down, game paddles are often the favorite controller. Game paddles provide a more realistic feeling of driving in auto racing games, for example. Although they are less sophisticated than other controllers, the bonus with paddles is that they come in pairs and sell for about $35. Apple sells them for $34.95; Kraft offers a more elegant pair with trim adjustments for $49.95; and Tech Designs makes a $34.95 pair of paddles called Adam and Eve I that also include trim adjustments.

You might think of a trackball, such as the WICO Smartball in Figure 8-3, as an upside-down mouse: Instead of rolling a box around the desktop, you roll a ball that sits in a stationary housing. Trackballs are older than mice, with roots that go back to medical and military applications in the 1950s and 1960s. Trackballs have been the favored controllers for games in which the object you control must be moved quickly for long distances in any direction. The enduring advantage of trackballs is that they don't need an area to move in, as mice do, and they cost less. The WICO Smartball for the Apple, for example, costs $69.95, whereas WICO's mouse costs $260 to $300 (including the required interface card). The bad news about using a trackball, however, is that the palm of one hand must constantly be rolling the ball to control an object, so you have to use your other hand to hit the fire button(s).

For games that require maximum flexibility, however, I think the mouse is the controller of the future. Pointing with a mouse is a more intuitive (and therefore more easily learned) skill than is rolling a track-ball. And because your fingertip covers the fire button, you can operate a mouse with one hand. The popular mice for Apples contain a large ball underneath. As you roll the mouse about the desktop, the ball controls the cursor by translating its own relative position into a signal the software understands.

Figure 8-3
The WICO Smartball

Opinions differ about the number of buttons a mouse should have, but the chances are that for games you'll only need one button, which means any mouse will do. Apple's AppleMouse II has one button and costs $149. WICO's three-button mouse, which has contoured styling that is said to be more comfortable to hold, sells for $59, but requires the $199 to $249 WICO interface. As mice grow in popularity for use in every type of application, you can expect to see more competition and, hopefully, lower prices.

Touch tablets are yet another way to control games. The major advantage of these devices is response time, because you control the game simply by moving your finger around the tablet's membrane surface, instead of by moving a joystick or rolling a mouse or a trackball. Touch tablets are a particularly good control method for games that require rapid, flexible, and fairly wide-ranging control of your game piece. Zaxxon or Choplifter are good examples of such games, because to play them well you must move the object you control all around the screen as quickly as possible; Lode Runner and Ultima III, on the other hand, are examples of games in which control doesn't need to be this flexible or rapid. If your particular game requires a lot of accuracy in addition, you may want to use a stylus on the touch tablet instead of a blunt fingertip.

The drawback to a touch tablet is that the fire buttons are on the border of the tablet, off the touch surface, so you'll need both hands (one for cursor control and one to fire) to play games. The KoalaPad ($125) and the PowerPad ($100) are touch tablets for the Apple.

Socket Extenders

If you're a real game aficionado, you may well have more than one type of controller, to suit the demands of various games in your collection. If this is the case, you may find that switching controllers can be tedious: The 16-pin connector is the most common connector used for game controllers, but on all Apples, this connector, or port, is located inside the case, so you have to remove the top of the computer whenever you want to switch controllers. Several companies, however, sell external game connectors that include a 16-pin connector that hooks inside the Apple, a ribbon cable long enough to reach to the outside front of the computer, and a circuit board with one or more 16-pin sockets mounted on it. These devices ease the situation considerably, in effect bringing that internal port outside the computer, where changes from one controller to another are far easier.

If you own a IIe or IIc, however, there's another wrinkle to consider in switching game controllers. Beginning with the Apple IIe, Apple began using a 9-pin connector for its own game controllers. This connector is located on the back panel of the IIe and the IIc (the IIc, which is a sealed unit, has no 16-pin connector). The existence of two different types of game-controller sockets has led to some compatibility problems between control devices and Apples, since some manufacturers (such as Koala, with the KoalaPad) have continued producing 16-pin products. Others have either gone along with Apple's newer 9-pin connector, or they now offer 16- to 9-pin adapters.

Some external game connectors, however, solve the problem by offering both 16-pin and 9-pin sockets on the external circuit board. The fanciest of these products is the WICO Apple Expander, which plugs into the internal 16-pin port in the II, II+, and IIe (another version connects to the 9-pin port on the IIc) and offers four 9-pin and four 16-pin ports at the other, external end. The WICO product automatically activates whichever controller you happen to be using, whereas with other external connectors, you must flip a switch to activate different sockets. The Apple Expander retails for $49.

For less money, you can buy less sophisticated products with one or two 9-pin sockets. Happ Electronics sells its Game-Socket Extender, with two connectors, for $34.95, and Southern California Research Group sells its Paddle-Adapple extender, with three connectors, for $29.95.

OUTPUT ENHANCEMENTS

Once you've customized game inputs to your satisfaction, you may want to enhance the audio or video outputs of your system with some of the products we'll look at next. Unlike the Commodore 64, Atari 800XL, or Coleco computers, the Apple II doesn't have a built-in, programmable sound-generator chip, so the Apple's own sound-generating capabilities are quite limited. To get sounds out of a standard Apple, your software has to use special routines that interrupt the action of a game while a sound is generated, thereby slowing things down considerably. With an add-in sound-generator board, however, the board can produce the sounds, while the Apple simultaneously handles the graphics. Games that support sound boards also have wider ranges of sound and can produce more "voices," or tones, at one time.

Along with the limited built-in ability for sound generation, the Apple also has a small speaker. But if the volume of your games is a major issue, there are products that can amplify your computer's audio signal through a home stereo system.

In the graphics-enhancement department, you can buy boards that enable your Apple to produce Sprite graphics, like those popularized by the Commodore 64. These boards have a separate graphics chip that allows objects to move over a fixed background, essentially creating animation by putting two planes of graphics on the screen at once. The Commodore 64 and Atari 800 computers both have separate graphics-generation chips built in; with a graphics board, your Apple can have one, too.

Sound Generators

The Apple's 2-inch speaker doesn't pack much punch, so the game-playing experience can sometimes be improved simply by raising the volume or quality of the sounds put out by the software. Happ Electronics sells an internal hi-fi adapter for $25 that fits inside the Apple's case. The board has a single audio socket, so you won't get stereo sound, but you can still connect your Apple to your stereo system for single-channel amplification through larger speakers. There's also a product called the Sound Master from Clover Microsystems, which is an external box that contains connectors for two speakers and has its own volume-adjustment control. With this device, you bypass your home stereo and have the volume control within easy reach at all times. The Soundmaster costs $35.

At a more sophisticated level, there are speech- and sound-generating boards from various companies. The best-known sound-generating board for the Apple is the Mockingboard from Sweet Micro Systems. There are actually three versions of this product: The Mockingboard A converts your Apple's audio signal to stereo, and it provides hookups for two 8-ohm speakers; the Mockingboard B, a plug-in upgrade for the Mockingboard A, adds speech synthesis capabilities to the package; the Mockingboard C offers the combined abilities of the A and B boards. There's also a Mockingboard D, which is an external box (that contains the Mockingboard board and two speakers) made for the newer Apple IIc.

The Mockingboard is widely promoted through beautifully designed advertisements, and it has also gathered the support of several software manufacturers whose products it enhances significantly. Electronic Arts' Music Construction Set, for example, is really made to generate ranges and combinations of sounds that are well beyond the Apple's own capabilities. In fact, only two of the eleven pre-stored scores that come with the Music Construction Set can be played without the Mockingboard. Other games that can take advantage of the Mockingboard's music or voice-generating abilities are Ultima III, Zaxxon, and One on One. On the other hand, if you want to explore on your own, you can create music and speech with ease from the Mockingboard manual. The Mockingboard A sells for $129, and the speech upgrade costs an extra $99. The Mockingboard C and the Mockingboard D sell for $195 and $229, respectively.

If you want speech synthesis alone, you can go with the ECHO II speech synthesizer from Street Electronics. It comes with the speech-generating board, a small speaker, a diskette of software utilities, and a complete manual for $129.

Graphics Boards

The major graphics-enhancement boards that come to mind are the Sprite boards from Synetix. The Sprite I, which retails for $149, offers high-resolution color graphics, with software that lets you create and move color objects on the screen. The Sprite II adds sound-generation abilities and programming software to the Sprite I, and sells for $249. The SuperSprite adds an ECHO II voice synthesizer to the Sprite II, and it includes software that lets you easily program voices, music, and sound effects, as well as animated graphics.

If you long for the ability to create and animate objects easily on the screen, with or without sound effects, these products will give you capabilities well beyond those of most other personal computers. Be forewarned, though, that using a Sprite board by itself will require some patience and a yen for computer exploration. These boards are being supported increasingly by Synetix, which offers eight different Sprite-compatible game and educational programs and is working on more, but it's doubtful that the amount of software supporting Sprite boards now or in the near future will justify the expense of owning one if you don't enjoy experimenting for its own sake. (Refer to Chapter 7 for more on Sprite boards.)

Color Monitors

NOTE: *Color monitors are discussed in more detail in Chapter 7.*

Perhaps the most dramatic enhancement to graphic output from games comes from the use of a color monitor. It seems obvious, but graphically oriented games are meant to be displayed in color, and seeing them on a monochrome monitor detracts from their greatest appeal.

Many people who use Apples primarily for business-oriented tasks don't feel it's worth the extra expense to have a color monitor sitting around for game use. While it's probably true that spending $400 to $800 on a high-resolution RGB monitor is excessive for game-playing, you can buy a used color television and an RF modulator for less than $200 and get most of the impact of color games. On the other hand, if you're planning to upgrade your monitor anyway, you might want to opt for a color monitor with an interface that lets you switch between monochrome and color modes. Amdek's DVM 80e interface, for example, costs $195, and will provide either RGB color or 40- or 80-column monochrome displays on the $529 Amdek RGB monitor.

A MATTER OF TASTE

Game-playing options and game-players' tastes vary so widely that I won't presume to limit them by offering a few Showcase Systems here. If you want more information, you'll find a selection of game software, hardware products, and vendors in the List of Products at the back of the book.

C H A P T E R

9

PORTABILITY AND CONVENIENCE

In the old days it was enough for a microcomputer simply to work—for it to perform useful functions without requiring you to have a programmer's skills. But today, with that software hurdle safely out of the way, consumers are demanding more physical convenience in their computers, and manufacturers are using technological advances to provide it. An Apple IIc, for example, is about 35 percent smaller and lighter than an Apple II or IIe. And when you consider its built-in disk drive, serial ports, RGB output, and its special 80-column display, the IIc is probably closer to half the size and weight of either similarly equipped older brother. The smaller IIc package uses less desktop space, is far easier to move from one place to another, creates less clutter, and is more aesthetically pleasing.

While the idea of aesthetics entering into one's opinion of a computer may curl the hair of many long-time Apple owners, few of us can deny that the IIc and the Macintosh inspire thoughts of simplicity and convenience that are rarely stirred by our older machines. Since Apple's goal is for its computers to serve us handily as our personal needs require, it's not surprising that the same machines should occupy a similarly unobtrusive physical niche in our lives as well. When you think about it, the computing power of the Apple is what we want, but the easier and less obtrusive the computer is to have and use, the better off we are.

Physical convenience, as approached by an increasing number of computer manufacturers, breaks down into two distinct areas: portability and the absence of desktop clutter. In a product such as the Macintosh, these two attributes are combined, because the Mac is a single-unit, fully functional computer system that manages to occupy very little desktop space. Its single processor/monitor/disk-drive unit takes the place of three such devices in an Apple II system.

The efficient use of a desktop, however, doesn't necessarily have to be synonymous with portability. Wang, for example, makes a desktop computer with a central processing unit (CPU) that sits on the floor beside the desk and a monitor that mounts on an arm above the desktop and can easily be swiveled out of the way. Digital Equipment's personal computers are also set up so the disk drives and CPU are off the desk entirely, and only a small monitor and the keyboard occupy desk space. Both of these products use desk space efficiently, but neither is portable in even the remotest sense of the word. On the other hand, mobile units such as the Compaq, IBM Portable PC, and Kaypro require as much desk space as many non-portable computers.

As an Apple owner, you can satisfy your needs for portability, space-saving, or general convenience in a variety of ways. The modular design of the Apple may seem old-fashioned to some, but it allows remarkable flexibility in the way you configure your system. Somewhere amid the data-storage alternatives, furniture, external slot-switching devices, carrying cases, power strips, disk drives, and organizers available for your Apple, you'll probably find the configuration that suits you to a T.

PORTABILITY

I have yet to be convinced of the broad need for portable computers. The IIc and the Macintosh are portable because they're small; they're not small because they're portable. In both machines, portability is an added benefit of designs that seek to minimize usage of desk space; portability is not itself the main goal of the design. And you'll find that even computers (such as the Compaq or Kaypro) whose portability or transportability is the main goal of the manufacturer are often sold more because they're a good price/performance value. Many of them never leave their first desktop.

At first blush, portability does seem like a great idea: The computer you use at home in the den can go to the office, or to a friend's house, or to your vacation rental in the mountains. But when you think about it, the number of times you will really be transporting the computer to those places is probably so small that portability isn't a major buying consideration. Most people buy a computer to perform a limited set of specific tasks, and those tasks are more than likely performed in one place. A computer bought for the office stays at the office. A computer bought for the home stays there. Despite the testimonials of people who haul their computers back and forth between home and office, or between one office and another, such mobility remains the exception to the rule.

The first question to ask yourself, then, before seeking to make your Apple portable (or succumbing to an advertisement for a more portable computer) is whether or not you really need a computer in more than one place. If you have a particular second location where you know you'll need the computer on a regular basis, then it makes sense to configure your system so it's easier to move. But buying or converting for portability on the assumption that you'll find places to take the computer is like buying a computer on the assumption that you'll find things to do with it. Without a specific need, you should concentrate on desktop convenience. Whatever extra hassle you go through during the few times you need to move the computer will be comparatively minor.

Portable Data

Once you've made a realistic assessment of your need for portability, there are a lot of options that can mobilize your computing. The first (and simplest) is to shuttle diskettes between two Apples. This is a fairly obvious solution, and it doesn't need much clarification, except to say that you must be sure both Apples are similarly configured. For example, don't expect to take a double high-resolution graphics program or data disk from home and run it on the Apple II+ at the office (Chapter 7 discussed the graphics gulf between the II+ and the later IIe computers). Likewise, if you're going to use an 80-column display, make sure both computers have 80-column cards; or, if a program calls for a certain amount of RAM (64K or 128K), make sure both computers have it. Once you've taken care of these details, you're home free (or office free, as the case may be). Even if you have to spend an extra hundred dollars or so—on extra memory or an 80-column display card—to ensure compatibility between two Apples, it's still a lot easier and cheaper than taking drastic steps to make your own computer portable.

If you have an Apple II at home and a different kind of computer at the office, you can still "transport" some kinds of information through a modem. Some programs store data in a plain ASCII format (recall from Chapter 2, that just means unformatted information coded in the widely used ASCII convention). If the software on both computers deals with data in this way, you can simply send the information between computers over the phone line. Of course, a lot of software stores and uses data differently, so modem transmission won't be the answer in many cases. If you have modems for both computers anyway, and you think the data-storage format of the software on both computers is the same, this method is certainly worth a try.

A related technique for data transfer is to use an intermediary computer as a translator. Again, the file structure of the data you send will have to meet the requirements of the intermediary computer, but if it does, you're in business: You send your Apple file to an information or mailing utility, such as THE SOURCE or MCI Mail, and your other, otherwise incompatible, computer at the office retrieves the file. It may take some determination to get this transfer method working smoothly, because of quirks in the intermediary computer's way of receiving or storing files. Some systems, for example, will stop receiving a file when they encounter two carriage returns in a row. But these problems are far from insurmountable. The monthly membership fees for such services are nominal, and along with the data-exchange channel, you might also get access to lots of information data bases.

Portable Hardware

A more expensive and potentially complex way of getting portable computing with your Apple is to make your Apple portable. This process can be as simple as putting most of your system (CPU, monitor, and disk drives) in a case you can lug around, or it can be a more complex variation on the same theme. For maximum performance anywhere, with minimum disruption to your normal computing routine, a computer case is the best alternative. Cases come in a variety of sizes for different system configurations. Computer Case Co., for example, makes cases to accommodate an Apple with one drive ($109), an Apple with two drives ($119), and an Apple with two drives and a 9-inch monitor ($129). These cases are made of hard plastic; soft cases cost about $50.

If your arms are strong enough, the ideal setup is to take along two disk drives and a 9-inch monitor, so you can simply remove the lid of the case, plug in the system, and begin computing. Of course, a 12-pound Apple, two 3-pound disk drives, a 15-pound monitor, and a 5-pound case are a lot to carry around and, naturally, the fewer components you carry, the less the package will weigh.

As you try to lighten the load, though, you'll discover something portable computer makers have known for years: You have to trade functionality for weight. If you leave one disk drive behind, you have to swap your program and data disks more often, unless your program loads completely into RAM when you start up. If you leave the monitor behind, you must either have a monitor at the other end, or you must use an RF modulator and a television set as a display.

The display is the heaviest part of the system and should be the first thing you consider leaving behind, but if you're going to substitute a television set, read on. An RF modulator will cost you about $15 and can easily and permanently be installed inside your Apple, but a television set may cause some configuration problems with your software. If you normally use a monochrome monitor with an 80-column card, you've no doubt configured your software for an 80-column display. Television sets don't have enough resolution to display 80 columns of text clearly, however, so you'll have to reconfigure your software to display 40 columns. If you're using unprotected software, you can simply make another copy of the program, set it up for 40-column display, and keep one copy for each configuration. But if your program is copy protected, you'll have to use the backup copy (if there is one) or reconfigure the program every time you hit the road. In addition, some software, such as AppleWorks, requires an 80-column display and won't work with a television set at all.

Disk storage

Whether or not you leave your display at home, some alternative disk storage options can also help make your load smaller and lighter.

One alternative is a smaller disk drive. Amdek, for example, makes a drive called the AMDISK I (shown in Figure 9-1) that uses 3-inch, rather than 5¼-inch diskettes, and is thus a smaller, lighter unit than your Apple's normal disk drives. The AMDISK I sells for $299 and can use the Apple's Disk II controller card, so you can buy the AMDISK I and use it exactly as if you were using a larger drive.

The AMDISK I also offers some other advantages in the diskettes themselves. Unlike 5¼-inch diskettes, which are covered by thin plastic, 3-inch diskettes are encased in hard plastic shells that afford them more protection against bending, dust, and moisture. The extra protection is especially important when you're moving your computer and diskettes from place to place. Another nice plus about the 3-inch diskettes is that they're double sided; you get 143K of storage on each side and, when one side of a diskette is full, you simply flip the diskette over to use the other 143K. So in addition to being smaller, each 3-inch diskette gives you the equivalent of two 5¼-inch, 143K floppies.

One potential problem with the AMDISK I, however, is that Apple software comes on 5¼-inch diskettes. If you want to take only the 3-inch AMDISK I with you on a trip, you'll have to copy the software you need onto the smaller diskettes beforehand. This, naturally, will be a problem with copy-protected software. Still, if you *can* get your programs onto the smaller diskettes, you'll find you get identical performance in a smaller package. Actually, since the diskettes are smaller in diameter, you'll probably get slightly faster access times with the AMDISK I than you do with a standard Apple drive.

If you want to lighten your load without changing disk formats, you could opt for half-height, 5¼-inch disk drives. Apple's new DuoDisk drive system contains two half-height drives, and makes a more compact unit than a pair of the older Disk II drives. These drives are also sold individually by such companies as TEAC and ALPS. Half-height drives are smaller (from top to bottom) and somewhat lighter than the Disk II drives, and they sell for about $300 each. Like the AMDISK I, half-height drives can use the Apple's Disk II controller card.

An even lighter and more portable storage option than half-height drives or the AMDISK I is a bubble memory card, which plugs inside your Apple and stores information in the form of magnetized bubbles. Access time is about 50 percent faster than it is with a disk drive and, unlike RAM cards, bubble cards don't "forget" what they contain when the power goes off. The best thing about bubble cards, however, is that they

Figure 9-1
The AMDISK I 3-inch disk drive

let you replace a disk drive with a very rugged alternative. The people at MPC Peripherals, the best-known manufacturer of bubble cards, say they sell about 75 percent of their cards to industrial clients whose computers are being used in dusty locations that would cause nothing but problems for regular disk drives.

The trouble with the bubble, though, is that it's expensive. MPC Peripherals sells its 128K BUBDISK card for the Apple for $599, including software that allows your Apple to treat the card as if it were a normal disk drive. And, while you benefit from permanent and extremely rugged storage, using the BUBDISK to help make your Apple more portable raises the same software-copying problem you would have with the AMDISK I disk drive: You would have to find a way to get your software onto the

BUBDISK before you hit the highway, if you wanted to leave the disk drives behind.

The BUBDISK's 128K limit will be a problem with storage-filling applications and files, such as database management or spreadsheets, but you can manage very nicely with less expansive applications, such as word processing. A small word-processing program, such as PIE: Writer, for example, which occupies only about 30K of memory, leaves you nearly 100K for files on a BUBDISK. That much storage would probably serve you fine for as much as a week on the road.

Of course, the absolute best solution to Apple portability also happens to be the most expensive: Buy a portable Apple. If you reach the point at which you're doing a lot of traveling with your Apple, the $1300 you'd spend for a IIc will be more than offset by its convenience. While you could, at best, reduce the weight of a II+ or IIe to about 13 pounds by using a 128K BUBDISK, you get a built-in disk drive with the IIc in an 8-pound package. Sure, the IIc costs more money, but it's also easier to carry, and you don't face the potential problem of copying your favorite software onto a bubble or a smaller disk.

CONVENIENCE

Without a doubt, the major disadvantage of having so many hardware and software options with an Apple is clutter. If you buy even a fraction of the hardware products available for the Apple, your computing area can easily be transformed from a showcase of computing efficiency into a Kludge Kloset. And the worst part is that the transformation can happen so slowly that you barely notice.

ONE THING AFTER ANOTHER

Suppose you started out with a dual drive IIe system. Just like the illustration in Figure 9-2, you had a CPU, with a 12-inch monitor and a pair of disk drives standing neatly together. It wasn't long before you realized you needed a printer, and that was no problem, because you could set it next to the computer. But then you decided you really wanted a hard disk. It wouldn't fit beside the drives on top of your Apple, so you set it off to the side. Expansion mania was upon you, and you didn't realize you could well be on your way to a kludge like the one in Figure 9-3. You were like a kid in a candy store: You got an external

Figure 9-2
A basic Apple IIe system

Figure 9-3
A kludge

modem, a few RAM boards for your spreadsheet work, a clock card, and a sound/graphics board. And with the graphics-enhancement board, you decided you really wanted to add a color monitor alongside the green monitor, for use with games and graphics, and then a mouse to help your drawing.

Suddenly, seemingly out of nowhere, the Kludge Effect had struck: You were out of desk space, you were out of slots, and it was necessary to move the monitor, open the Apple, and change boards whenever you switched applications.

If you've explored the enhancement of your Apple with any vigor at all, it's quite possible you now have a classic kludge; it's a desk-eating mass of wires and boxes that requires at least a few minutes of wire-connecting, board-swapping, or switch-throwing just to get started. The very act of computing has become almost more trouble than it's worth, and the room in which you compute is not only an embarrassment, it's a potential fire hazard. It's a shame, because the quality of your computing may well have declined considerably as a result of this tangle, and you may be tempted to start afresh with a new system, when all that's needed is a little housecleaning and organization.

GETTING STARTED

We all have our own notions about the ideal computer setup, but problems associated with desktop convenience can be divided into three major areas: organization, hookups, and power.

Organization

Clutter is the most common problem computer owners face, because even the simplest computer system has at least two components, and most have somewhere between four and six. A two-drive Apple system, for example, typically has five components, including a printer, and if you've added an in-line printer buffer, a modem, or other products, you have more than that. Each component is connected to the computer by a cable that's either too long or too short, and in any case seems bent on getting in the way. Computer furniture seeks to solve these organizational problems, but often the furniture seems to be designed to make things easy on your computer system instead of on you: Your system looks nice, and is easy to store, but few of the components are where you want them.

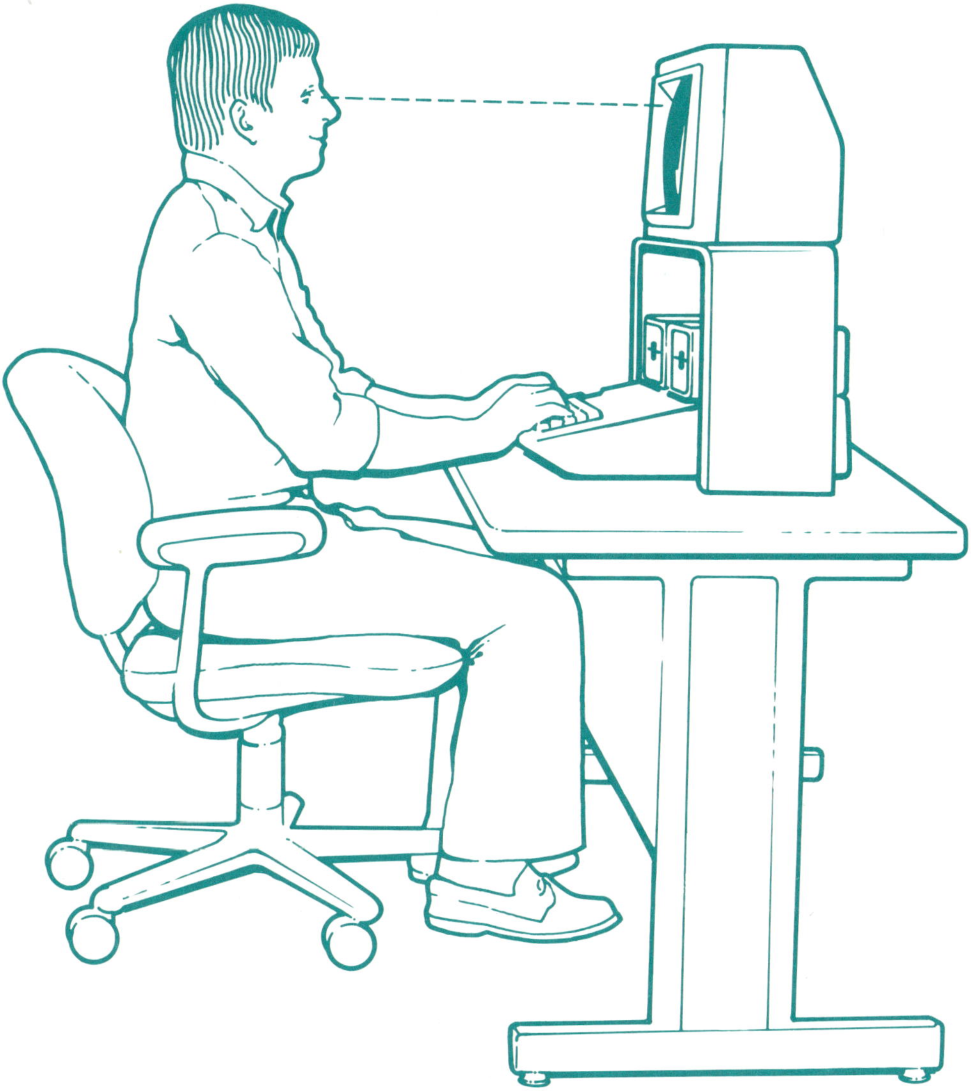

Figure 9-4
The optimum location for your keyboard and monitor

Comfort

In getting your system organized, your comfort, as you can see in Figure 9-4, should be the most important consideration. So the most crucial element in setting up a system is your position in relation to the display and the keyboard. The suggested relationships discussed in this section are usually cited as optimum for heavy keyboard work by ergonomic studies, but remember, there's always room for modifications to suit your eyesight, posture, or the application you are using. If you don't do a lot of heavy typing, for example, you might want—or need—to alter the keyboard placement suggested here.

When you're sitting upright in your chair, you should just be able to touch the surface of the display screen by extending your arm, but without turning your body toward the screen. Preferences about the height of the display vary, but if you look straight ahead, you should be looking at roughly the upper third of the display. If you see the lower part of the display, you're likely to develop a stiff neck or sore eyes from reading the upper part of the screen; if you can see over the top of the monitor, you'll have the same results from trying to see the bottom of the screen.

As for the keyboard, your chair should be close enough to it that your upper arms hang straight down. When your forearms are extended, the heels of your hands should rest on the front edge of the keyboard. This position should put your fingers, when semi-bent in a relaxed position, on the home (middle) row of the keyboard. Ideally, your forearms should slope downward one or two inches to the keyboard.

You'll notice from these descriptions and the illustration in Figure 9-4 that the keyboard unit should be on a lowered surface, not a normal table, and the monitor should be six to ten inches (depending on your height) above the keyboard. The monitor stand once supplied with an Apple starter system won't fill the bill in these respects: It puts the display surface too close to your eyes, and it also places the monitor lower than it should be for maximum comfort. For the same reasons, you should think twice about any organizing device that locks the monitor directly above the keyboard. The setup may look neat, but it will be harder on you than necessary.

Good computer furniture, on the other hand, has a lowered surface at the correct keyboard height, and often features a shelf that puts the monitor at the right height. Such furniture also gives you enough room to slide the keyboard well forward of the display, so that the distances to the screen and to the keyboard are appropriate. You can see a good layout in Figure 9-5.

Beyond ensuring proper placement of your display and keyboard, your decisions about where to put your disk drives, modems, and printers

Figure 9-5
A well-designed Apple workstation

can be as arbitrary as you like. Some people like their disk drives on top of the computer, while others like them beside the unit or on a shelf underneath. If you don't swap disks a lot, moving the drives off the desk can give you more space for books and paper, or for a mouse or a graphics tablet.

If you want even more space, you can use a detached keyboard or a keyboard-detaching housing (like those discussed in Chapter 2), so that the keyboard alone is on the typing surface, while the computer is out of the way on a lower shelf. The computer part of the Apple isn't too particular about where it's put—even whether it lies flat on a table or stands up on its side—as long as it's close enough for all the cables to reach your other equipment.

Furniture

From a clutter-reducing standpoint, the idea behind putting all the parts of the system on the same piece of furniture (or workstation) is to keep all the cables out of the way. With everything side by side or stacked on one workstation, all the cables can fall harmlessly behind the unit. If you want to have a modem in the same place as everything else, you need access to a telephone line, but a 25-foot telephone extension cord can usually fix that problem. And with such a workstation, all your peripherals are well within reach, and the cables are out of the way. The components you use a lot, such as the keyboard, are in the best possible location, and the items you seldom have to touch, such as the CPU or the modem, can be out of your way.

A good piece of furniture for your computer can cost anywhere from a hundred to several thousand dollars, depending on how fancy you want to get. Some of the fanciest workstations have adjustable typing surfaces, or a keyboard shelf that slides under a normal desktop, like a drawer, so that the unit can double as a standard desk. Most of these units, however, are designed to be used exclusively with a computer and don't easily double as normal desks. You can also buy computer tables that don't feature a raised shelf for the monitor, but you should definitely look for something that has a higher surface for the display, if you don't want to find yourself rigging something up with bricks and boards.

Even though there are dozens of furniture manufacturers, your best chance of getting a workstation that holds everything exactly where you want it is either to build one yourself or have one custom made. The "building" of a dream workstation could mean doing your own carpentry, or it might simply be a matter of finding a combination of furnishings that give you the surfaces you want, in the arrangement you want. A typing table is the right height for the keyboard, for example, and it can be placed alongside a desk, so that the computer/keyboard goes on the typing table, while the monitor, disk drives, and printer sit behind it on the desk (you could use a monitor stand to hold the display above the disk drives). If you don't want to buy a typing table, an ordinary TV tray (if it's a sturdy one) is also typing height.

As another do-it-yourself alternative, an old wooden desk from a used furniture store might easily be converted to a workstation by sawing three inches off its legs. You would then have a typing-height surface that would also be wide enough and deep enough for the monitor to go on a raised shelf behind the keyboard. The printer and disk drives could sit at either side, and you'd have the added bonus of several drawers that could hold supplies or could be removed for conversion to shelves for software. But by now you get the idea: The key to building the right system is your imagination.

Hookups

The second of our three convenience problems, known primarily to the true hardware aficionado, is the need to change from one input device, card, or peripheral to another. The game player who has both trackballs and joysticks swaps them all the time. The card collector who has filled the Apple's seven internal slots may have to remove a graphics card and replace it with a sound card and thereby change functions. The person with two printers has to hassle with constant cable switching. Ideally, you want any of your options to be available at any time, and fortunately, there are several simple and fairly inexpensive ways to have this capability.

Suppose, for example, you're hooked on games and you regularly use several different kinds of input devices. As Chapter 8 described, you can buy a game-paddle connector that plugs into your Apple's internal, 16-pin connector and "moves" it outside the computer via a ribbon cable. Since most of these connectors give you a bonus by multiplying the one internal slot into two, four, or even eight external ones, you can have several different controllers hooked up at all times, and switching between them will be a simple matter. (Of course, finding a convenient place to store all those paddles, joysticks, and trackballs is another matter.) These connectors cost about $30 to $50.

As for cards, by now you know that there are dozens of different cards that add new functions to your Apple, but you can have only seven of them connected at any one time. Seven seems like a large number, but by the time you hook up a printer interface, a modem interface, a CP/M card, a disk-drive controller, and an 80-column card, you've already used five slots. That leaves only two for sound cards, graphics cards, mouse interfaces, clocks, RAM cards, hard-disk controllers, RGB cards, accelerator cards, and everything else.

A partial solution is to bring one of the slots outside your Apple, with a product such as Extend-A-Slot, which is offered by the Southern

California Research Group and sells for $35. If you have this type of connector, when you have to switch cards, you don't have to open up the computer to do it. If you have several favorite cards that you use regularly, though, a neater solution that can do away with card-swapping entirely is a device that connects to one internal slot at one end and offers several external slots at the other, any of which you can select with a dial. One such product, again from the Southern California Research Group, is called Switch-A-Slot. It holds up to four cards, any of which you can select by turning a knob on the front of the card housing, and sells for $180. The Extend-A-Slot and Switch-A-Slot devices are shown in Figure 9-6.

Finally, if you use two different printers and want to switch between them, there's a product called the Printer Switch from Intra Computer that lets you run two printers off one parallel interface card. This switch sells at retail for $165.

Power Problems

The last of our three major considerations in terms of convenience is power and its by-product, heat. Let's look at heat first. Every add-in card for an Apple generates a certain amount of heat that adds to the heat given off by the Apple's own circuitry. The more cards you have, the more your Apple's interior heats up. Heat shortens the lives of electronic components.

Your Apple is vented on both sides, and with a standard complement of cards (one printer interface card, one disk-controller card, and one 80-column card, for example), the venting should be adequate for heat to be borne away by the normally circulating air in the room. But if you add more cards, or if you store your Apple in a tight place where there isn't much room for air to circulate around it, you should invest in a fan to prolong the computer's life. Fans are particularly important with Apple II and II+ models, as these computers have nearly three times as many chips as the Apple IIe, and thus generate that much more heat.

Cooling fans, which usually cost from $75 to $100, simply hang on the left side of your Apple, over the vents, and work by drawing air in through the vents on the opposite side. The constantly changing air keeps the internal components cool. Most fans sold today also offer some bonuses along with better air circulation. The Kensington Microware System Saver, for example, lets you plug your computer, monitor, and printer into the back of the fan, and turn them all on at once with a front-mounted switch. This fan, as well as many others, also contains a surge suppressor, which filters out fluctuations in the power supply that could

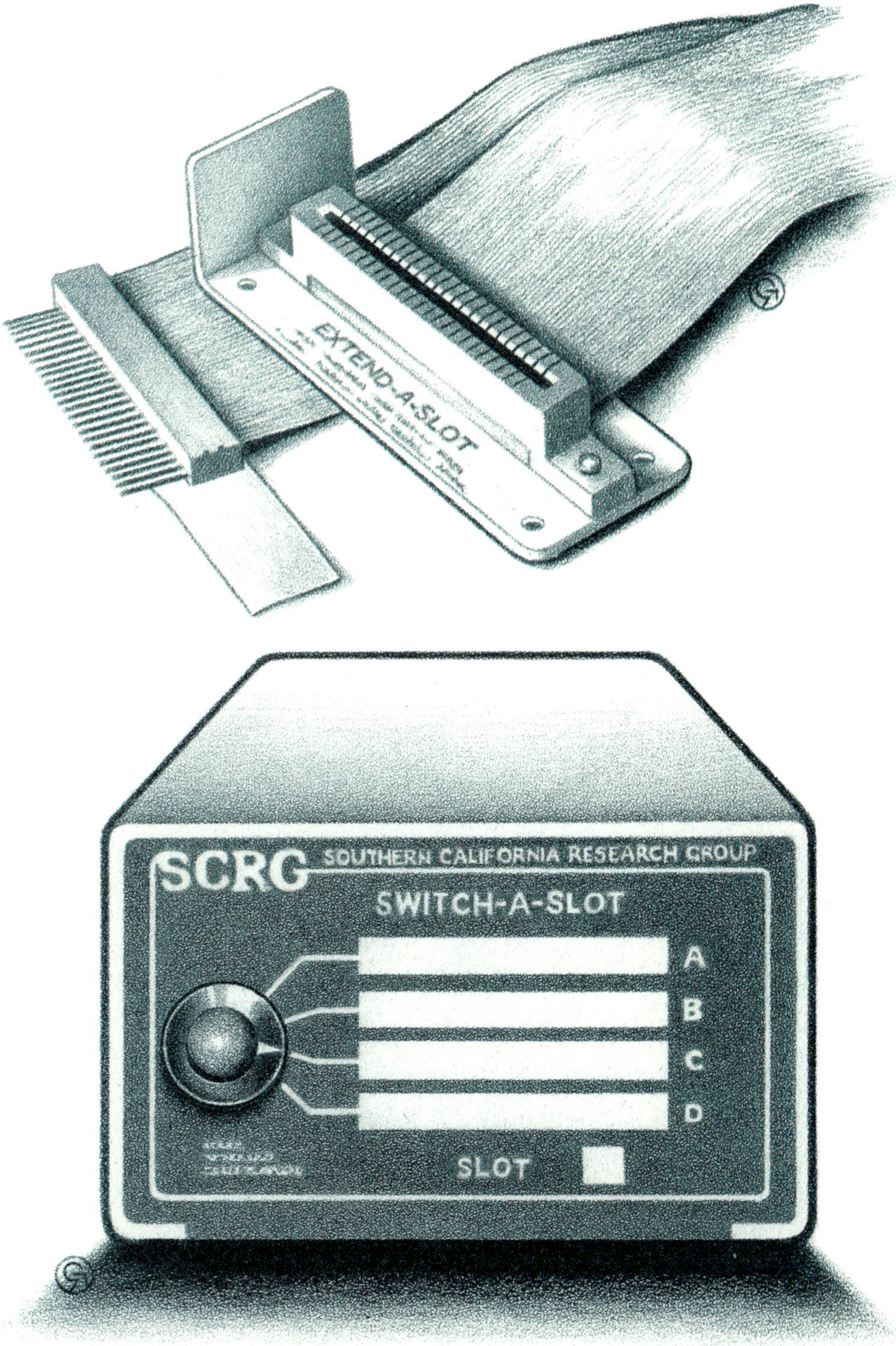

Figure 9-6
Extend-A-Slot and Switch-A-Slot

otherwise damage your computer or cause you to lose valuable data files. With the cooling, the surge suppression, and the convenient power switch, a fan like this one is well worth having. Another variation on this theme is the Cool-Time fan from Tencal, Inc., which sells for $90 and offers surge suppression, two extra outlets, a fan, and a built-in digital clock.

A single, easy-to-reach power switch is a real plus in terms of computing convenience, because the Apple, like most other personal computers, has its on/off switch at the back. You end up reaching behind the machine and fumbling for the switch each time you turn it on. The rear location is only moderately inconvenient if the computer is on a flat surface, all by itself, but when (as is often the case in workstations) the printer or computer is in a confined area, surrounded by a monitor, disk drives, modem, or just shelving, reaching that switch can be a real nuisance. And insult can be added to injury if you have to go through the same contortions not only once for the computer, but once for a hard disk, and once for the printer as well. So, the single switch on a cooling fan is a blessing both because of its more convenient location and because of its ability to control all three devices.

If you do your computing on a windy terrace and don't feel a fan is necessary, you should still invest in a combination power switch and a surge suppressor like the ones on fans. First of all, you can save yourself a lot of reaching and groping by spending $15 or so on a six-outlet power strip, especially one that has a single switch that controls power to the whole strip, as well as a built-in circuit breaker that will trip if you're trying to run more power through the strip than the single circuit it's connected to can handle. You'll need a strip with at least six outlets because, along with your computer equipment, you'll probably want to plug in a clock or radio, a desk lamp, and a power supply for the modem (if it's external). Power strips are available at any hardware store.

Surge suppressors are made necessary by the capricious nature of our electrical system and the strict demands of computer circuitry. Power surges can be caused by lightning, changes in the routing of electricity, problems at the power plant, periods of heavy demand (such as summer), and other wholly uncontrollable situations. And when power surges occur, your computer won't like them. A sudden increase in the level of power could overload some of the circuits or chips and force you to make some expensive repairs.

If you don't get one in a fan, you can buy a separate in-line surge suppressor that goes on the power line between the wall socket and your computer. There are different price ranges, depending on the sensitivity of the suppressor and its ability to handle surges of varying intensity. Some computer dealers will offer to sell you an in-line suppressor on top of the one that's built into the fan you're buying, but in most cases, this extra protection isn't necessary.

One other way you can ensure the quality of your electrical power is to use a grounded, three-prong wall outlet. You may dimly remember your computer's manual saying something about the importance of using a grounded outlet, and you may well have dismissed the warning, just as you did when plugging in your microwave oven or electric drill. But failing to ground a computer is potentially more serious than failing to ground a normal appliance, because the computer circuitry is more sensitive. Even the presence of static electricity can make computer chips do strange things, so grounding the power supply helps your Apple deal with such problems. If your house has only two-prong outlets, you should replace at least the outlet for your computer. In a pinch, you can ground the third terminal in the new socket by running a wire from it to a nearby water or gas pipe. Your hardware store will have other suggestions.

If you live in an area where a steady supply of electricity is particularly "iffy," it's important to protect yourself against power outages. When the power goes, so does everything in your Apple's memory. This loss can be a heartbreaking experience, particularly when the information is as complex as a large spreadsheet model or an accounts receivable file. The best protection against such a disaster is to back up the contents of your RAM regularly. Every twenty minutes or so, just save the updated file to disk. The backup takes only a few seconds, and this way, you'll only be out twenty minutes' work at the most, if the power goes out.

Making regular backups is a good idea, but if you can't seem to make yourself do it, and your information is irreplaceable, you may want to invest in an uninterruptable power supply (UPS) unit. These units come from the mainframe and minicomputer world, where loss of data is particularly catastrophic because of the large amounts of RAM involved; the UPS units sold for personal computers are downsized versions, offering less power for less money.

A UPS designed for microcomputers contains a 12-volt battery and the circuitry to detect the loss of electrical current. You plug your computer into the UPS, and plug the UPS into the wall. If the wall power cuts out, the battery in the UPS takes over and continues to supply your Apple with power for anywhere from five minutes to an hour, depending on the size of the battery and the price of the unit. In either case, you have plenty of time to save all the data in RAM.

Although they're not as big and expensive as their larger relatives, UPS units for personal computers are still expensive and they take up a fair amount of room. Most units are at least as high and as wide as two disk drives put together, and some are larger. A lower-end unit that offers six minutes of backup power at 150 watts, called the Guardian Angel from RH Electronics, Inc., retails for $595. Other units offer up to 1000 watts of power and cost up to $2795. Since your computer and monitor don't require more than 100 watts between them, a low-end UPS will be more than adequate.

SHOWCASE SYSTEMS

There aren't any Showcase Systems in this chapter, since convenience is in the eye (and the body) of the beholder and there are so many ways to meet your specific needs. Thanks to its flexibility and the wide selection of convenience products available, you can make your Apple system as physically convenient as any computer on the market.

C H A P T E R

10

WHAT'S DIFFERENT ABOUT THE IIc

Since its introduction at the start of 1984, the Apple IIc has been getting more attention than the IIe, and not without good reason. The IIc offers all the capabilities of a significantly expanded IIe, in a package that's 35 percent smaller and lighter. Apple spent more than $20 million to promote the IIc during the computer's first six months on the market. And while it was grabbing the public eye,

Figure 10-1
An Apple IIc system

this newest Apple was generating considerable excitement in the hardware- and software-development communities as well.

A lot of people, Apple owners as well as those new to computing, are curious about the functional differences between the IIc and its older brothers: If the IIc is really meant to enhance the Apple II product line, rather than replace the IIe, what are the differences that permit both machines to coexist in the marketplace, and which product is best for which applications? This chapter will compare the IIc and IIe on the basis of function and price, and it will look at the differences in using a IIc to

Figure 10-2
An Apple IIe system

perform the major applications discussed in earlier chapters. (The IIc is illustrated in Figure 10-1, the IIe in Figure 10-2.)

NUTS AND BOLTS

While the IIc and IIe do many things identically, they are significantly different inside and out, as you can see from the table in Figure 10-3. Although the statistics don't tell the whole story, they do point to some obvious differences, which give you a logical starting point in evaluating the two machines.

The IIc's smaller size, of course, is a big bonus in its favor. It's so small and light that you can carry it anywhere, set it up in a small space, and easily stash it out of the way when you're not using it.

From a hardware standpoint, the IIc is a fully equipped, ready-to-use computer system with 128K of RAM, built-in interfaces for popular peripherals, an RF modulator for use with a television, a switchable, 40-/80-column display, and a disk drive built into the side of the unit. You can take this little Apple out of the box, plug it into your TV, and be computing in minutes. The IIc also comes with some nice extras, such as RGB video output capability, an earphone jack, a mouse port, and a volume control for the audio output.

The basic IIe, in contrast, has no serial interfaces, it has no built-in disk drive, it doesn't include an RF modulator, it has only 64K of RAM, and it produces only a 40-column display. Based on the manufacturer's suggested price of $795 for this basic IIe, and assuming you purchased all the enhancements separately, you would have to spend close to $2000 to get a IIe with the same interfaces, display, and RAM capabilities as the $1295 IIc. (It's worth pointing out, though, that a IIe system with two disk drives, an 80-column display, and a 12-inch monitor can often be found for about $1400, and that the basic IIe, alone, usually costs closer to $500 than $800.)

On the design front as well, the IIc offers some incidental benefits over the IIe. The IIc's motherboard uses fewer chips and the circuits are more highly integrated, so it gives off less heat than the IIe's motherboard does. Since heat isn't much of a problem, the IIc can be used in a wider variety of locations—on carpeted floors, for example—without fear of damage to its insides. The IIc contains fewer parts, so the computer is easier (and cheaper) to assemble. The IIc also features a redesigned keyboard that, while laid out almost identically to the IIe's (the reset key has been moved to the left side), has a significantly improved feel. Aesthetically, the IIc has a more pleasing design, with the italicized lettering on its keyboard and case, its new color, and its sleek, modern lines. And finally, in line with so much else, the documentation has been completely redone, and there's an expanded set of tutorial disks (five, to the IIe's one).

Where the IIe outdistances the IIc, however, is in expandability. The IIc has two general-purpose serial ports that will doubtless be used with a variety of products from printers and modems to hard disks and sound generators—but it has only two of them. The IIe, on the other hand, has six expansion slots (if you don't count the auxiliary slot normally occupied by the 80-column card). Theoretically, serial ports can provide a gateway

Specification	IIc	IIe
Width	12 inches	15 inches
Length	11 ¼ inches	17 ¾ inches
Height	2 ¼ inches	4 ½ inches
Weight	7 ½ pounds	12 pounds
Processor	65C02	6502
RAM (standard)	128K	64K
Serial ports	2	0
Audio port	Yes	Yes
Audio volume control	Yes	No
Headset jack	Yes	No
Cassette ports	No	No
Mouse port	Yes*	No
9-pin game port	Yes	Yes
16-pin game port	No	Yes
Numeric keypad port	No	Yes
Composite video port	Yes	Yes
RGB video port	Yes	No
RF modulator	Yes	No
Built-in disk drive	Yes	No
Second disk-drive port	Yes	No
Expansion slots	0	7
40-/80-column display	Yes	40 only

*The IIc mouse connects through its 9-pin game port, while the IIe mouse requires a separate interface card.

Figure 10-3
A comparison of the Apple IIc and IIe

into the IIc system for just about any kind of hardware but, in actuality, they probably won't. Their 19,200-baud maximum data transfer rate is fine for use with peripherals, such as printers and modems, which exchange data fairly slowly, but it's too slow for devices, such as coprocessors, RAM boards, and certain hard disks, which rely on high-speed data transfer. No one can say positively that there will never be a Z-80 card for the IIc, or that you'll never be able to add RAM to handle bigger spreadsheet models, but the IIc's market niche and design say the odds are heavily against such enhancements. And the bottom line right now is that the IIc's lack of expansion slots makes it fine for some users, and too restrictive for others.

As far as compatibility goes, the IIc's 65C02 processor could pose some problems, as might its standard 128K of RAM and double high-resolution graphics. At this point, Apple says that 90 percent of available IIe software will run on the IIc. The 65C02 processor in the IIc, however, has a slightly different instruction set from that of the IIe's 6502. If developers take advantage of the 65C02's newer instruction set to gain better performance in their products, then IIe owners will be out of luck with this processor-specific software. Conversely, II+ or IIe software that has been souped up at the expense of ignoring Apple's software-development guidelines (the program accesses non-standard memory locations, for example) won't run on the IIc.

Another factor that will affect compatibility is memory. With its 128K of RAM, the IIc has twice the standard memory of the IIe. Before the IIc came out, developers were reluctant to write programs that required 128K of RAM, because they didn't want to leave the owners of unenhanced IIe's out in the cold. But since the IIc will add substantially to the number of machines with 128K, the minimum RAM requirements could move upward. This situation is similar to the earlier situation between the 48K II+ and the 64K IIe: For a while, all software ran on the smaller amount of RAM, but as the IIe's sales surpassed those of the II+, 48K programs grew fewer and fewer. Of course, some programs simply don't need 128K of RAM (or 64K, for that matter). But since the spreadsheet and graphics applications have the biggest appetites for RAM, you can expect products in these areas to expand quickly into the larger RAM environment.

Speaking of graphics, the IIc is the first Apple that has offered a double high-resolution display mode from the very beginning. The IIe, as explained in Chapter 7, was initially produced with standard high-resolution graphics, and it was only after some 70,000 IIe's had been produced that the double high-resolution mode was incorporated in the Revision B motherboard.

For a long time, developers stayed away from using the double high-resolution graphics mode, in deference to owners of those first 70,000 IIe's, and because this mode could only be used by Revision B IIe owners who had installed an Extended 80-column card. From the day the IIc was announced, however, double high-resolution graphics programs and games were on the market, and the use of this mode will undoubtedly expand into every application, as screen windowing and graphics interfaces grow in popularity. If you are a II+ owner, or a IIe owner and haven't swapped your Revision A motherboard for a Revision B motherboard, you will not be able to use these programs. If you own a Revision B IIe, compatibility is simply a matter of installing an Extended 80-column card in your computer. (See Chapter 7 for information about upgrading your IIe motherboard.)

APPLYING THE IIc

Both the IIc and the IIe are capable of the same kinds of applications, but the IIc is better at some applications and not as good at (or incapable of) others. If you're a new user, you'll have to decide which level of function is acceptable for the applications you have in mind. If you're thinking of using a IIc as an enhancement to your Apple II system, the issue is whether the differences in levels of function will prevent you from having the compatibility you want.

Spreadsheets

The possibilities for enhancing spreadsheet work on the IIc are very limited. While its 128K of memory is double that of a standard IIe, and thus will accommodate larger models, 128K is the upper limit of the IIc's capacity. If you want, you can add extra RAM cards to a II+ or a IIe that will allow you to create spreadsheets that fill up to 512K of memory, but the IIc's lack of expansion slots eliminates this type of enhancement.

Display is another IIc limitation. An 80-column display is standard on the IIc, but 80 columns is the limit. With a II+ or a IIe, you can install an UltraTerm card to generate displays up to 128 columns wide, and thus view larger portions of spreadsheets at once. Again, the lack of expansion slots precludes this sort of enhancement on the IIc.

For users dissatisfied with spreadsheet recalculation times, the II+ or the IIe can be speeded up with a faster 6502 coprocessor, a Z-80 coprocessor, or even the Rana 8086/2 system. But again, all of these devices interact with the computer through the internal expansion bus, so the IIc can't use them.

The final restriction in the spreadsheet arena is the IIc's lack of a port that allows you to add a numeric keypad. Since the IIc is designed primarily for home use, the circuitry to handle keypad input would have been a luxury that took up precious space on the IIc's motherboard. Apple has no announced plans to market a keypad for the IIc, but some enterprising developer may well find a way to use one of the serial ports or the mouse/joystick port to provide this option.

If you're concerned with compatibility between a IIc and a II+ or a IIe, the key issue in terms of spreadsheets will be RAM use. For example, if you create models larger than 128K, you won't be able to work with them on the IIc because of its 128K limitation. On the other hand, enhanced spreadsheet software that uses the IIc's full 128K of RAM may not be compatible with other II computers. You can duplicate the IIc's memory on a IIe by installing the Extended 80-column card, but this card only fits a special slot in the IIe, so the solution will not work on a II+. So, either you won't have enough RAM to match the IIc environment, or (if you've increased your II+ RAM to 128K) the IIc software won't know how to access the extra RAM without pre-boot software.

Word Processing

Word-processing software doesn't have the same heavy RAM requirements spreadsheet programs do, so the RAM problem won't be as acute in this application if you want compatibility between the IIc and an older Apple. Most programs will offer the option of using either 128K or 64K of RAM, and your old 48K word processor will run fine on the IIc (unless the author told it to use offbeat memory addresses).

On the hardware side, you'll encounter some difficulties because of the IIc's limited expansion capability. You can't go beyond an 80-column by 24-line display with the IIc so, for example, if you normally use an UltraTerm board to get a 48-line display, you'll have to revert to the smaller 24-line format when you use your word processor on the IIc. Fortunately, the change from an expanded display to the normal display doesn't require any reconfiguration of the software. You have to use an UltraTerm pre-boot diskette to get the bigger display, so you would just boot your word processor directly when using the IIc.

If you've installed a high-capacity disk drive on your II+ or IIe, however, you won't be able to use either it or your high-capacity diskettes on the IIc. ProDOS, the IIc's standard operating system, doesn't care about the capacity of the disk drive you're using, but the IIc's disk controller currently supports only the standard 143K Apple disk drives. It's the controller that informs ProDOS about the size of the disk drive, and since any external drive, Apple or otherwise, must be plugged into the port run by the controller, you can only add a 143K drive to the IIc.

Rana or another manufacturer of disk drives may find it worthwhile to make a higher-capacity drive that would work with the IIc, but such a drive would have to have its own internal controller card that enabled it to work with the IIc's controller. Since such a drive would have to send data through both controllers, it would offer much slower data transfer than a standard drive does.

This same problem applies to hard disks, too. There are hard disks available for all Apple II models, but the ones for the II+ and IIe work through their own controllers that connect directly with the computer by way of its internal expansion slots. Since they don't have to use the II+ or IIe's controller as an intermediary, these drives can transfer data at a faster rate than the one that must hook up to the IIc's internally controlled disk-drive port.

Aside from these restrictions, the IIc and the IIe or II+ should work fine together for word processing. Other word-processing enhancement products, such as printer buffers or alternate printers, will work with the IIc as easily as they will with any other member of the family. You won't be able to use a detached keyboard, but since the IIc is so small, it's easy enough to consider the whole unit a detached keyboard.

Database Management

The requirements of personal (as opposed to business) file management are small enough that the IIc can handle them with ease. Such products as PFS: File and QuickFile will work fine on the IIc. When you get into high-end software, however, the IIc looks less attractive. You can't use coprocessors to speed up sorting or to run more sophisticated CP/M or MS-DOS software; access to a hard disk will be slower than it is with another II-series computer; and some software won't run at all or will require an unreasonable amount of disk-swapping.

The IIc's closed design allows you to add one external disk drive (currently, either Apple's external floppy drive or Quark's hard disk), but one extra device is the limit. That's no problem if all you need are two floppy disk drives, but this limit does make it impossible to connect a traditional hard-disk backup device to the IIc, because such devices generally operate as additional disk drives and are connected directly to the Apple's internal expansion bus. Manufacturers might enable you to connect a tape backup device if they include a port on the hard disk itself (as Corvus does with its Omnidrives), but adding this capability to a hard disk will increase its price.

Integrated Software

The IIc's 128K of RAM, built-in mouse port, and double high-resolution graphics all create an excellent environment for integrated programs, such as Jane and AppleWorks. For example, you get about four times as much AppleWorks file space with 128K of RAM as you get with 64K. In addition, split-screen windows, pull-down menus, and mouse-oriented command selection are all becoming hallmarks of integrated software, and the IIc is better equipped to handle them than the standard IIe or II+ are. As this trend toward integration continues, you can expect increasing use of double high-resolution graphics, too—for example, in Macintosh-like, pull-down menus, improved text displays, and integrated text and graphics packages.

But suppose you take the hard-disk approach to integration, where you store several separate, but related, programs on a hard disk for fast and convenient access. Here, you're better off with a IIe or a II+, because the hard disk for the IIc is much slower than are the hard disks for the other computers, and there's the added problem of mounting copy-protected software onto the hard disk.

As for compatibility between the IIc and the IIe or II+, the only likely problems will be the amount of RAM and the Open Apple and Closed Apple function keys, which are on the IIe and IIc keyboards, but not on the II+ keyboard. AppleWorks won't work at all on a II+, because it uses the function keys so heavily, and future products that insist on 128K of RAM won't work on machines with less. Mouse-driven software, such as Jane, is probably most convenient to use if you have a mouse for each Apple you own. Unfortunately, the IIc mouse won't work on the IIe or II+ without an extra interface card, and conversely, the WICO mouse, which requires WICO's SmartCard, won't work on the IIc at all because the IIc has no expansion slots to accommodate the card.

Communications

Because communications, like word processing, is another application in which varying amounts of RAM are not a problem, there's really very little you can't do on a IIc in the way of communications that you can do on another 8-bit Apple. You'll have to have an external modem with the IIc, of course, but you won't have to spend any extra money on an interface card. And if you want a clock, you'll have to buy a modem that contains one, as there can be no clock cards for the IIc.

The IIc's built-in 40-/80-column display, however, eliminates any software compatibility problems, too. And as for networking, you can use one of the IIc's serial ports for the network connection, although you will still require additional interfacing circuitry (doubtless in an external box) to make the necessary connection. In other respects, the IIc is compatible enough with other 8-bit Apples to coexist on the same network with no problems.

Graphics

The IIc's home orientation makes it likely that a variety of graphics input devices will be made available for it, although your choices will probably be more limited than they are with a IIe. Touch tablets, mice, and light pens will certainly be available for the IIc, but such things as digitizing tablets and digitizing cameras look like longshots, because they're so expensive for a computer in this market niche.

The double high-resolution graphics capability of the IIc is a plus, though, and you'll see a lot of software that takes advantage of it. The IIc's built-in RGB port also saves you a little money, because you don't have to spend $150 on a separate interface, as you do for the IIe. It looks like double high-resolution graphics will be limited to software, though. You can't install a Sprite graphics board, which lets you animate your own graphics, in the slotless IIc, and such products exchange information with the processor too quickly to make connection through a relatively slow serial port a practical alternative.

Printers and plotters are no problem for the IIc, and again you'll save the expense of a separate interface card. If you want to use the same printer or plotter with both a IIc and a IIe or II+, though, you'll probably need an adapter or a different cable, because the serial connections on the IIc differ from those on the interface cards used with other Apples.

Entertainment

You can expect games for the IIc to make good use of double high-resolution graphics, and the IIc has the advantage of a volume control and an earphone jack, both of which will probably be well received by the families of arcade-game enthusiasts. External sound-generating devices, such as the Mockingboard D and the Cricket, are already available for the IIc.

Because of its home-oriented marketing, the IIc will be generally attractive to makers of entertainment software or enhancement products. Joysticks, trackballs, and touch tablets can all connect to the IIc's 9-pin port, directly or through an adapter. Game-connection expanders,which turn one 9-pin socket into an assortment of 9- and 16-pin sockets, should also be available. High-speed 6502 boards and Sprite graphics boards are other entertainment enhancements for the II+ and IIe, but they won't be available for the IIc, because they need internal expansion slots.

Portability

There's no question that the IIc is easier to move about than the IIe. Companies have already announced combination battery packs and carrying cases for the IIc that let you pack it up with an LCD display and compute anywhere for a few hours. This portability is an attractive benefit but, as discussed in Chapter 9, real utility is another question. If you're trying to decide between a IIc or a IIe as your only computer, don't decide on the basis of one machine's size versus the other's. Size is the first thing you'll notice, and it's one of the things that will arouse a strong emotional response, but it's really the least important feature of a well-designed computer. Long after size and visual appeal have ceased to matter, the computer's level of function will remain foremost in your mind. As an adjunct to an existing II+ or IIe system, on the other hand, the IIc offers the best, though not the cheapest, solution to a need for mobility.

TO EACH ITS OWN

Despite Apple's pledge of peaceful coexistence between the IIc and the IIe, you'll probably get the impression that everything new and wonderful is being made for the IIc. You'll see little stickers on software packages or little banners on advertisements that say, "Works on the IIc" or "For Apple IIc." But this labeling is merely an acknowledgment of the heightened consumer awareness of the IIc as a vehicle for new products, and it's an attempt to assure current and future IIc owners that the computer isn't all that different in terms of compatibility.

Stickers that proclaim compatibility with the IIc don't necessarily mean that the product is incompatible with the IIe or II+. Some manufacturers will use the IIc's 128K of RAM or its superior graphics capabilities in a way that leaves standard IIe or II+ owners out in the cold, but most manufacturers won't, and for good reason: Apple's goal was to sell 350,000 IIc's during the machine's first eight months on the market; but even at that rate (which takes a heavy promotional campaign into account) it would take about four years for the IIc's installed base to equal that of the IIe and II+. Manufacturers won't settle for such a limited part of the market unless absolutely necessary, and in most cases they won't have to, because of the IIc's compatibility with the other II-series computers.

So, if you're trying to decide whether to invest in a IIc, one guidepost by which to make your decision is Apple's marketing approach, which tags the IIc as for the "serious home user"—someone who is primarily concerned with home applications, whether they're for entertainment or education, or are scaled-down versions of traditional productivity applications.

The productivity area is where the IIc's main functional differences—its limited mass storage capabilities and its inability to use extra RAM or coprocessors—really matter the most. If your use of productivity programs is home oriented (you use word processing for letter writing, or spreadsheets for home budgets), then the IIc will probably be all the computer you'll ever need. If your productivity applications involve large amounts of office-like work (you sort data bases, build large spreadsheet models, or need software that is compatible with MS-DOS machines), then you'll need a IIe.

And even after you've determined your needs in terms of hardware and software, one other way to measure the appeal of either computer is to assess your own level of involvement in computing, for there's a basic philosophical difference between a IIc and a IIe. The IIc is a packaged solution; it requires less knowledge of computing, and less desire to know about the subject. It's great for people who are interested in getting something done as quickly and easily as possible. On the other hand, the IIe is characterized by its potential but, like anything with a lot of potential, the IIe requires some imagination and determination, and an interest not only in the destination, but in your means of getting there.

It's probable that 60 to 70 percent of the people shopping for Apple II computers can have their present and future needs met nicely by the IIc. But if you prefer to research the features, specifications, and performance histories of different computers and take an interest in the machine for its own sake, rather than for its ability to perform specific tasks, then the IIe is the computer for you.

11

IS IT REALLY ENDLESS?

The question of just how long Apple will continue to build and support its 8-bit computers looms large in any decision about enhancing one. Obviously, you'll be more reluctant to spend $1500 on a hard disk for your IIe if Apple seems to be losing interest in its II-series of computers. But while it may seem so, the matter of continued support for the II-series isn't entirely in Apple's hands.

Other factors, from the state of computing itself to the tastes of consumers, and from the average price of a computer to the continued enthusiasm of third-party hardware and software developers, all contribute to the equation. After all, Apple won't keep making these things if no one wants to buy them or develop new products for them. And even if Apple continues to generate enthusiasm and sales with redesigned products, such as the IIc, how long will it be before such refinements, made in the quest for more power and convenience, result in new computers that really aren't Apple IIs anymore at all?

EIGHT-BIT UPGRADES

The dilemma Apple faces about how far it can advance the state of 8-bit computing while maintaining the closest possible compatibility with earlier machines is becoming more acute with each new product. With the introduction of the IIc, standard Apple equipment has become 128K of RAM, two function keys, and double high-resolution graphics—a far cry from the II/II+ world. An increasing number of programs will take advantage of these refinements too, and create a growing compatibility gap between the II/II+ and the IIe and IIc.

Apple could offer some kind of conversion program for II/II+ owners wanting to upgrade their units to the IIc level, but such a program would be costly for both Apple and Apple owners alike. Upgrading such a large number of computers would also be an interesting exercise in logistics, whether it involved upgrading existing II+ computers or simply exchanging the older computers at a nominal price for IIe's.

For a while, rumors circulated that Apple was working on a "IIe board" for the II+ that would take care of an upgrade with ease, but a faithful conversion to the higher capabilities of a IIe would mean replacing the II+ motherboard. With the installed base of IIe and IIc computers now greater than the base of II/II+ computers, Apple's energies are probably better directed elsewhere.

If you are a II or II+ owner, perhaps you're beginning to feel left behind. Technologically, that may be true—the whole industry is rushing ahead. But you *have* gotten several years of service from your computer by now, and if you're still satisfied with it, you have no problem. On the other hand, if you want to upgrade, you can buy a new, "stripped" IIe for about $500. Since most of your other equipment will work with the IIe, $500 doesn't seem like much money to spend to stay current with the state of Apple art, especially given the cost of some peripherals you might buy.

Apple II and II+ computers will still be used for less demanding applications, such as educational programs, but continuing improvement of the II and II+ will probably be limited to software upgrades. Since a lot of new Apple software is using IIe and IIc features, such as function keys and more memory, it may well be that the enhancement possibilities of the II and II+ are very nearly over.

Beyond the II+, however, Apple seems to have settled on a 128K, double high-resolution graphics configuration that will prove to be an adequate foundation upon which to build for several years. Apple's introduction of the IIc in 1984 underscores the company's commitment to this configuration. Products that use these RAM and graphics capabilities are growing in number, but this new environment still offers a lot of possibilities that will take a few years to explore completely.

Within the limits of 8-bit processing, the IIe/IIc environment has been used only to about half of its capabilities, so there's a lot of room for more enhancements. What sorts of enhancements? Graphics interfaces are certainly on the way. Pull-down menus, multiple-image windows, and mice will be featured more and more on the IIe and IIc. Some 300 developers are currently working on new software for this environment, and by using more efficient programming and heretofore unused powers of the circuitry, they will make some astounding things possible. MousePaint is only the first of the software products that will make the Apple IIe closely resemble the more advanced Macintosh.

Apple's peripherals for the IIe will also improve. The old 143K disk drives will be replaced, probably by 3½-inch microfloppies that offer disk compatibility with the Macintosh (more on this later). The ProFile hard disk, now limited to five megabytes, will be replaced either by a higher capacity 5¼-inch drive offering up to 40 megabytes of storage or by a 3½-inch hard disk with a 10- to 20-megabyte capacity. Apple is also exploring combination units containing a hard disk and a floppy disk drive. In the display area, look for an RGB monitor from Apple in the near future. Monochrome monitors should offer improved resolution and nicer-looking character sets when they are next upgraded.

Apple is also continuing research on other output devices. A laser printer costing about $3500 to $4000 will be announced soon, with the price probably falling to about $3000 by the end of 1985. Laser printers will be used almost exclusively in network installations. An Apple ink-jet printer will soon offer exquisite color printing with good text resolution for about $500.

From a manufacturing standpoint, Apple will continue to try and integrate more of the circuits in its products for the II-series, making these devices smaller, more reliable, and less expensive. This approach should result in better liquid-crystal, flat-panel displays and less expensive RAM chips that require less power. Such products should, in turn, result in a more truly portable computer than the IIc within a year or so.

SIXTEEN-BIT UPGRADES

The limit of 8-bit computing is still a few years in the future, but it will be reached eventually. Long before that, though, Apple will probably have arrived at a 16-bit upgrade for the IIe. Such a 16-bit processor will allow direct access to far more RAM, and that will result in smarter and more elegant software. It will also provide a bridge to the 16-bit world of the Lisa and the Macintosh.

Apple is currently looking at several 16-bit processors for the IIe, and at several ways of using them. Despite its early enthusiasm for Western Design Center's 65816 chip, Apple has decided to wait and see how it is received by the rest of the computer industry. Understandably nervous about using a product available from only one source, Apple is waiting to see whether the 65816 becomes popular enough—either with another current user of the 6502, such as Commodore or Atari, or with a new company—that semiconductor manufacturers other than Western Design Center begin making the new processor.

Another distinct 16-bit possibility for the IIe is the Motorola MC 68000 processor that is used in the Lisa and Macintosh computers. Some very clever engineering would be needed to put the processor, its related hardware, and enough RAM to make 16-bit computing worthwhile on one board designed for one IIe expansion slot, but Apple has produced more than its share of innovations in this department. There's also an attractive alternative to this approach, and that is putting the MC 68000 processor in an external box with a 3½-inch microfloppy disk drive, or with a microfloppy and a 3½-inch hard disk. This approach could also provide disk compatibility, as well as software compatibility, with the Macintosh and Lisa. The current Rana 8086/2 coprocessor system sets a promising precedent for this type of setup.

AN APPLE IN YOUR FUTURE

The future looks bright for the Apple IIe and IIc, because of the combination of design flexibility and corporate innovation for which Apple is famous. Flexibility alone is a powerful agent for stimulating endless upgrades, but the types of expansion a company encourages are just as important as flexibility in keeping a product current. Apple has gracefully and effectively managed to enhance an eight-year-old product by being as much of a technological innovator as any other company in this business, and its enhancements to the Apple II line have often been made to further technology.

If you're at the leading edge, there's little danger of being outdistanced by your competition, although there's a far greater risk of advancing in a direction where no one else will follow. Apple has accepted that risk. So far, Apple has been highly successful in bringing technologically advanced products to market, and in making that technology available for its earlier computers. While there have been some false starts (and even a notable disappointment in the Apple III), Apple has generally made and kept an important promise: That it will propel the microcomputer market into the future, and that, as one of its customers, you are guaranteed a seat on its rocket.

LIST OF PRODUCTS

The products in this appendix are listed alphabetically, both by product category and within product category. Prices listed are approximate retail, and are subject to change. This list is by no means complete; some categories contain most or all of the known manufacturers of a product, while other categories provide only a sampling of the manufacturers and products. Furthermore, some of the manufacturers mentioned in this appendix make more products than the ones listed here. If you want to look at a broader listing of hardware and software products, I recommend either *The Blue Book for the Apple Computer* ($25), published by WIDL Video, 5245 W. Diversey Ave., Chicago, IL 60639, (312) 622-9606; or *The Addison-Wesley Book of Apple Software* ($20), published by Addison-Wesley, 6 Jacob Way, Reading, MA 01867, (617) 944-3700.

BUBBLE MEMORY CARDS

BUBDISK ($599), MPC Peripherals, 9466 Black Mtn. Rd., San Diego, CA 92126, (619) 578-9222.

CARRYING CASES

Apple II Case ($75 and $245), Fiberbilt Computer Cases, 601 W. 26th St., New York, NY 10001, (212) 675-5820.

C-Series Carry Case and Flight Form Transit Case ($110 to $330), Cases, Box 33820, Seattle, WA 98133, (206) 365-5210.

Protective Case ($110), P.C.A., 901 49th NW, Seattle, WA 98107, (206) 789-1888.

Soft Padded Carrying Case ($135), The Madson Line, 228 Harrison St., Oakland, CA 94607, (800) 851-1551.

Various cases (custom made), Anvil Cases, Inc., 4128 Temple City Blvd., Rosemead, CA 91770, (213) 575-8614.

Various cases ($109 to $130), Computer Case Co., 5650 Indian Mount Ct., Columbus, OH 43213, (614) 868-9464.

CLOCK CARDS

ProClock ($149), Practical Peripherals, Inc., 31245 La Baya Dr., Westlake Village, CA 91362, (213) 991-8200.

Thunderclock ($150), Thunderware, Inc., 44 Hermosa Ave., Oakland, CA 94618, (415) 652-1737.

Timemaster II ($129), Applied Engineering, P.O. Box 470301, Dallas, TX 75247, (214) 492-2027.

COMMUNICATIONS SOFTWARE

ACCESS II ($75), Apple Computer, Inc., 20525 Mariani Ave., Cupertino, CA 95014, (408) 996-1010.

ASCII Express Professional ($129), United Software Industries, 1880 Century Park East, Suite 311, Century City, CA 90067, (213) 556-2211.

DataCapture ($90), Southeastern Software, 6414 Derbyshire Dr., New Orleans, LA 70126, (504) 246-7937.

Era 2 ($499 including modem), Microcom, Inc., 1400A Providence Highway, Norwood, MA 02062, (617) 762-9310.

Smartcom I ($119), Hayes Microcomputer Products, 5923 Peachtree Industrial Blvd., Norcross, GA 30092, (404) 449-8791.

Terminus IIe ($89), Quark, Inc., 2525 West Evans, Suite 220, Denver, CO 80219, (303) 934-2211.

Transend 1, 2, and 3 ($79, $119, and $220), Transend Corp., 2190 Paragon Dr., San Jose, CA 95131, (408) 946-7400.

COPROCESSORS

Accelerator IIE ($599), Titan Technologies, Inc., 310 West Ann St., Ann Arbor, MI 48104, (313) 662-8542.

AD8088 Processor Card ($345), Alf Products, 1315F Nelson, Denver, CO 80215, (303) 234-0871.

Appli-Cards, several ($375 to $595), Personal Computer Products, Inc., 16776 Bernardo Center Dr., San Diego, CA 92128, (619) 485-8411.

Booster Card ($599), Number Nine Computer Corp., 691 Concord Ave., Cambridge, MA 02138, (617) 492-0999.

CP/M Gold Card ($495 to $775), Digital Research, Inc., 160 Central, P.O. Box 579, Pacific Grove, CA 93950, (408) 649-3896.

8086/2 ($1895), Rana Systems, 21300 Superior St., Chatsworth, CA 91311, (800) 421-2207.

SoftCards, various ($345 to $395), Microsoft Corp., 10700 Northup Way, Bellevue, WA 98004, (206) 828-8080.

SpeeDemon ($295), MCT, 1745 21st St., Santa Monica, CA 90404, (213) 829-3643.

Z-Card II and CP/M Card ($169 and $399), Advanced Logic Systems, 1195 E. Arques Ave., Sunnyvale, CA 94086, (408) 730-0306.

Z-80 Plus ($139), Applied Engineering, P.O. Box 470301, Dallas, TX 75247, (214) 492-2027.

DATABASE SOFTWARE

Aladin ($595), Advanced Data Institute of America, 1215 Howe Ave., Sacramento, CA 95825, (916) 925-2229.

Business Savvy ($950 including coprocessor card), Excalibur Technologies Corp., 800 Rio Grande Blvd. N.W., Mercado 21, Albuquerque, NM 87104, (800) 551-5199.

DB Master ($350), Stoneware, Inc., 50 Belvedere St., San Rafael, CA 94901, (415) 454-6500.

PFS: File and PFS: Report ($125 each), Software Publishing Corp., 1901 Landings Dr., Mountain View, CA 94043, (415) 962-8910.

Qbase and VersaForm ($189 and $389), Applied Software Technology, 170 Knowles Dr., Los Gatos, CA 95030, (408) 370-2662.

Quick File II ($100), Apple Computer, Inc., 20525 Mariani Ave., Cupertino, CA 95014, (408) 996-1010.

DIGITIZERS

Diplomat Video Digitizer ($295), Computech Systems, 168 Finchley Rd., London NW3 6HP, England, 01-794-0202.

DS-65 Digisector ($350), The Micro Works, Inc., P.O. Box 1110, Del Mar, CA 92014, (619) 942-2400.

MicronEye Bullet ($295), Micron Technology, Inc., Vision Systems Group, 2805 E. Columbia Rd., Boise, ID 83706, (208) 383-4106.

DIGITIZING TABLETS

Apple Graphics Tablet ($795), Apple Computer, Inc., 20525 Mariani Ave., Cupertino, CA 95014, (408) 996-1010.

Digitizing Tablets, various ($395 to $1300), Summagraphics Corp., 35 Brentwood Ave., Fairfield, CT 06430, (203) 384-1344.

HiPlot ($1995), Houston Instruments, 8500 Cameron Rd., Austin, TX 78753, (512) 835-0900.

Space Tablet Graphics System ($795), Micro Control Systems, Inc., 143 Tunnel Rd., Vernon, CT 06066, (203) 872-0602.

DISPLAY CARDS

Apple Extended 80-Column Card ($295), Apple Computer, Inc., 20525 Mariani Ave., Cupertino, CA 95014, (408) 996-1010.

Neptune Card ($249 with 64K of RAM), Titan Technologies, 310 West Ann St., Ann Arbor, MI 48104, (313) 662-8542.

Smarterm II ($179), Advanced Logic Systems, 1195 E. Arques Ave., Sunnyvale, CA 94086, (408) 730-0306.

Sup 'R' Term ($195), M&R Enterprises, 910 George St., Santa Clara, CA 95050, (408) 980-0160.

VideoTerm and UltraTerm ($279 and $379), Videx, Inc., 897 NW Grant Ave., Corvallis, OR 97330, (503) 758-0521.

ViewMaster 80 ($169), Applied Engineering, P.O. Box 470301, Dallas, TX 75247, (214) 492-2027.

Vision-80 ($195), Action-Research Northwest, 11442 Marine View Dr., Seattle, WA 98146, (206) 241-1645.

FLOPPY DISK DRIVES

AMDISK I ($299), Amdek Corp., 2201 Lively Blvd., Elk Grove Village, IL 60007, (312) 964-1180.

A2 and A80 ($345 to $465), Microsci Corp., 2158 S. Hathaway St., Santa Ana, CA 92705, (714) 241-5600.

DuoDisk ($795), Apple Computer, Inc., 20525 Mariani Ave., Cupertino, CA 95014, (408) 996-1010.

Elite One, Two, and Three ($379 to $749), Rana Systems, 21300 Superior St., Chatsworth, CA 91311, (818) 709-5484.

Solo ($300), Vista Computer Company, Inc., 1317 E. Edinger St., Santa Ana, CA 92705, (714) 953-0523.

GAME-SOCKET EXTENDERS

Apple Expander ($49), WICO Corp., 6400 W. Gross Point Rd., Niles, IL 60648, (312) 647-7500.

Bosmerco Multiport ($50), Alpha Logic Business Systems, Inc., 4119 N. Union Rd., Woodstock, IL 60098, (815) 568-5166.

Game-Socket Extender GS-4 ($35), Happ Electronics, Inc., 4640 Island View, Oshkosh, WI 54901, (414) 231-5128.

Joyport ($50), Sirius Software, 10364 Rockingham Dr., Sacramento, CA 95827, (916) 366-1195.

Paddle-Adapple ($30), Southern California Research Group, P.O. Box 2231, Goleta, CA 93118, (805) 685-1931.

Paradise Ports ($40), Tech Designs, 3638 Grosvenor Dr., Ellicott City, MD 21043, (301) 953-4818.

Select-A-Port ($40), TG Products, 1104 Summit Ave., Suite 110, Plano, TX 75074, (214) 424-8568.

Swapper Stopper ($26), A B Computers, 252 Bethlehem Pike, Colmar, PA 18915, (215) 822-7727.

GAME SOFTWARE

The Arcade Machine ($60), Broderbund Software, 17 Paul Dr., San Rafael, CA 94903, (415) 479-1170.

Castle Wolfenstein ($30), Muse Software, 347 N. Charles St., Baltimore, MD 21201, (301) 659-7212.

EXODUS: ULTIMA III ($55), Origin Systems, Inc., 18100 Upper Bay Rd., Suite 202, P.O. Box 48009, Houston, TX 77058, (713) 333-2539.

Flight Simulator II ($50), SubLogic Corp., 713 Edgebrook Dr., Champaign, IL 61820, (217) 359-8482.

Lode Runner ($35), Broderbund Software, 17 Paul Dr., San Rafael, CA 94903, (415) 479-1170.

Maze Craze Construction Set ($40), DTI Data Trek, Inc., 621 2nd St., Encinitas, CA 92024, (619) 436-5055.

Night Mission Pinball ($35), SubLogic Corp., 713 Edgebrook Dr., Champaign, IL 61820, (217) 359-8482.

Pinball Construction Set ($40), Electronic Arts, 2755 Campus Dr., San Mateo, CA 94403, (415) 571-7171.

Wizardry ($50), Sir-Tech Software, Inc., 6 Main St., Ogdensburg, NY 13669, (315) 393-6633.

Zork I, II, and III ($40 each), Infocom, 55 Wheeler St., Cambridge, MA 02138, (617) 492-1031.

GRAPHICS BOARDS

Arcade Board ($175), Third Millennium Engineering Corp., 1015 Gayley Ave., Suite 394, Los Angeles, CA 90024, (213) 473-2102.

Sprite I, Sprite II, and SuperSprite ($149, $249, and $395), Synetix, Inc., 10635 N.E. 38th Pl., Kirkland, WA 98033, (206) 828-4884.

GRAPHICS SOFTWARE

Dazzle Draw ($50), Broderbund Software, 17 Paul Dr., San Rafael, CA 94903, (415) 479-1170.

Fontrix 1.0 ($75), Data Transforms, 616 Washington St., Suite 106, Denver, CO 80203, (303) 832-1501.

Graphics Department ($125), Sensible Software, Inc., 6619 Perham Dr., West Bloomfield, MI 48033, (313) 399-8877.

Graphics Exhibitor ($40), Koala Technologies, Inc., 3100 Patrick Henry Dr., Santa Clara, CA 95052-8100, (408) 986-8866.

The Graphics Magician ($60), Penguin Software, 830 Fourth Ave., Box 311, Dept. 8, Geneva, IL 60134, (312) 232-1984.

MousePaint ($149 with AppleMouse II), Apple Computer, Inc., 20525 Mariani Ave., Cupertino, CA 95014, (408) 996-1010.

PFS: Graph ($125), Software Publishing Corp., 1901 Landings Dr., Mountain View, CA 94043, (415) 962-8910.

Pixit ($50), Baudville, 1001 Medical Park Dr., S.E., Grand Rapids, MI 49506, (616) 957-3036.

The Print Shop ($49), Broderbund Software, 17 Paul Dr., San Rafael, CA 94903, (415) 479-1170.

Zoom Grafix ($40), Phoenix Software, Inc., 64 Lake Zurich Dr., Lake Zurich, IL 60047, (312) 438-4850.

HARD-DISK BACKUP SYSTEMS

The Mirror ($790), Corvus Systems, Inc., 2100 Corvus Dr., San Jose, CA 95124, (408) 559-7000.

Streaming Tape Backup System ($1795), Davong Systems, 217 Humboldt Ct., Sunnyvale, CA 94086, (408) 734-4900.

HARD DISK DRIVES

Apple 5-megabyte ProFile ($1295), Apple Computer, Inc., 20525 Mariani Ave., Cupertino, CA 95014, (408) 996-1010.

Corvus 5-, 11-, 20- and 45-megabyte Omnidrives ($1995, $2495, $3195, and $4995), Corvus Systems, Inc., 2100 Corvus Dr., San Jose, CA 95124, (408) 559-7000.

Davong 5-, 10-, and 15-megabyte Hard Disks ($1995, $2395, and $2795), Davong Systems, 217 Humboldt Ct., Sunnyvale, CA 94086, (408) 734-4900.

Infax 101A ($2595), Vufax, Inc., 5301 Covington Highway, Decatur, GA 30035, (404) 981-6778.

Mini-mega Series Hard Disk (6-megabyte fixed and 6-megabyte removable cartridge, $3995), Santa Clara Systems, Inc., 1860 Hartog Dr., San Jose, CA 95131, (408) 287-4640.

Mountain Computer 5- and 10-megabyte Hard Disks ($2495 and $2995), Mountain Computer, Inc., 300 El Pueblo Rd., Scotts Valley, CA 95066, (408) 438-6650.

QC10 (under $2500), Quark, Inc., 2525 West Evans, Suite 220, Denver, CO 80219, (303) 934-2211.

Rana 5- and 10-megabyte Hard Disks ($995 and $1495), Rana Systems, 21300 Superior St., Chatsworth, CA 91311, (213) 709-5484.

INTEGRATED SOFTWARE

AppleWorks ($250), Apple Computer, Inc., 20525 Mariani Ave., Cupertino, CA 95014, (408) 996-1010.

Incredible Jack and Jack2 ($179 and $259), Business Solutions, Inc., 60 E. Main St., Kings Park, NY 11754, (516) 269-1120.

Jane ($295 with mouse, $179 without), Arktronics, 520 East Liberty, Ann Arbor, MI 48104, (313) 769-7253.

INTERFACE CARDS

Apple Super Serial Card ($195), Apple Computer, Inc., 20525 Mariani Ave., Cupertino, CA 95014, (408) 996-1010.

Orange Interface and Grappler+ ($100 and $175), Orange Micro, Inc., 1400 N. Lakeview, Anaheim, CA 92807, (714) 779-2772.

PPC-100 and TAC-200 ($100 and $120), Tymac Controls Corp., 127 Main St., Franklin, NJ 07416, (201) 827-4050.

Printerface and Graphicard ($75 and $100), Practical Peripherals, 31245 La Baya Dr., Westlake Village, CA 91362, (213) 991-8200.

Printermate and Dispatcher ($99 and $139), Advanced Logic Systems, 1195 E. Arques Ave., Sunnyvale, CA 94086, (408) 730-0306.

Printmax and Graphmax standard ($80 and $119), Micromax Systems, 6868 Nancy Ridge Dr., San Diego, CA 92121, (619) 457-3131.

PSIO Board ($200), Intra Computer, 101 W. 31st St., New York, NY 10001, (212) 947-5533.

PSIO Board ($229), Videx, Inc., 897 NW Grant Ave., Corvallis, OR 97330, (503) 758-0521.

Various interfaces ($60 to $185), PC Ware, Inc., 4883 Tonino Dr., San Jose, CA 95136, (408) 978-8626.

Various interfaces ($130 to $225), Transend Corp., 2190 Paragon Dr., San Jose, CA 95131, (408) 946-7400.

JOYSTICKS

Apple Joystick ($50), Kraft Systems, 450 W. California Ave., Vista, CA 92083, (800) 854-1923.

Mach II and Mach III Joysticks ($45 and $55), Hayes Products, 1558 Osage St., San Marcos, CA 92069, (619) 744-8546.

MAGstik ($65), Tech Designs, 3638 Grosvenor Dr., Ellicott City, MD 21043, (301) 953-4818.

Mimco Stick ($55 to $69), Mimco, Inc., 1547 Cunard Rd., Columbus, OH 43227, (614) 237-3380.

TG Joystick ($45), TG Products, 1104 Summit Ave., Suite 110, Plano, TX 75074, (214) 424-8568.

WICO Analog Joystick ($50), WICO Corp., 6400 W. Gross Point Rd., Niles, IL 60648, (800) 323-4258

LIGHT PEN

Gibson Light Pen ($250), Koala Technologies, Inc., 3100 Patrick Henry Dr., Santa Clara, CA 95052-8100, (408) 986-8866.

MICE

AppleMouse II ($149), Apple Computer, Inc., 20525 Mariani Ave., Cupertino, CA 95014, (408) 996-1010.

SummaMouse ($300), Summagraphics Corp., 35 Brentwood Ave., Fairfield, CT 06430, (203) 384-1344.

WICO Mouse ($59 without interface, $260 to $310 with interface), WICO Corp., 6400 W. Gross Point Rd., Niles, IL 60648, (312) 647-7500.

MODEMS

AMC 300 Modemcard ($275 to $399 with software), Transend Corp., 2190 Paragon Dr., San Jose, CA 95131, (408) 946-7400.

Apple Modem ($495), Apple Computer, Inc., 20525 Mariani Ave., Cupertino, CA 95014, (408) 996-1010.

Era 2 and PCS 2000 ($499 including modem and $1195 including software), Microcom, Inc., 1400A Providence Highway, Norwood, MA 02062, (617) 762-9310.

J-Cat, Apple-Cat II, 212 Apple-Cat II, and others ($149, $319, $595 with software), Novation, 20409 Prairie St., Chatsworth, CA 91311, (213) 996-5060.

Micromodem IIe, Smartmodem 300, and Smartmodem 1200 ($329, $388, and $798, including software), Hayes Microcomputer Products, 5923 Peachtree Industrial Blvd., Norcross, GA 30092, (404) 449-8791.

Networker ($129 and $179 including software), Zoom Telephonics, Inc., 207 South St., Boston, MA 02111, (800) 631-3116.

Password ($449 including software), US Robotics, Inc., 1123 W. Washington, Chicago, IL 60607, (312) 733-0497.

Pro-Modem 1200 ($495 to $750), Prometheus Products, Inc., 45277 Fremont Blvd., Fremont, CA 94538, (415) 490-2370.

MONITORS

CPD-120 ($280), SONY Corp. of America, Office Products Division, 1 Sony Dr., Park Ridge, NJ 07656, (201) 930-1000.

CRT-36 and CRT-70 ($179 and $699), Sanyo Business Systems Corp., 51 Joseph St., Moonachie, NJ 07074, (201) 440-9300.

JB 1201, JC1415P2, JC1460, and others ($199, $249, $499), NEC Home Electronics, (U.S.A.), Inc., 1401 Estes St., Elk Grove Village, IL 60007, (312) 228-5900.

Monitor II, Monitor III, and Monitor IIc ($229, $249, and $199), Apple Computer, Inc., 20525 Mariani Ave., Cupertino, CA 95014, (408) 996-1010.

P3 and A3 ($199 and $225), USI International, 71 Park Lane, Brisbane, CA 94005, (415) 468-4900.

Quadchrome CH8400 ($795), Quadram Corp., 4355 International Blvd., Norcross, GA 30093, (404) 923-6666.

RGBvision 210 ($399), Taxan Corp., 18005 Cortney Ct., City of Industry, CA 91748, (213) 810-1291.

Video 300A, Color-I, Color-II Plus, and others ($199, $379, $529), Amdek Corp., 2201 Lively Blvd., Elk Grove Village, IL 60007, (312) 364-1180.

NETWORK HARDWARE AND SOFTWARE

Corvus Omninet (price depends on configuration), Corvus Systems, Inc., 2100 Corvus Dr., San Jose, CA 95124, (408) 559-7000.

Davong Network System (price depends on configuration), Davong Systems, Inc., 217 Humboldt Ct., Sunnyvale, CA 94086, (408) 734-4900.

NUMERIC KEYPADS AND AUXILIARY KEYBOARDS

Apple Numeric Keypad ($99), Apple Computer, Inc., 20525 Mariani Ave., Cupertino, CA 95014, (408) 996-1010.

Keywiz Numeric Keypad, Keywiz 83, and others ($89, $369), Creative Computers, Inc., Aztec Environmental Center, 1044 Lacey Rd., Forked River, NJ 08731, (609) 693-0002.

Numeric Keypad ($125), Advanced Business Technology, 12333 Saratoga-Sunnyvale Rd., Saratoga, CA 95110, (408) 446-2013.

IIe Tender ($199), Track House, 625 Trailwood Ct., Garland, TX 75043, (214) 270-0922.

PADDLES

Adam and Eve I ($35/pair), Tech Designs, 3638 Grosvenor Dr., Ellicott City, MD 21043, (301) 953-4818.

Apple Game Paddles ($35/pair), Apple Computer, Inc., 20525 Mariani Ave., Cupertino, CA 95014, (408) 996-1010.

Kraft Paddle Pair ($50), Kraft Systems, 450 W. California Ave., Vista, CA 92083, (800) 854-1923.

TG Game Paddles ($35/pair), TG Products, 1104 Summit Ave., Suite 110, Plano, TX 75074, (214) 424-8568.

PLOTTERS

Apple Color Plotter ($779), Apple Computer, Inc., 20525 Mariani Ave., Cupertino, CA 95014, (408) 996-1010.

DXY-100 and Amplot-II Plotters ($750 and $1300), Amdek Corp., 2201 Lively Blvd., Elk Grove Village, IL 60007, (312) 364-1180.

DXY 101 and DXY 800 ($750 and $995), Roland Corp., 7200 Dominion Cir., Los Angeles, CA 90040, (213) 685-5141.

Model 100 and Six Shooter ($795 and $1095), Enter Computer, Inc., 6867 Nancy Ridge Dr., Suite D, San Diego, CA 92121, (619) 450-0601.

Pixy ($795), Mannesmann Tally, 8301 S. 180th St., Kent, WA 98032, (206) 251-5524.

7470A and 7475A Plotters ($1575 and $1895), Hewlett-Packard Co., Personal Computer Group, 974 E. Arques Ave., Sunnyvale, CA 94088, (408) 720-3000.

PRINTER BUFFERS

Buffered Grappler+ ($239 and up), Orange Micro, Inc., 1400 N. Lakeview, Anaheim, CA 92807, (714) 779-2772.

Microbuffers, several ($159 to $349), Practical Peripherals, Inc., 31245 La Baya Dr., Westlake Village, CA 91362, (213) 991-8200.

P/S Buffer Card ($125 to $249), Prometheus Products, Inc., 45277 Fremont Blvd., Fremont, CA 94538, (415) 490-2370.

PRINTERS (Dot-Matrix, Unless Otherwise Stated)

Gemini-10X and Gemini-15X ($499 and $645), Star Micronics, Inc., 2803 E. 12th, Dallas/Ft. Worth Airport, TX 75261, (214) 456-0052.

Micro Prism and Prism 80 color ($795 and $1995), Integral Data Systems, Inc., Rt. 13 S., Milford, NH 03055, (603) 673-9100.

Microline Printers, several ($549 to $1495), Okidata Corp., 532 Fellowship Rd., Mt. Laurel, NJ 08054, (609) 235-2600.

MT 160I ($700), Mannesmann Tally, 8301 S. 180th St., Kent, WA 98032, (206) 251-5524.

P-1340 and P-1351 ($995 and $2195), Toshiba America, Inc., 2441 Michelle Dr., Tustin, CA 92680, (714) 730-5000.

PC-8023A Dot-Matrix Printer, 5510 Spinwriter Daisy-Wheel Printer, and others ($650 to $3000), NEC Home Electronics (U.S.A.), Inc., 1401 Estes Ave., Elk Grove Village, IL 60007, (312) 228-5900.

Prowriter 8510A ($795), C. Itoh Electronics, Inc., 5301 Beethoven St., Los Angeles, CA 90066, (213) 306-6700.

PT-88 and PT-89 Ink-Jet Printers ($895 and $1150), Siemens Communication Systems, Inc., 5500 Broken Sound Pkwy. NW, Boca Raton, FL 33431, (305) 994-8100.

Quadjet Color Ink-Jet Printer ($895), Quadram Corp., 4335 International Blvd., Norcross, GA 30093, (404) 923-6666.

RX 80, FX 80, LQ 1500, and others ($399, $699, $1395), Epson America, Inc., 3415 Kashiwa St., Torrance, CA 90505, (213) 539-9140.

Scribe Color Thermal-Transfer Printer and Imagewriter ($299 and $599), Apple Computer, Inc., 20525 Mariani Ave., Cupertino, CA 95014, (408) 996-1010.

Series C Color Ink Jet, various daisy-wheel printers ($1295 and up), Diablo Systems, Inc., P.O. Box 5030, Fremont, CA 94537, (415) 498-7000.

Sprint 11/40 Plus, others ($1776), Qume Corp., 2350 Qume Dr., San Jose, CA 95131, (408) 942-4000.

Style Writer and DTC 380Z Daisy-Wheel Printers ($899 and $1495), Data Terminals and Communications, 590 Division St., Campbell, CA 95008, (408) 378-1112.

ThinkJet Printer ($495), Hewlett-Packard Co., Personal Computer Products Group, 974 E. Arques Ave., Sunnyvale, CA 94088, (408) 720-3000.

TI 855 ($995), Texas Instruments, Inc., P.O. Box 402430, Dallas, TX 75240, (800) 527-3500.

Transtar 315 Color Dot-Matrix Printer and 130 Daisy-Wheel Printer ($600 and $900), Transtar/Vivitar, P.O. Box C-96975, Bellevue, WA 98009, (206) 454-9250.

RAM CARDS

Memory Master IIe ($249), Applied Engineering, P.O. Box 470301, Dallas, TX 75247, (214) 492-2027.

Neptune and Saturn Cards, various ($219 to $499), Titan Technologies, 310 W. Ann St., Ann Arbor, MI 48104, (313) 662-8542.

Ramex 16K and 128K ($140 and $500), Omega Microware, Inc., 222 S. Riverside Plaza, Chicago, IL 60606, (312) 648-4844.

S' Cards, 64K and 256K ($399 and $725), Legend Industries, Ltd., 2220 Scott Lake Rd., Pontiac, MI 48054, (313) 674-0953.

RAM-DISK DRIVES

Disco RAM ($239), Orbital Systems, Inc., 2929 E. Jasmine, Mesa, AZ 85203, (602) 830-6457.

Flashcards, several ($395 and up), Synetix, Inc., 10635 N.E. 38th Pl., Kirkland, WA 98033, (206) 828-4884.

RAMDISK 320K ($995), Axlon, Inc., 70 Daggett Dr., San Jose, CA 95134, (408) 945-0500.

REPLACEMENT KEYBOARDS AND KEYBOARD DETACHMENT KITS

D-TACH ($99), Innovative Micro Goodies, 34732 Calle Fortuna, Capistrano Beach, CA 92624, (714) 661-0435.

KB 200 Keyboard ($298), Key Tronic Corp., P.O. Box 14687, Spokane, WA 99214, (509) 928-8000.

SHIFT-KEY MODIFIERS

Enhancer II ($149), Videx, Inc., 897 NW Grant Ave., Corvallis, OR 97330, (503) 758-0521.

Repeaterrrr and Repeaterrrr + ($28 and $40), High Order Micro Electronics Corp., 17 River St., Chagrin Falls, OH 44022, (216) 247-3110.

SLIDE AND PRINT MAKERS

Instagraphic CRT ($190), Eastman Kodak Co., 343 State St., Rochester, NY 14560, (716) 724-4000.

Pallette ($1500), Polaroid Corp., Industrial Marketing Dept., 575 Technology Square, Cambridge, MA 02139, (617) 577-2000.

VFR 2000 ($2500), Celtic Technology, 6265 Variel Ave., Woodland Hills, CA 91367, (213) 884-6767.

Video Slide 35 ($2800 to $3500), Lang Systems, Inc., 1010 O'Brien Dr., Menlo Park, CA 94025, (415) 328-5555.

SLOT EXTENDERS AND SWITCHES

Extend-A-Slot ($35), Southern California Research Group, P.O. Box 2231, Goleta, CA 93118, (805) 685-1931.

Interchange Switch ($80), SouthWest EdPsych Services, Inc., Box 1870, Phoenix, AZ 85007, (602) 253-6528.

MacSwitch ($99), Computer Friends, 6415 SW Canyon Ct., Suite 10, Portland, OR 97221, (503) 297-2321.

Printer Switch ($165), Intra Computer, 101 W. 31st St., New York, NY 10001, (212) 947-5533.

Switch-A-Slot ($180), Southern California Research Group, P.O. Box 2321, Goleta, CA 93118, (805) 685-1931.

SOUND GENERATORS

ECHO II, ECHO GP and ECHO-PC ($130, $250, and $250), Street Electronics Corp., 1140 Mark Ave., Carpinteria, CA 93013, (805) 684-4593.

Mockingboard A and B ($125 and $225), Sweet Micro Systems, 50 Freeway Dr., Cranston, RI 02920, (401) 461-0530.

Sprite II and SuperSprite ($249 and $395), Synetix, Inc., 10635 NE 38th Pl., Kirkland, WA 98033, (206) 828-4884.

SPREADSHEET SOFTWARE

FlashCalc ($99), VisiCorp, 2895 Zanker Rd., San Jose, CA 95134, (408) 946-9000.

MAGICALC ($150), Artsci, Inc., 5547 Satsuma Ave., North Hollywood, CA 91601, (213) 985-2922.

Multiplan ($195), Microsoft Corp., 10700 Northup Way, Bellevue, WA 98004, (206) 828-8080.

UltraPlan ($170), Videx, Inc., 897 NW Grant Ave., Corvallis, OR 97330, (503) 758-0521.

VisiCalc and VisiCalc Advanced Version ($179 for both), Software Arts, 27 Mica Lane, Wellesley, MA 02181, (617) 237-4000.

SURGE PROTECTORS AND COOLING FANS

Cooling Fan ($38), PC Kingdom, P.O. Box 51600, San Jose, CA 95151, (408) 286-4651.

Cool-Time ($90), Tencal, Inc., 9525 DeSoto Ave., Chatsworth, CA 91311, (213) 998-4850.

Hibernator ($145), Innovative Measurements, Inc., P.O. Box 3879, San Clemente, CA 92672, (714) 492-9690.

MACC Master AC Control Console ($80), Alpha Delta Communications, P.O. Box 571, Dayton, OH 45459, (513) 435-4772.

Stedi Watt 118 and Stedi Watt 618 ($65 and $90), National Field Sales, 2458 Central Ave., St. Petersburg, FL 33712, (800) 345-1280.

Super Fan II ($75 to $110), RH Electronics, Inc., 566 Irelan Dr., Buellton, CA 93427, (805) 688-2047.

Surge Sentry, several models ($90 to $150), RKS Industries, Inc., 4865 Scotts Valley Dr., Scotts Valley, CA 95066, (408) 438-5760.

System Saver ($90), Kensington Microware, 919 Third Ave., New York, NY 10022, (212) 486-7707.

TOUCH TABLETS

KoalaPad ($125), Koala Technologies, Inc., 3100 Patrick Henry Dr., Santa Clara, CA 95052-8100, (408) 986-8866.

PowerPad ($100), Chalk Board, Inc., 5470 D Oakbrook Pkwy., Norcross, GA 30090, (404) 447-6711.

TRACKBALLS

TG Trackball ($40), TG Products, 1104 Summit Ave., Suite 110, Plano, TX 75074, (214) 424-8568.

WICO Smartball ($70), WICO Corp., 6400 W. Gross Pt. Rd., Niles, IL 60648, (312) 647-7500.

UNINTERRUPTIBLE POWER SUPPLIES

Datasaver ($695), Cuesta Systems, Inc., 3340 Roberto Ct., San Luis Obispo, CA 93401, (805) 541-4160.

Guardian Angel ($595), RH Electronics, Inc., 566 Irelan Dr., Buellton, CA 93427, (805) 688-2047.

Mayday UPS ($240 to $2795), Sun Research, Inc., P.O. Box 210, New Durham, NH 03855, (603) 859-7110.

WORD-PROCESSING SOFTWARE

Bank Street Writer ($70), Broderbund Software, 17 Paul Dr., San Rafael, CA 94903, (415) 479-1170.

Format-II ($150), Kensington Microware, 919 Third Ave., New York, NY 10022, (212) 486-7077.

Homeword and Screen Writer II ($50 and $130), Sierra On-Line, Inc., Sierra On-Line Bldg., Coarsegold, CA 93614, (209) 683-6858.

Magic Window II ($170), Artsci, Inc., 5547 Satsuma Ave., North Hollywood, CA 91601, (213) 985-5763.

Megawriter and Megaspell ($100 and $60), Megahaus Corp., 5703 Oberlin Dr., San Diego, CA 92121, (619) 450-1230.

PFS: Write ($125), Software Publishing Corp., 1901 Landings Dr., Mountain View, CA 94043, (415) 962-8910.

PIE: Writer and The Speller ($150 and $50), Hayden Software Co., 600 Suffolk St., Lowell, MA 01853, (800) 343-1218.

SENSIBLE SPELLER IV ($125), Sensible Software, 6619 Perham Dr., West Bloomfield, MI 48033, (313) 399-8877.

Super-Text Home/Office and Super-Text Professional ($125 and $175), Muse Software, 347 N. Charles St., Baltimore, MD 21201, (301) 659-7212.

Word Juggler IIe and Lexicheck IIe ($189 for both), Quark, Inc., 2525 W. Evans, Suite 220, Denver, CO 80206, (303) 934-2211.

Zardax ($210), Action-Research Northwest, 11442 Marine View Dr., Seattle, WA 98146, (206) 241-1645.

WORKSTATIONS AND FURNITURE

Apple Cart and Workstation ($475 and $665), Williams and Foltz Computer Furniture, 1816 Fourth St., Berkeley, CA 94710, (415) 644-2022.

Basic Comfort SL ($189), Picture House, 166 Boynton Blvd., Daytona Beach, FL 32018, (904) 252-7970.

Compucart ($595), VersaTech Corp., P.O. Box 2095, Tampa, FL 33601, (813) 251-2431.

Compu-Mate and Compu-Corner ($240 and $399), John James Furnishings, Inc., P.O. Box 501321, Houston, TX 77250, (713) 462-5533.

CT710 and CT720 Series Computer Furniture ($150 and $170), O'Sullivan Industries, Inc., 19th and Gulf Sts., Lamar, MO 64759, (417) 682-3322.

50-inch Personal Computer Desk ($190), Atlantic Cabinet Corp., P.O. Box 100, Williamsport, MD 21795, (301) 223-8900.

Workstations, various ($160 and up), The Wood Works, 11th and Haskell, Rt. 2, Box 407, Lawrence, KS 66044, (913) 842-7797.

GLOSSARY

A

Addressability: The ability of a computer's processor to use a certain amount of memory at one time. The Apple's 8-bit processor has a maximum addressability of 64K of RAM, while the IBM PC's 8088 has a maximum addressability of 1024K.

Alphanumeric: Consisting of letters, numbers, and symbols.

Analog device: A device that operates by comparing physical relationships, such as the distance between two objects (as in the hands of a clock) or the relative amount of electricity passing through a circuit (as in a dimmer switch). *Compare* Digital device.

Architecture: The internal design of a computer chip or a circuit board.

ASCII: American Standard Code for Information Interchange. The most widely used coding scheme for microcomputer information, ASCII assigns a specific string of zeros and ones (the language a computer understands) to each letter, number, and symbol that the keyboard can produce.

Asynchronous: A method of transmitting computer data that does not use a timing signal. *Compare* Synchronous.

B

Bank switching: The exchange of one area, or bank, of memory for another one. In the Apple, bank switching lets the computer use more than 64K of RAM, which is the limit of its processor's addressability. Bank switching is often used to increase the storage space available for large spreadsheet models. *See also* Addressability.

Baud rate: The speed, usually in bits per second, at which a modem transmits data.

Bit: A binary digit which, in a computer, represents one on/off state in one circuit.

Bit-mapped graphics: A graphics display in which each dot of light on the computer's screen display is controlled by a specific bit, or binary digit, in the computer's memory. Bit-mapped graphics are high quality, because the computer has precise control over the image (via the individual dots that make it up).

Bubble memory: A collection of circuits that stores data in the form of tiny magnetized bubbles. Unlike RAM, bubble memory doesn't need constant electrical power to maintain its contents. Bubble memory, however, is slower at storing and retrieving data than RAM is, and it is more expensive.

Buffer: A section of memory, either in the computer itself or in an external device, such as a printer or a modem, that temporarily stores incoming or outgoing data so the computer's main memory and processor can be freed for other operations.

Bus: The electrical pathway that connects the CPU with the computer's memory, input/output ports, and other devices that the CPU controls.

Byte: A group of eight bits, which is the smallest number of bits that can represent one character of information. *See also* Bit.

C

Card: Alternate name for a circuit board, as in "video display card," or "80-column card." *See* Circuit board.

Chip: A small sliver of silicon, etched with electrical pathways, that is encased in a protective plastic housing. Depending on the circuits etched on it, a chip can perform various computer tasks, such as processing information, storing data, or producing a video display. *See* Integrated circuit.

Circuit board: A thin plastic sheet that (depending on its function) contains chips and other electrical components, and the metallic connections linking them. Depending on its components, a circuit board may control disk drives, produce a video display, transmit or receive data, or convert an Apple so it can run software designed for other computers. Also simply called a board or a card.

Clock: A circuit board, containing the circuitry of a digital clock, which keeps track of the time and date and makes this information available to the computer. A clock gives the computer the ability to "tell time" and thus label information with the current time and date, or perform specified tasks automatically at certain times or on certain days.

Clock speed: The speed, in megahertz (MHz), at which electricity passes through a microprocessor and across its input/output bus. The Apple's processor, the 6502, has a clock speed of 1 MHz.

Communications parameter: A user-adjustable setting for a communications program. Communications parameters include the rate at which data is sent (baud rate) and the transmission mode (duplex). These settings can be varied, but usually remain the same during any given transmission.

Communications protocol: A set of rules governing the way in which data are transferred between computers. In order for two computers to communicate, both must use the same protocol, which includes the number of data bits in a byte of transmitted information, the number or presence of stop (end-of-character) bits, and the presence or type of parity (error-checking) bit.

Composite video: A video signal or video display method in which several colors are mixed together and must be sorted out by the monitor (a composite monitor) that displays them. Because the colors are mixed together and must be deciphered by the monitor, this video display method doesn't produce as many colors, or colors as sharp, as those produced by the alternate, RGB video method. *See* RGB video.

Configure: To instruct a program about a specific hardware setup, such as the type of printer being used, the type of display, and the number of disk drives.

Coprocessor: A second, often auxiliary, microprocessor that either assists the computer's main processor or takes over all of its functions. The most popular coprocessor for the Apple is the Z-80, which permits an Apple to run the CP/M operating system and CP/M programs. Other coprocessors (such as the 6502C coprocessor) either speed up the execution of Apple programs or they enable the Apple to produce better sound or graphics.

Copy protected: Protected against unauthorized duplication. Much of the commercial software used with microcomputers is copy protected by the manufacturer, so it can't be duplicated and distributed for free.

Co-resident: Stored in RAM with other programs or data. For example, when you use a program written in Integer BASIC, the program is co-resident in RAM with the Integer BASIC language itself.

CPU: Central Processing Unit. The data-processing part of a computer. In a microcomputer, the CPU is the computer's microprocessor chip itself. The 6502, 65802, 65816, Z-80, 8088, 8086, and MC68000 are all microprocessors. The term CPU is also often used to describe the hardware component that contains the microprocessor chip. Thus, the unit that contains the expansion slots, keyboard, RAM, and processor in the Apple is sometimes called the CPU. *See also* Processor, Microprocessor.

CRT: Cathode-Ray Tube. The most common type of computer display. A CRT displays characters or graphics by means of an electron gun, which fires electrons at a sheet of phosphor, causing the phosphor to glow. The pattern in which electrons are fired at the phosphor is controlled by the computer, and this pattern determines the shapes of characters and graphics produced on the screen.

Cursor: The marker on a computer display that shows where information typed on the keyboard will appear. On the Apple, the cursor is usually a blinking rectangle.

D

DIF: Data Interchange Format. A specific way of storing files on disk that makes it easier for one program to exchange data files with another program. DIF is the data interchange format used by VisiCalc, VisiPlot, and many other products; it enables files from these programs to be used by many word-processing and database management programs.

Digital device: A device that operates by converting physical relationships to numeric ones. A digital watch, for example, converts a relative measurement (time) into specific numbers. In computers and peripheral equipment, digital technology uses on/off states, or switches, to represent physical relationships, such as the position of a joystick or the amount of current passing through a circuit. *Compare* Analog device.

Digitizer: A device, usually a circuit board connected to a video camera, that converts images into digital information the computer can understand. A digitizer breaks a camera's image into a series of tiny dots, each of which has a numeric representation that can be manipulated, stored, or reproduced by the computer.

Digitizing camera: A video camera connected to a digitizing interface, which allows for the conversion of visual images into strings of computer data that can be stored, manipulated, or re-created by the computer later.

Digitizing tablet: A drawing tablet with a stylus, connected to a digitizing interface, that converts a drawn image into strings of computer data. The surface of the tablet is covered with a grid of dots, each of which represents a specific digital address in the computer's memory. As a light-sensitive stylus is passed over the dots, the computer "reads" the shape of the object drawn and then, usually, reproduces it on a video screen.

DIP switch: Dual In-line Package switch. Any of a series of tiny switches built into the housing of a computer chip. By manipulating the switches, you can alter the function of the chip. DIP switches are often used in printers and modems to change type faces or transmission speeds.

Disk: A thin, round recording medium, usually coated with magnetic oxide, used for the storage of computer data. Disks come in various sizes, from 3½ inches to 14 inches in diameter, and are either made of flexible mylar (floppy disks) or aluminum (hard disks).

Disk cache: A part of a computer's RAM used temporarily to store data or instructions that are needed by a program. The computer's ability to use a disk cache depends on whether its operating system knows how to use such a cache, whether there is enough RAM to make up a cache area, and whether the program being run needs to use a cache. Spreadsheet and database management programs, which often sort or perform calculations on large files, can benefit from a disk cache, because it speeds the manipulation of information by providing an intermediate storage area that can be accessed by the computer much more quickly than the disk can be.

Disk controller: A circuit board to which disk drives are connected. The disk controller is the pathway through which data are transferred between the computer and the disk drives. It also turns the disk drives on and off when the computer accesses the disk.

Disk drive: A device that reads information from, or writes information to, a disk. Depending on the type of disk (floppy disk or hard disk) and the type of computer used, disk drives can store 100 kilobytes to about 40 megabytes of information on a single disk.

Display memory: A specific part of a computer's memory, which is set aside for the storage of video-display information. The Apple was the first microcomputer to use built-in display memory; earlier machines kept display information on a separate circuit board, rather than in the computer's main memory.

Duplex: A way of transmitting data through a modem. Half-duplex transmissions permit computers to exchange information in only one direction at a time, while full-duplex transmissions allow them to exchange information in both directions simultaneously.

E

Electronic mail: The automatic transmission of typed messages from one computer to one or more others, either over telephone lines or within a computer network.

Emulate: To mimic, or to act like, something else. When a computer is instructed by a special program to act like another kind of computer or a data terminal, it is said to emulate the other. The Apple III, for example, is capable of emulating an Apple II for the purpose of running the II's software.

Environment: A software concept that involves either the creation of a new operating system or the modification of an existing one in order to unify the workings of several different application programs under a fairly uniform set of commands. Unlike integrated software, an environment permits the use of several different programs from different manufacturers.

Error checking: Ensuring the accuracy of data being transmitted between one computer and another.

Expansion slot: An internal slot in the Apple II, II+, or IIe that accommodates additional circuit boards that either enhance the computer's abilities or enable it to connect with peripheral devices, such as modems, special monitors, printers, and scientific instruments. Apple II-series computers, except for the IIc, have seven expansion slots.

F

Fast-phosphor monitor: A monitor in which the phosphor that lights up to produce characters and graphics (as a result of charges from an electron gun) doesn't glow very long. Because the glow of the phosphor fades quickly after each charge from the electron gun, fast-phosphor monitors tend to last longer than slow-phosphor monitors, on which the glow lingers. *Compare* Slow-phosphor monitor.

Field: In a database program, a specific item of information in a record. In a customer record, for example, the customer name, street address, and telephone number each are fields. *Compare* Record.

File server: A device used in a computer network that controls the data traffic between a hard disk drive and the several computers that access the drive for programs and data files. A file server can either be built into the hard disk or placed in a separate unit outside the hard disk. Sometimes, a single computer is set aside to handle file-serving chores on a network.

G

Ground: To connect an electrical device with the ground in order to channel static electricity harmlessly away from delicate electrical circuits. Grounded electrical outlets have three holes instead of two—the third hole is used to connect the electrical device with the ground. Grounding is usually achieved by connecting a wire from the electrical system to a rod in the ground or to a water pipe.

H

High-resolution graphics: A relative term indicating visual images made up of a larger-than-usual number of individual dots, or pixels, in a computer display. In the Apple, for example, standard resolution is 140 by 192 dots, while high resolution is 280 by 192 dots. Newer Apples also have a double high-resolution mode, which uses 560 by 192 dots to display images.

I

Icon: A representative image. Icons are being used increasingly in computer software to represent commands on the display screen. In integrated software, for example, a filing cabinet icon may represent the database management part of the program.

Information utility: A mainframe computer that contains various kinds of information that can be accessed for a fee by microcomputer users. Information utilities, such as THE SOURCE, CompuServe, and Dow Jones News/Retrieval, offer current news, financial data on companies, an encyclopedia, airline schedules, and other subjects of interest to consumers. More specialized information utilities offer summaries of scientific articles, research data, and the like.

Input/Output: The movement of data or program instructions to and from the CPU in a computer. Also called I/O, for short. *See also* Bus, CPU.

Instruction set: The basic machine-language instructions a CPU understands. Instruction sets are unique to each series of processor. The 6502 processor, for example, has a different instruction set from that of the 8088. *See also* Machine language.

Integrated circuit: An electronic circuit, often containing several thousand feet of electric pathways, that has been reduced to microscopic size and placed on a silicon chip. Integrated circuits vary in their density (the size and complexity of the circuit that has been squeezed onto a chip), and denser circuits are said to be more highly integrated. Integrated circuits are also called ICs.

Integrated software: A single software program, often on more than one disk, that combines several applications (or functions) under a similar set of commands and that usually permits the exchange of data among the applications. AppleWorks, Jane, Jack2, and Lotus 1-2-3 are all examples of integrated software.

Interface: A circuit board or built-in circuitry that allows the transmission of data between a computer and its peripheral devices (monitor, modem, printer, and so forth). The most common interfaces for microcomputers are the serial interface, which allows data to be transmitted one bit at a time, and the parallel interface, which allows data to be transmitted eight bits at a time.

K

K: Kilobyte. A unit of measurement equal to one thousand bytes of storage in a computer's RAM or on a disk. The Apple's RAM is typically 64K, and Apple disks will store a maximum of 143K of data. Because a computer converts all data to binary (base-2) notation, however, one K is actually 1024 bytes (2^{10}), rather than an even 1000 bytes. Thus, a 64K computer actually has 65,535 bytes of RAM.

L

LCD: Liquid Crystal Display. A display that produces characters and graphics by reflecting ambient light, rather than by generating light from within, as a CRT monitor does. LCD displays are used mainly in portable computers, where their light weight and low power requirements are an advantage.

LED: Light-Emitting Diode. A type of display that uses a network of tiny light sources to form characters. LED displays are usually found in peripheral devices, such as modems, where they are used to display small amounts of data, such as the time or date.

Light pen: An input device that absorbs the light from a CRT display and transmits the locations of individual pixels to the computer. The advantage of a light pen is that the user can simply point to an item on the screen to make a menu selection, or move the pen across the screen to draw a line by lighting a series of pixels. A light pen is most often used with graphics and educational programs.

M

Machine language: The programming language that is directly understood by a computer. Machine language is composed exclusively of binary digits (zeros and ones), which represent the on/off electrical states in the computer.

Macro: A user-defined command or set of keystrokes that represents a series of commands or more than one set of keystrokes. Macros allow users to issue long, repetitive commands more easily by consolidating them under a shorter, more easily used command or set of keystrokes.

Matrix: A grid. On a display monitor, the character matrix is the grid of pixels that contains an individual character; such a matrix is usually 7 pixels by 9 pixels. On a dot-matrix printer, the matrix is a grid of pins in the printhead. The pins are extended by the printer in various patterns; these patterns then transfer the different character shapes through the ribbon and onto the paper. The matrices in dot-matrix printers range from 5 by 7 dots up to 12 by 24 dots. With any matrix of dots, whether on a printer or monitor, more dots will produce sharper and clearer characters than will fewer dots.

Memory address: A numbered location in the computer's memory. A 64K computer has 65,535 individual memory locations, each of which has its own number, so that the computer can easily refer to it.

Menu: A listing of program options, identified by numbers or letters, with which the user controls the program. Menus simplify the use of software because they display a set of program options on the screen for easy access. Without a menu, the user must remember both the options and the commands for selecting them. Programs that use menus heavily are said to be menu driven.

Microprocessor: A CPU on a chip. While the processor on a minicomputer or a mainframe computer may consist of circuits spread across several circuit boards or across several chips, the processor in a microcomputer is called a microprocessor because it is contained entirely on one chip. *See also* CPU, Processor.

Monitor: A display device that reads a computer's video output signal directly. Usually, monitors can receive a signal only via a wire connection—they don't contain a receiver that lets them display programs like a television does.

Motherboard: In a microcomputer, the main circuit board, which contains the CPU, RAM, ROM, input/output bus, and most other essential circuitry. Because computers like the Apple contain expansion slots into which small, auxiliary circuit boards can be plugged, the term motherboard is used to distinguish the computer's main circuit board from these smaller boards.

Mouse: A small, rolling box that can be used to control the location of the cursor on a computer screen or to select menu options. Most computer mice are about the size of a cigarette package. They roll on a ball bearing, either on a desktop or on a special tablet containing a grid of dots, and have one or more buttons on the top surface that are used to select menu options or to highlight data on the screen. Mechanical mice control the position of the cursor by transmitting information about the movement of the ball bearing relative to a set of contacts it rolls against; optical mice transmit information by absorbing light reflected from dots on a grid that correspond to the dots on a computer screen.

N

Network: A group of computers linked by a cable and by circuitry that enables them to exchange information and to share storage and printing devices.

Node: One hardware device and its connection on a network. A computer, a printer, a hard disk, and a modem could each be nodes on a network.

O

Off line: Not directly or immediately available to a computer. Data stored on a disk that isn't loaded in a disk drive is off line. A printer that isn't connected to the computer or that isn't turned on is off line.

On line: In direct contact with, or immediately available to, a computer. On-line help, for example, is a help file in the computer's RAM or on a disk in a disk drive, which is immediately available for use. A computer's printer is on line when it is connected and the power is turned on. Data stored in a computer's RAM or on a disk in one of its disk drives are on line. When a personal computer is communicating with an information utility, it remains on line as long as the connection continues.

Operating system: A set of software programs that tell a computer how to store files, access disk drives, and otherwise interact with peripheral devices. Different operating systems instruct a computer in different ways, so application software must be written to interact with a specific operating system. On the Apple, the two most widely used operating systems are DOS 3.3 (DOS stands for Disk Operating System), and the newer, more powerful, ProDOS. Other popular operating systems for microcomputers include CP/M, CP/M-86, and MS-DOS.

P

Peripheral: An external device used to get information into or out of a computer. Printers, monitors, modems, and disk drives are all peripherals.

Picture packing: A data-storage technique used by developers of graphics software to compress the sizes of graphics files so that more files can be stored on one disk. A typical Apple graphics file normally occupies about 8K of disk space, so only about twelve such files can be stored on one Apple disk. Picture packing can compress graphics files so that three or four times as many can be stored on one disk.

Pixel: An individual dot on a computer monitor. The quality of a computer's display is measured by the number of pixels that can be lit horizontally and vertically on the monitor. Control of individual pixels requires the use of individual memory locations in the computer, so the number of pixels on a monitor is limited by the display memory available. The best (double high-resolution) display an Apple can produce is 560 pixels across by 192 pixels down. *See also* CRT.

Port: A channel for transmitting data that connects peripheral devices with the main computer unit through a socket or a plug. Port connections are distinguished by the kind of device they are made for, by the number of pins or socket holes they have, or by the way data are transmitted through them. A standard Apple IIe without extra circuit boards contains a composite video port, a cassette-recorder port, a 9-pin game controller port, a 16-pin game controller port, an RF modulator port, and a numeric keypad port. With the addition of extra circuit boards, the Apple IIe can also accommodate serial or parallel interface ports, or an RGB video interface port. *See also* Interface.

Potentiometer: A device used to measure or control electrical current by comparing it to a known voltage. Household dimmer switches and volume controls on radios and televisions all use potentiometers. For computers, game paddles and the most accurate joysticks use potentiometers that maneuver an object on the screen by transmitting the movements of the paddle or joystick control relative to a fixed position.

Pre-boot software: Software that instructs a computer to convert standard input from a specific program for use with an enhancement product. Pre-boot software for VisiCalc, for example, tells the computer to create large spreadsheet files by using additional RAM. Pre-boot software for Apple Writer II converts that program's standard 24-line display instructions and generates a 48-line display with the Videx UltraTerm card.

Processor: The circuit or set of circuits that allows a computer to follow program instructions, manipulate information, and interact with input, output, and storage devices. *See also* CPU.

Programmable: Capable of being altered with program instructions. Microprocessors are programmable, because they respond in different ways to different sets of program instructions.

R

RAM: Random Access Memory. The largest memory segment in a microcomputer, RAM is important because its contents can easily be changed under instructions from the CPU. RAM is the main place where programs and data are stored for immediate use in the computer, because information can be both written to it and read from it. RAM is volatile: It retains its contents only as long as it is supplied with electric power. When you turn your computer off, whatever is in RAM is lost. RAM is measured in K, or kilobytes. A standard Apple IIe contains 64K of RAM.

Record: In a database program, a record is a collection of related data. In a data base of employee information, for example, the collection of data about any individual employee, such as name, date of hire, salary, and so forth, is a record. *Compare* Field.

Relational database: A database program that permits the manipulation of more than one file of information at one time. Relational databases encourage the creation of several files, from which specific records or fields can be selected and merged in new files when necessary.

Resolution: The quality of a computer display, measured by the horizontal and vertical numbers of pixels that make up the screen. The Apple's high-resolution display is 280 pixels across by 192 pixels down.

RF modulator: Radio Frequency modulator. A device that converts, or modulates, the standard video signal generated by a computer into a radio frequency that can be received by a standard television set through its antenna connection. An RF modulator lets you use an ordinary television to display your computer's output, instead of having to buy a special computer display, or monitor.

RGB video: Red, Green, Blue. A color video signal that separates colors into red, green, and blue signals. RGB video can only be displayed by an RGB monitor. It is superior to composite video, which mixes the colors in a single signal, because colors can be displayed individually on the screen, rather than as a mixture of different colored dots. This makes for sharper images with a wider variety of colors. The standard Apple IIe produces only a composite color video signal—an extra circuit board is needed to produce an RGB signal. The Apple IIc has a built-in RGB video output port.

Ribbon cable: A cable used to connect a parallel device to the computer. A ribbon cable carries data eight bits at a time in individual wires that are arranged side by side. This setup results in a cable that is about 1¼ inches wide and as thin as a small wire. It looks like a ribbon, hence the name.

ROM: Read-Only Memory. Unlike RAM, which can have information either read from it or written to it, a computer's ROM can only have information read from it. A set of instructions stored in ROM cannot be changed by the computer. Although ROM is less useful than RAM in this respect, it has one redeeming quality: It is non-volatile. Whereas RAM loses any program or data stored in it when the computer's power is turned off, ROM retains its contents at all times. Because of this permanence, ROM is used to store the start-up instructions the computer needs when it is turned on. Without ROM, the computer wouldn't know how to access a disk drive or understand the keyboard input you gave it to load and run an application program. Because this particular ROM helps the computer start itself up, it is often called the start-up, or bootstrap ROM.

S

Screen dump: The transfer of the exact contents of a display screen to a printer for reproduction on paper.

Slide maker: A peripheral device that reproduces a color screen image on a photographic slide. A slide maker is usually a long box with a tiny RGB monitor at one end and a camera at the other end. Using an RGB video interface, the monitor reproduces the image from the computer's display, the camera photographs the image, and the photograph is later developed as a color slide.

Slow-phosphor monitor: A monitor in which the type of phosphor used to generate light maintains its glow for a relatively long time after it is charged by the monitor's electron gun. Slow-phosphor monitors are best for certain types of character displays, but because the phosphor glows longer, these monitors don't last as long as their fast-phosphor counterparts. *Compare* Fast-phosphor monitor.

Speech synthesis: The creation of human-like speech using the sound-generating capabilities of a computer. Speech-synthesis circuit boards usually contain enhanced sound-generating functions that mirror the range of human speech. They are sold with software that translates keyboard input into spoken sounds.

Sprite: A type of graphic character, made popular by Commodore, that can be moved across a computer screen by software commands. Sprite graphics are superior to an Apple's standard graphics because they can be moved over a static graphic background. Hobbyists who want to create a background and then move Sprites over it need only draw the background once and then move the Sprites on a second, independent, graphic plane. In contrast, the standard Apple produces only one plane of graphics, and the object is actually part of the background itself. Moving an object under this system requires that the entire background be redrawn each time the object moves to a new position.

Surge suppressor: An electrical circuit placed between a computer's power supply and the wall outlet, which filters or equalizes fluctuations in the amount of power being delivered. The circuitry in computers is very sensitive to power surges, or fluctuations, and a surge suppressor helps ensure a relatively constant level of power.

Synchronous: A means of transmitting data between computers in which a timing signal is used to prevent fluctuations in the transfer rate. Synchronous communications are generally required for fast, reliable data transfers between a microcomputer and a mainframe computer.

T

Touch tablet: A pressure-sensitive, rectangular device that is used as an alternative input and control method for computers. A plastic membrane on the tablet responds to the pressure of a fingertip or stylus, and relays this movement to the computer, which uses the information to move the cursor.

Trackball: A control device most often used with game software. A trackball consists of a stationary plastic housing in which is seated a palm-sized, movable ball. When the ball is rotated, mechanical or optical sensors inside the housing relay the movement to the computer, which uses the information for cursor control.

U

Utility: A type of program that makes other software easier to use. A graphics utility, for example, may convert the binary screen-address locations required by the computer into simpler and less cumbersome codes, so the user can program images more quickly. An operating system utility may contain simple programs to facilitate file naming, file copying, or other kinds of file management.

V

Virtual memory: A program feature that makes it possible to use data files that are larger than a computer's available RAM. A virtual-memory system permits the creation of files as large as a whole disk, and then swaps sections of the file on and off the disk as they are needed by the program.

Volume: The name given to a disk's worth of files under ProDOS. On most Apples, a volume is equal to a 143K disk, but under ProDOS, a volume can be equal to a disk of any size, whether it's a 143K floppy disk or a five-megabyte hard disk.

W

Window: An area of the display screen used to present a specific type of information. Most Apple programs have only one window—the entire screen area. Some word-processing programs or integrated programs, however, let you split the screen into two or more windows, with a different file in each window.

Index

D

E

F

G

H

I

J

K

L

M

S

T

U

V

W

Z

CHARLES RUBIN

After growing up in Los Angeles, California, Charles Rubin attended Antioch College, the University of Southern California, and San Francisco State University. He holds both a Bachelor's and a Master's degree in English and has been writing about microcomputers since 1981. He is a former associate editor of *Personal Computing* and *Personal Software* magazines, and is currently a contributing editor for these publications. His work has also appeared in other technological and general-interest magazines, including *Newsweek Access* and *InfoWorld*. His first book, *Thinking Small: The Buyer's Guide to Portable Computers,* was recently published by Addison-Wesley. He lives in Oakland, California, and has been using an Apple IIe since early 1983.

THE MANUSCRIPT for this book was word processed using PIE:Writer on an Apple IIe and submitted to Microsoft Press in electronic form via modem. Text files were processed and formatted using Microsoft Word on an IBM PC.

COVER AND TEXT design by Ted Mader and Associates. Airbrush cover illustration by Steven Peringer. Interior renderings by Rick van Genderen.

TEXT COMPOSITION in Sabon and Helvetica Bold Extended, using CCI Book and the Mergenthaler Linotron 202 digital phototypesetter.

COVER ART separated by Color Masters, Phoenix, Arizona. Printed on 12 pt. Carolina by Strine Printing Company, York, Pennsylvania. Text stock, 60 lb. Glatfelter Offset, supplied by Carpenter/Offutt. Book printed and bound by Fairfield Graphics, Fairfield, Pennsylvania.

Other Titles from Microsoft Press

THE IBM ENVIRONMENT

Discovering the IBM PCjr
PETER NORTON
ISBN 0-914845-01-2 *$15.95*

Exploring the IBM PCjr
PETER NORTON
ISBN 0-914845-02-0 *$18.25*

Getting Started with Microsoft WORD
A Step-by-Step Guide to Word Processing
JANET RAMPA
ISBN 0-914845-13-6 *$16.95*

Managing Your Business with Multiplan
How to Use Microsoft's Award-Winning Electronic Spreadsheet on Your IBM PC
RUTH K. WITKIN
ISBN 0-914845-06-3 *$17.95*

Running MS-DOS
The Microsoft Guide to Getting the Most Out of the Standard Operating System for the IBM PC and 50 Other Personal Computers
VAN WOLVERTON
ISBN 0-914845-07-1 *$19.95*

THE APPLE ENVIRONMENT

The Apple Macintosh Book
CARY LU
ISBN 0-914845-00-4 *$18.95*

Learning Apple Logo Together
An Activity Book for Creative Parents, Teachers, and Kids
KENNETH P. GOLDBERG
ISBN 0-914845-25-X *$14.95*

MacWork MacPlay
Creative Ideas for Fun and Profit on your Apple Macintosh
LON POOLE
ISBN 0-914845-22-5 *$18.95*

Presentation Graphics on the Apple Macintosh
How to Use Microsoft Chart to Create Dazzling Graphics for Professional and Corporate Applications
STEVE LAMBERT
ISBN 0-914845-11-X *$18.95*

GENERAL

Learning Commodore 64 Logo Together
An Activity Book for Creative Parents, Teachers, and Kids
KENNETH P. GOLDBERG
ISBN 0-914845-24-1 *$14.95*

Silicon Valley Guide
DAVID REMER, PAUL REMER, and ROBERT DUNAWAY
ISBN 0-914845-09-8 *$19.25*

Available wherever fine books are sold.